EATING THE DRAGON

EATING THE DRAGON
A Study Guide to HSK and Supplemental Chinese Vocabulary

VOLUME 1: ELEMENTARY AND INTERMEDIATE

Michael Burkhardt

Monkeywalk Multimedia Press
Columbus, Ohio, USA

Copyright © 2011 Michael H. Burkhardt
First Edition, July 2011
All rights reserved.

This book contains information derived from the CC-CEDICT Chinese-English dictionary data (cc-cedict.org), which is licensed under a Creative Commons Attribution-Share Alike 3.0 License.

10 9 8 7 6 5 4 3 2 1

ISBN: 978-1-257-92187-4

Updates and errata can be found online at monkeywalk.com.

The author can be reached by e-mail at michael@monkeywalk.com.

How do you eat an elephant? One bite at a time!
ORIGIN UNKNOWN

Preface

I have faced the feeling many times, that feeling of no end in sight, like eating an elephant. When it comes to studying Chinese language, though, the beast is not an elephant, but a dragon with thousands of characters for scales, and breathing the fire of a seemingly endless vocabulary.

I am not an expert in linguistics or pedagogy, so I can't make any sweeping statements about methodology, psychology, or learning plateaus; all I can give you is my own experience. As an intermediate learner, I have struggled mightily to build my vocabulary without the benefit of immersion. (I live and work in the United States, and my obligations make living in China impossible, at least for now.) I listen to podcasts, and watch CCTV4, and I have examined many, many books.

One way of analyzing the Chinese language is by counting the number of times individual characters appear in a very large body of Chinese text. The characters having the highest rate of occurrence, or highest relative frequency, are considered the most common. Lots of books have been written on the basis of character frequency, and they all—the ones I've seen, anyway—take the same approach: present the next most common character in line, along with a list of "common" words that use that character. Since most of the words in the list use characters that have lower relative frequencies, I quickly become lost in a barrage of characters and words without any good way to prioritize. As interesting as character frequency is, I haven't found it all that helpful in acquiring new vocabulary.

Another useful tool available to learners is the Hanyu Shuiping Kaoshi (HSK) word lists, which were newly revised in 2009. The lists are divided into 3 major parts, two each at the elementary, intermediate, and advanced levels. Each of the six lists contains from just over 100 to several thousand (!) new characters, words, and phrases, in no particular order. I find this a bit overwhelming. On top of all that, the HSK lists omit a lot of common vocabulary, even at the lowest levels.

With the *Eating the Dragon* series, I have attempted to apply the technique of frequency-based analysis to the hierarchically arranged HSK lists in order to produce a unified set of lessons that present a large body of Chinese characters and vocabulary in a methodical, progressive way. Designed to be consumed in order, each of the 198 lessons contains a list of new characters, HSK vocabulary, and non-HSK vocabulary at a comparable level. New terms are only introduced once all the component characters have been introduced in the same or earlier lesson.

While this book is not intended as a textbook or comprehensive course of study, I do hope that it will find a useful place on the shelves of some learners who, like me, struggle with eating the dragon.

Michael Burkhardt
July 2011

Introduction

In all, the *Eating the Dragon* series presents over 11,000 new Chinese characters, words, and phrases drawn from both the HSK word lists and a news-based corpus of modern informational Chinese. I've compared the contents and skill levels of the HSK terms with the relative frequency data derived from the corpus to produce an organized set of lessons that satisfy the following goals:

1. Present all of the HSK vocabulary in some meaningful order—specifically, by level and then relative frequency.

2. Present relevant supplemental vocabulary at a level and pace commensurate with the HSK vocabulary.

3. Introduce all new unique characters as they are used.

4. Present new terms only after new characters have been introduced.

5. Divide it all up into lessons small enough in size to be easily consumed.

The result, contained in this book and its companion volumes, is a working modern Chinese vocabulary in 198 lessons.

About the HSK Word Lists

The Hanyu Shuiping Kaoshi is a standardized exam designed to rate a person's Chinese language skill level. The current exam structure, revised in 2009, has three levels (elementary, intermediate, and advanced), each having two sub-levels ("acceptable" and "with honors"). A summary of the six HSK word lists is given in the table below.

HSK Level	Single Character	Multi-Character	Total Entries	Unique Characters
1. A1 Elementary	80	68	150	176
2. A2 Elementary with Honors	67	78	145	200
3. B1 Intermediate	95	204	299	395
4. B2 Intermediate with Honors	112	474	586	718
5. C1 Advanced	193	1,118	1,311	1,229
6. C2 Advanced	152	2,360	2,512	2,070
Totals	699	4,302	5,003	* 4,788

* The total number of unique single-character entries in the HSK word list (699) is not the same as the number of unique characters (4,788) since some entries contain characters that do not appear as standalone single-character entires in the HSK list.

About the Frequency Ratings

The relative frequency ratings (that is, the measure of "common-ness" of a particular character or word) come from analysis of a news-based corpus drawn from over 21,000 pages of the *People's Daily* web site. Within the corpus, some 10,245,000 (over 60,000 unique) terms of varying length, including single character terms, were identified and counted. Terms appearing more frequently have a higher rating than those appearing less frequently.

About the Lessons

Each lesson is divided into four parts, as follows:

- New Characters — These are characters that have not yet appeared in any prior lesson. Characters marked with a dagger (†) appear in the HSK lists as a single-character entry. Characters having an asterisk (*) are supplemental, and do not appear anywhere in the HSK lists. Occasionally, a character appears in the HSK list as part of a word at a level lower than when it appears as a standalone character. (For example, 对 is a level 2 term, but 对不起 is a level 1 term.) In these cases, I present the character in question at the earlier level.

- HSK Vocabulary — These are multicharacter words and phrases that appear in the HSK lists.

- Non-HSK Vocabulary — These are terms drawn from the news-based corpus. Supplemental vocabulary terms are chosen if they (a) have only characters that have appeared in the current or a prior lesson, and (b) have a relative frequency rating at or below the median frequency rating of the lesson's HSK vocabulary terms.

- Glossary — As a convenience, the dictionary definitions, as they appear in CC-CEDICT, are given for each of the terms from the first three sections.

The table below gives a summary of the lesson contents:

Vol.	HSK Level	Lessons	New Chars	HSK Vocab	Non-HSK Vocab	Total
1	1. A1 Elementary	1-6 (6)	193	68	77	338
	2. A2 Elementary	7-12 (6)	180	78	96	354
	3. B1 Intermediate	13-24 (12)	315	204	218	737
	4. B2 Intermediate	25-47 (23)	511	474	460	1,445
2	5. C1 Advanced	48-98 (51)	795	1,118	1,009	2,922
3	6. C2 Advanced	99-198 (100)	1,277	2,360	2,337	5,974
	Totals		**3,271**	**4,302**	**4,197**	**11,770**

Known Problems

Corpus bias is the tendency of the relative frequency ratings to favor certain terms over others, relative to the particular corpus at hand. For example, using a news-based corpus (as I have done) leads to frequency ratings that favor, among other things, people and place names over, say, bookish terms that one might find in a a fiction-based corpus.

Web page bias is special kind of corpus bias unique to web-based corpora, in which certain informational and navigational terms, such as 首页, 下页, and 推荐 are found much more frequently than what would otherwise be natural. Although I have gone to some lengths to ensure most such terms unrelated to the content have been omitted, some have inevitably slipped through.

Overlap occurs when more than one valid "word" of the same length overlap within a given string of characters. For example, the string 走出去 may be interpreted as 走出 + 去 or 走 + 出去. Without a complex set of rules for resolving such overlaps, I have taken the easy way out and simply ignored them. I found that fewer than 0.26% of the distinct n-grams counted were affected.

Part 1
HSK I (A1) ELEMENTARY
Lessons 1-6

Lesson 1

New Characters

1 †	2 †	3 †	4 †	5 †	6 †
的	在	是	和	了	一

7 †	8 †	9 †	10	11 †	12 †
年	个	有	中	月	这

13 †	14 †	15 †	16 †	17 †	18 †
他	大	多	我	日	人

19 †	20 †	21 †	22 †	23 †	24
都	会	不	很	三	国

25	26	27
们	作	工

Lesson 1

HSK Vocabulary

28 中国 30 工作

29 我们

Lesson 1

Glossary

1 的 (†) [de] of; structural particle: used before a noun, linking it to preceding possessive or descriptive attributive ◆ [dí] really and truly ◆ [dì] aim; clear

2 在 (†) [zài] (located) at; (to be) in; to exist; in the middle of doing sth; (indicating an action in progress)

3 是 (†) [shì] is; are; am; yes; to be

4 和 (†) [hé] surname He ◇ and; together with; with; sum; union; peace; harmony; Japanese related; Taiwan pr. [hàn] ◆ [hè] cap (a poem); to respond in singing ◆ [hú] to complete a set in mahjong or playing cards ◆ [huó] soft; warm ◆ [huò] to mix together; to blend

5 了 (†) [le] (modal particle intensifying preceding clause); (completed action marker) ◆ [liǎo] to finish; to achieve; to understand ◇ (of eyes) bright; clear-sighted; to understand clearly

6 一 (†) [yī] one; 1; single; a (article); as soon as; entire; whole; all; throughout; "one" radical in Chinese characters (Kangxi radical 1)

7 年 (†) [nián] year; CL: 个 [gè]

8 个 (†) [gè] individual; this; that; size; classifier for people or objects in general ◇ variant of 个 [gè]

9 有 (†) [yǒu] to have; there is; there are; to exist; to be

10 中 [zhōng] China; Chinese; surname Zhong ◇ within; among; in; middle; center; while (doing sth); during ◆ [zhòng] to hit (the mark); to be hit by; to suffer; to win (a prize, a lottery)

11 月 (†) [yuè] moon; month; CL:个 [gè], 轮 [lún]

12 这 (†) [zhè] this; these; (commonly pr. [zhèi] before a classifier, esp. in Beijing)

13 他 (†) [tā] he or him; (used for either sex when the sex is unknown or unimportant); (used before sb's name for emphasis); (used as a meaningless mock object); other; another

14 大 (†) [dà] big; huge; large; major; great; wide; deep; oldest; eldest ◆ [dài] see 大夫 [dàifu]

15 多 (†) [duō] many; much; a lot of; numerous; more; in excess; how (to what extent); multi-; Taiwan pr. [duó] when it means "how"

16 我 (†) [wǒ] I; me; my

17 日 (†) [rì] sun; day; date, day of the month; abbr. for 日本 Japan

18 人 (†) [rén] man; person; people; CL: 个 [gè], 位 [wèi]

19 都 (†) [dōu] all, both; entirely (due to) each; even; already ◆ [dū] surname Du ◇ capital city; metropolis

20 会 (†) [huì] can; be possible; be able to; will; be likely to; be sure to; to assemble; to meet; to gather; to see; union; group; association; CL: 个 [gè]; a moment (Taiwan pr. for this sense is [huǐ]) ◆ [kuài] to balance an account; accountancy; accounting

21 不 (†) [bù] (negative prefix); not; no

22 很 (†) [hěn] (adverb of degree); quite; very; awfully

23 三 (†) [sān] surname San ◇ three; 3

24 国 [guó] surname Guo ◇ country; nation; state; national; CL: 个 [gè]

25 们 [men] plural marker for pronouns, and nouns referring to individuals

26 作 [zuò] to do; to grow; to write or compose; to pretend; to regard as; to feel; writings or works

27 工 [gōng] work; worker; skill; profession; trade; craft; labor

28 中国 [zhōngguó] China; Middle Kingdom

29 我们 [wǒmen] we; us; ourselves; our

Lesson 1

30 工作 [gōngzuò] job; work; construction; task; CL: 个 [gè], 份 [fèn], 项 [xiàng]

Lesson 2

New Characters

1 †	2 †	3 †	4 †	5 †	6 †
好	来	下	做	能	家

7 †	8 †	9 †	10 †	11 †	12 †
小	你	五	里	她	二

13 †	14 †	15 †	16 †	17 †	18 †
去	本	四	点	水	想

19 †	20 †	21	22	23	24
岁	开	学	院	北	京

25	26	27	28	29
现	医	习	什	么

Lesson 2

HSK Vocabulary

30 北京

31 现在

32 学习

33 医院

34 什么

Non-HSK Vocabulary

35 他们

36 这个

Lesson 2

Glossary

1 好 (†) [hǎo] good; well; proper; good to; easy to; very; so; (suffix indicating completion or readiness) ◆ [hào] to be fond of

2 来 (†) [lái] to come; to arrive; to come round; ever since; next

3 下 (†) [xià] down; downwards; below; lower; later; next (week etc); second (of two parts); to decline; to go down

4 做 (†) [zuò] to do; to make; to produce; to write; to compose; to act as; to engage in; to hold (a party); to be; to become; to function (in some capacity); to serve as; to be used for; to form (a bond or relationship); to pretend; to feign; to act a part; to put on appearance

5 能 (†) [néng] surname Neng ◇ to be able to; to be capable of; ability; capability; able; capable; can possibly; (usually used in the negative) to have the possibility of

6 家 (†) [jiā] surname Jia ◇ home; family; classifier for families or businesses; refers to the philosophical schools of pre-Han China; noun suffix for specialists in some activity such as musician or revolutionary, corresponds to English -ist, -er, -ary or -ian; CL: 个 [gè]

7 小 (†) [xiǎo] small; tiny; few; young

8 你 (†) [nǐ] you (informal, as opposed to courteous 您[nín])

9 五 (†) [wǔ] five; 5

10 里 (†) [lǐ] lining; interior; inside; internal ◇ Li (surname) ◇ li (Chinese mile); 500 meters (modern); home; hometown; village; neighborhood; administrative unit

11 她 (†) [tā] she

12 二 (†) [èr] two; 2; stupid (Beijing dialect)

13 去 (†) [qù] to go; to go to (a place); to cause to go or send (sb); to remove; to get rid of; (when used either before or after a verb) to go in order to do sth; to be apart from in space or time; (after a verb of motion indicates movement away from the speaker); (used after certain verbs to indicate detachment or separation); (of a time or an event etc) just passed or elapsed

14 本 (†) [běn] roots or stems of plants; origin; source; this; the current; root; foundation; basis; classifier for books, periodicals, files etc; originally

15 四 (†) [sì] four; 4

16 点 (†) [diǎn] drop (of liquid); stain; spot; speck; jot; dot stroke (in Chinese characters); decimal point; point; mark (of degree or level); a place (with certain characteristics); iron bell; o'clock; a little; a bit; some; (point) unit of measurement for type; to touch on briefly; to make clear; to light; to ignite; to kindle; period of time at night (24 minutes) (old); a drip; to dibble; classifier for small indeterminate quantities

17 水 (†) [shuǐ] surname Shui ◇ water; river; liquid; beverage; additional charges or income; (of clothes) classifier for number of washes

18 想 (†) [xiǎng] to think; to believe; to suppose; to wish; to want; to miss

19 岁 (†) [suì] classifier for years (of age); year; year of crop harvests)

20 开 (†) [kāi] to open; to start; to turn on; to boil; to write out (a medical prescription); to operate (vehicle); abbr. for 开尔文 degrees Kelvin

21 学 [xué] learn; study; science; -ology

22 院 [yuàn] courtyard; institution; CL: 个 [gè]

23 北 [běi] north; to be defeated (classical)

24 京 [jīng] abbr. for Beijing; surname Jing; Jing ethnic minority ◇ capital city of a country; big; algebraic term for a large number (old); artificial mound (old)

Lesson 2

25 现 [xiàn] to appear; present; now; existing; current

26 医 [yī] medical; medicine; doctor; to cure; to treat

27 习 [xí] surname Xi ◇ to practice; to study; habit

28 什 [shén] what ◆ [shí] ten (used in fractions, writing checks etc); assorted; miscellaneous

29 么 [má] exclamatory final particle ◆ [ma] interrogative final particle ◆ [me] suffix, used to form interrogative 什么, what?, indefinite 这么 thus etc

30 北京 [běijīng] Beijing, capital of People's Republic of China; Peking; PRC government

31 现在 [xiànzài] now; at present; at the moment; modern; current; nowadays

32 学习 [xuéxí] to learn; to study

33 医院 [yīyuàn] hospital; CL: 所 [suǒ], 家 [jiā], 座 [zuò]

34 什么 [shénme] what?; who?; something; anything

35 他们 [tāmen] they

36 这个 [zhège] this; this one

Lesson 3

New Characters

1	2	3 *	4	5 *	6 †
时	天	刘	生	杨	那

7	8 †	9 †	10 †	11 †	12 †
先	太	吃	没	书	钱

13 †	14 †	15 †	16	17 †	18 †
十	少	六	电	呢	买

19 †	20 †	21 †	22 †	23 †	24 †
爱	七	住	写	请	八

25	26	27	28	29	30
校	今	视	影	候	昨

Lesson 3

HSK Vocabulary

31 学生   35 学校
32 时候   36 先生
33 今天   37 电影
34 电视   38 昨天

Non-HSK Vocabulary

39 没有   43 不能
40 今年   44 中的
41 我国   45 日电
42 不是

Lesson 3

Glossary

1 时 [shí] surname Shi ◇ o'clock; time; when; hour; season; period

2 天 [tiān] day; sky; heaven

3 刘 (*) [liú] surname Liu

4 生 [shēng] to be born; to give birth; life; to grow; raw, uncooked

5 杨 (*) [yáng] surname Yang ◇ poplar

6 那 (†) [nǎ] variant of 哪 [nǎ] ◆ [nà] that; those; then (in that case); commonly pr. [nèi] before a classifier, esp. in Beijing

7 先 [xiān] early; prior; former; in advance; first

8 太 (†) [tài] highest; greatest; too (much); very; extremely

9 吃 (†) [chī] to eat; to consume; to eat at (a cafeteria etc); to eradicate; to destroy; to absorb; to suffer ◆ [jí] stammer

10 没 (†) [méi] (negative prefix for verbs); have not; not ◆ [mò] drowned; to end; to die; to inundate

11 书 (†) [shū] book; letter; CL: 本 [běn], 册 [cè], 部 [bù]

12 钱 (†) [qián] surname Qian ◇ coin; money; CL: 笔 [bǐ]

13 十 (†) [shí] ten; 10

14 少 (†) [shǎo] few; little; lack ◆ [shào] young

15 六 (†) [liù] six; 6

16 电 [diàn] electric; electricity; electrical

17 呢 (†) [ne] particle indicating that a previously asked question is to be applied to the preceding word ("What about ...?", "And ...?"); particle for inquiring about location ("Where is ...?"); particle serving as a pause, to emphasize the preceding words and allow the listener time to take them on board ("ok?", "are you with me?"); (at the end of a declarative sentence) particle indicating continuation of a state or action; particle indicating strong affirmation ◆ [nī] this (Cantonese); see also 哩 [lī] ◆ [ní] woolen material

18 买 (†) [mǎi] to buy; to purchase

19 爱 (†) [ài] to love; affection; to be fond of; to like

20 七 (†) [qī] seven; 7

21 住 (†) [zhù] to live; to dwell; to stay; to reside; to stop; (suffix indicating firmness, steadiness, or coming to a halt)

22 写 (†) [xiě] to write

23 请 (†) [qǐng] to ask; to invite; please (do sth); to treat (to a meal etc); to request

24 八 (†) [bā] eight; 8

25 校 [jiào] to proofread; to check; to compare ◆ [xiào] school; military officer; CL: 所 [suǒ]

26 今 [jīn] today; modern; present; current; this; now

27 视 [shì] to look at; to regard; to inspect

28 影 [yǐng] picture; image; film; movie; photograph; reflection; shadow; trace

29 候 [hòu] wait

30 昨 [zuó] yesterday

31 学生 [xuésheng] student; schoolchild

32 时候 [shíhou] time; length of time; moment; period

33 今天 [jīntiān] today; at the present; now

34 电视 [diànshì] television; TV; CL: 台 [tái], 个 [gè]

35 学校 [xuéxiào] school; CL: 所 [suǒ]

Lesson 3

36 先生 [xiānsheng] Mister (Mr.) ◇ teacher; husband; doctor (topolect); CL: 位 [wèi]

37 电影 [diànyǐng] movie; film; CL: 部 [bù], 片 [piàn], 幕 [mù], 场 [chǎng]

38 昨天 [zuótiān] yesterday

39 没有 [méiyǒu] haven't; hasn't; doesn't exist; to not have; to not be

40 今年 [jīnnián] this year

41 我国 [wǒguó] our country; China

42 不是 [bùshì] no; is not; not ◆ [bùshi] fault; blame

43 不能 [bùnéng] cannot; must not; should not

44 中的 [zhòngdì] to hit the target; to hit the nail on the head

45 日电 [rìdiàn] NEC (Nippon Electronic Company); abbr. for 日电电子

Lesson 4

New Characters

1	2	3	4	5	6 *
上	老	分	东	西	吴

7 †	8 *	9 *	10 †	11 †	12 *
吗	徐	郭	谁	朱	亩

13 †	14 †	15 †	16 †	17 †	18 †
听	热	回	字	叫	九

19 †	20	21 †	22 †	23 †	24 †
坐	师	块	读	喝	菜

25	26	27	28	29	30
友	果	喜	钟	欢	认

31	32	33	34	35
识	午	朋	怎	苹

Lesson 4

HSK Vocabulary

36	认识		42	上午
37	朋友		43	东西
38	怎么		44	喜欢
39	分钟		45	老师
40	医生		46	多少
41	下午		47	苹果

Non-HSK Vocabulary

48	日本		57	有的
49	大学		58	一家
50	人们		59	昨日
51	不少		60	年来
52	那么		61	这么
53	大会		62	一下
54	不会		63	中国人
55	这里		64	有了
56	十二		65	一点

Lesson 4

Glossary

1 上 [shǎng] see 上声 [shǎngshēng] ◆ [shàng] on top; upon; above; upper; previous; first (of multiple parts); to climb; to get onto; to go up; to attend (class or university)

2 老 [lǎo] prefix used before the surname of a person or a numeral indicating the order of birth of the children in a family or to indicate affection or familiarity; old (of people); venerable (person); experienced; of long standing; always; all the time; of the past; very; outdated; (of meat etc) tough

3 分 [fēn] to divide; to separate; to allocate; to distinguish (good and bad); part or subdivision; fraction; one tenth (of certain units); unit of length equivalent to 0.33 cm; minute; a point (in sports or games); 0.01 yuan (unit of money) ◆ [fèn] part; share; ingredient; component

4 东 [dōng] surname Dong ◇ east; host (i.e. sitting on east side of guest); landlord

5 西 [xī] the West; abbr. for Spain 西班牙[Xī bān yá]; Spanish ◇ west

6 吴 (*) [wú] surname Wu; area comprising southern Jiangsu, northern Zhejiang and Shanghai; name of states in Southern China at different historical periods

7 吗 (†) [mǎ] see 吗啡, morphine ◆ [ma] (question tag)

8 徐 (*) [xú] surname Xu ◇ slowly; gently

9 郭 (*) [guō] surname Guo ◇ outer city wall

10 谁 (†) [shéi] who; also pr. [shuí]

11 朱 (*) [zhū] surname Zhu ◇ vermilion ◇ cinnabar; see 朱砂 [zhūshā]

12 亩 (*) [mǔ] classifier for fields; unit of area equal to one fifteenth of a hectare

13 听 (†) [tīng] to listen; to hear; to obey; a can (loanword from English "tin"); classifier for canned beverages ◆ [tìng] to let; to allow

14 热 (†) [rè] to warm up; to heat up; hot (of weather); heat; fervent

15 回 (†) [huí] to circle; to go back; to turn around; to answer; to return; to revolve; Hui ethnic group (Chinese Muslims); time; classifier for acts of a play; section or chapter (of a classic book) ◇ to curve; to return; to revolve

16 字 (†) [zì] letter; symbol; character; word; CL: 个 [gè]; courtesy or style name traditionally given to males aged 20 in dynastic China

17 叫 (†) [jiào] to shout; to call; to order; to ask; to be called; by (indicates agent in the passive mood)

18 九 (†) [jiǔ] nine; 9

19 坐 (†) [zuò] surname Zuo ◇ to sit; to take a seat; to take (a bus, airplane etc); to bear fruit

20 师 [shī] teacher; master; expert; model; army division; (old) troops; to dispatch troops

21 块 (†) [kuài] lump (of earth); chunk; piece; classifier for pieces of cloth, cake, soap etc; colloquial word for yuan (or other unit of currency such as Hong Kong or US dollar etc), usually as 块钱

22 读 (†) [dòu] comma; phrase marked by pause ◆ [dú] to read; to study; reading of word (i.e. pronunciation), similar to 拼音 [pīn yīn]

23 喝 (†) [hē] to drink; My goodness! ◆ [hè] to shout loudly

24 菜 (†) [cài] dish (type of food); vegetables; vegetable; cuisine; CL: 盘 [pán], 道 [dào]

25 友 [yǒu] friend

26 果 [guǒ] fruit; result; resolute; indeed; if really

27 喜 [xǐ] to be fond of; to like; to enjoy; to be happy; to feel pleased; happiness; delight; glad

Lesson 4

28 钟 [zhōng] surname Zhong ◇ handleless cup; goblet; to concentrate ◇ clock; o'clock; time as measured in hours and minutes; bell; CL: 架 [jià], 座 [zuò]

29 欢 [huān] joyous; happy; pleased

30 认 [rèn] to recognize; to know; to admit

31 识 [shí] to know; knowledge; Taiwan pr. [shì] ◆ [zhì] to record; to write a footnote

32 午 [wǔ] 7th earthly branch: 11 a.m.-1 p.m., noon, 5th solar month (6th June-6th July), year of the Horse

33 朋 [péng] friend

34 怎 [zěn] how

35 苹 [pín] marsiliaceae; clover fern ◆ [píng] (artemisia); duckweed ◇ apple

36 认识 [rènshi] to know; to recognize; to be familiar with; to get acquainted with sb; knowledge; understanding; awareness; cognition

37 朋友 [péngyou] friend; CL: 个 [gè], 位 [wèi]

38 怎么 [zěnme] how?; what?; why?

39 分钟 [fēnzhōng] minute

40 医生 [yīshēng] doctor; CL: 个 [gè], 位 [wèi], 名 [míng]

41 下午 [xiàwǔ] afternoon; CL: 个 [gè]; p.m.

42 上午 [shàngwǔ] morning; CL: 个 [gè]

43 东西 [dōngxī] east and west ◆ [dōngxi] thing; stuff; person; CL: 个 [gè], 件 [jiàn]

44 喜欢 [xǐhuan] to like; to be fond of

45 老师 [lǎoshī] teacher; CL: 个 [gè], 位 [wèi]

46 多少 [duōshǎo] number; amount; somewhat ◆ [duōshao] how much; how many; which (number); as much as

47 苹果 [píngguǒ] apple; CL: 个 [gè], 颗 [kē]

48 日本 [rìběn] Japan; Japanese

49 大学 [dàxué] the Great Learning, one of the Four Books 四书 [Sìshū] in Confucianism ◇ university; college; CL: 所 [suǒ]

50 人们 [rénmen] people

51 不少 [bùshǎo] many; a lot; not few

52 那么 [nàme] like that; in that way; or so; so; so very much; about; in that case

53 大会 [dàhuì] general assembly; general meeting; convention; CL: 个 [gè], 届 [jiè]

54 不会 [bùhuì] improbable; unlikely; will not (act, happen etc); not able; not having learned to do sth

55 这里 [zhèlǐ] here

56 十二 [shí'èr] twelve; 12

57 有的 [yǒude] (there are) some (who are...); some (exist)

58 一家 [yījiā] the whole family; the same family; the family... (when preceded by a family name); group

59 昨日 [zuórì] yesterday

60 年来 [niánlái] this past year; over the last years

61 这么 [zhème] so much; this much; how much?; this way; like this

62 一下 [yīxià] (used after a verb) give it a go; to do (sth for a bit to give it a try); one time; once; in a while; all of a sudden; all at once

63 中国人 [zhōngguórén] Chinese person

64 有了 [yǒule] I've got a solution!; to have a bun in the oven (abbr. for 有了胎[yǒu le tāi])

65 一点 [yīdiǎn] a bit; a little; one dot; one point

Lesson 5

New Characters

1	2	3	4	5	6
说	高	名	同	打	明

7	8	9	10	11	12
女	子	机	气	飞	话

13	14	15 †	16	17 †	18 *
亮	兴	茶	谢	零	曹

19 *	20 *	21 †	22 *	23 *	24
沈	暨	些	君	凤	儿

25 †	26 †	27	28	29 †	30
哪	冷	服	衣	猫	脑

31 †	32	33	34	35	36
狗	样	姐	妈	爸	漂

Lesson 5

HSK Vocabulary

37	儿子	43	名字	49	明天
38	女儿	44	妈妈	50	说话
39	电脑	45	同学	51	谢谢
40	高兴	46	衣服	52	漂亮
41	飞机	47	打电话	53	爸爸
42	天气	48	小姐	54	怎么样

Non-HSK Vocabulary

55	这些	64	大学生	73	不好
56	来说	65	十一	74	国有
57	电话	66	热点	75	东北
58	有些	67	小学	76	三国
59	有人	68	怎样	77	中学
60	多个	69	读书	78	多年来
61	同样	70	下来	79	有点
62	电子	71	有一些		
63	你们	72	医学		

Lesson 5

Glossary

1 说 [shuì] to canvass; to persuade; see 游说 [yóushuì], to canvass and 说客 [shuìkè], persuasive speaker ◆ [shuō] to speak; to say; a theory (usually in compounds such as 日心说 heliocentric theory)

2 高 [gāo] surname Gao ◇ high; tall; above average; loud; your (honorific)

3 名 [míng] name; noun (part of speech); place (e.g. among winners); famous; classifier for people

4 同 [tóng] like; same; similar; together; alike; with ◆ [tòng] see 胡同 [hútòng]

5 打 [dá] dozen ◆ [dǎ] to beat; to strike; to hit; to break; to type; to mix up; to build; to fight; to fetch; to make; to tie up; to issue; to shoot; to calculate; to play (a game); since; from

6 明 [míng] Ming Dynasty (1368-1644); surname Ming; Ming (c. 2000 BC), fourth of the legendary Flame Emperors, 炎帝 [Yándì] descended from Shennong 神农 [Shénnóng] Farmer God ◇ bright; opposite: dark 暗 [àn]; (of meaning) clear; to understand; next; public or open; wise; generic term for a sacrifice to the gods

7 女 [nǚ] female; woman; daughter ◆ [rǔ] archaic variant of 汝 [rǔ]

8 子 [zǐ] son; child; seed; egg; small thing; 1st earthly branch: 11 p.m.-1 a.m., midnight, 11th solar month (7th December to 5th January), year of the Rat; Viscount, fourth of five orders of nobility 五等爵位 [wǔděng juéwèi] ◆ [zi] (noun suffix)

9 机 [jī] surname Ji ◇ machine; engine; opportunity; intention; aircraft; pivot; crucial point; flexible (quick-witted); organic; CL: 台 [tái]

10 气 [qì] gas; air; smell; weather; vital breath; to anger; to get angry; to be enraged

11 飞 [fēi] to fly

12 话 [huà] dialect; language; spoken words; speech; talk; words; conversation; what sb said; CL: 种 [zhǒng], 席 [xí], 句 [jù], 口 [kǒu], 番 [fān]

13 亮 [liàng] bright; clear; resonant; to shine; to show; to reveal

14 兴 [xīng] surname Xing ◇ to rise; to flourish; to become popular; to start; to encourage; to get up; (often used in the negative) to permit or allow (topolect); maybe (topolect) ◆ [xìng] feeling or desire to do sth; interest in sth; excitement

15 茶 (†) [chá] tea; tea plant; CL: 杯 [bēi], 壶 [hú]

16 谢 [xiè] surname Xie ◇ to thank; to apologize; to wither (of flowers, leaves etc); to decline

17 零 (†) [líng] zero; nought; zero sign; fractional; fragmentary; odd (of numbers); (placed between two numbers to indicate a smaller quantity followed by a larger one); fraction; (in mathematics) remainder (after division); extra; to wither and fall; to wither

18 曹 (*) [cáo] surname Cao; Zhou Dynasty vassal state ◇ class or grade; generation; plaintiff and defendant (old); government department (old)

19 沈 (*) [chén] variant of 沉 [chén] ◆ [shěn] surname Shen; place name

20 暨 (*) [jì] and; to reach to; the limits

21 些 (†) [xiē] some; few; several; measure word indicating a small amount or small number (greater than 1)

22 君 (*) [jūn] monarch; lord; gentleman; ruler

23 凤 (*) [fèng] surname Feng ◇ phoenix

24 儿 [ér] son ◆ [r] non-syllabic diminutive suffix; retroflex final

25 哪 (†) [nǎ] how; which ◆ [na] (particle equivalent to 啊 after noun ending in -n) ◆ [něi] which? (interrogative, followed by classifier or numeral-classifier)

26 冷 (†) [lěng] cold

Lesson 5

27 服 [fú] clothes; dress; garment; to serve; to obey; to convince; to acclimatize; to take (medicine); mourning clothes; to wear mourning clothes ◆ [fù] dose (measure word for medicine)

28 衣 [yī] clothes; CL:件 [jiàn] ◆ [yì] to dress; to wear; to put on (clothes)

29 猫 (†) [māo] cat; CL: 只 [zhī]

30 脑 [nǎo] brain; mind; head; essence

31 狗 (†) [gǒu] dog; CL: 只 [zhī], 条 [tiáo]

32 样 [yàng] manner; pattern; way; appearance; shape; CL: 个 [gè]

33 姐 [jiě] older sister

34 妈 [mā] ma; mom; mother

35 爸 [bà] father; dad; pa; papa

36 漂 [piāo] to float; to drift ◆ [piǎo] to bleach ◆ [piào] elegant; polished

37 儿子 [érzi] son

38 女儿 [nǚ'ér] daughter

39 电脑 [diànnǎo] computer; CL: 台 [tái]

40 高兴 [gāoxìng] happy; glad; willing (to do sth); in a cheerful mood

41 飞机 [fēijī] airplane; CL:架 [jià]

42 天气 [tiānqì] weather

43 名字 [míngzi] name (of a person or thing); CL: 个 [gè]

44 妈妈 [māma] mama; mommy; mother; CL: 个 [gè], 位 [wèi]

45 同学 [tóngxué] to study at the same school; fellow student; classmate; CL: 位 [wèi], 个 [gè]

46 衣服 [yīfu] clothes; CL: 件 [jiàn], 套 [tào]

47 打电话 [dǎdiànhuà] to make a telephone call

48 小姐 [xiǎojie] young lady; miss; (slang) prostitute; CL: 个 [gè], 位 [wèi]

49 明天 [míngtiān] tomorrow

50 说话 [shuōhuà] to speak; to say; to talk; to gossip; to tell stories; talk; word

51 谢谢 [xièxie] to thank; thanks

52 漂亮 [piàoliang] pretty; beautiful

53 爸爸 [bàba] (informal) father; CL: 个 [gè], 位 [wèi]

54 怎么样 [zěnmeyàng] how?; how about?; how was it?; how are things?

55 这些 [zhèxiē] these

56 来说 [láishuō] to have one's say; to interpret a topic (from a certain point of view); now we come to talk about it, ...

57 电话 [diànhuà] telephone; CL:部 [bù]; phone call; CL: 通 [tōng]; phone number

58 有些 [yǒuxiē] some; somewhat

59 有人 [yǒurén] someone; people; anyone; there is someone there; occupied (as in restroom)

60 多个 [duōge] many; multiple; multi- (faceted, ethnic etc)

61 同样 [tóngyàng] same; equal; equivalent

62 电子 [diànzǐ] electronic; electron

63 你们 [nǐmen] you (plural)

64 大学生 [dàxuéshēng] university student; college student

65 十一 [shíyī] eleven; 11

66 热点 [rèdiǎn] hot spot; point of special interest

67 小学 [xiǎoxué] primary school; CL: 个 [gè]

68 怎样 [zěnyàng] how; why

69 读书 [dúshū] to read a book; to study; to attend school

70 下来 [xiàlai] to come down; (after verb of motion, indicates motion down and towards us, also fig.); (indicates continuation from the past towards us); to be harvested (of crops); to be over (of a period of time); to go among the masses (said of leaders)

71 有一些 [yǒuyīxiē] somewhat; rather; some

Lesson 5

72 医学 [yīxué] medicine; medical science; study of medicine

73 不好 [bùhǎo] no good

74 国有 [guóyǒu] nationalized; public; government owned; state-owned

75 东北 [dōngběi] northeast

76 三国 [sānguó] Three Kingdoms period (220-280) in Chinese history; several Three Kingdoms periods in Korean history, esp. from 1st century AD to unification under Silla 新罗 [Xīnluó] in 658

77 中学 [zhōngxué] middle school; CL: 个 [gè]

78 多年来 [duōniánlái] for the past many years

79 有点 [yǒudiǎn] a little

Lesson 6

New Characters

1	2	3	4	5	6
对	看	出	起	车	前

7	8	9	10	11	12
再	站	期	米	店	商

13	14	15	16	17	18
馆	面	见	系	客	火

19	20	21	22	23	24
星	关	雨	汉	杯	租

25	26	27	28	29	30 *
语	饭	睡	觉	桌	耶

31 *	32 *	33	34 †	35 *	36 *
淇	彬	椅	喂	骆	粪

Lesson 6

HSK Vocabulary

37 出租车	45 星期	53 再见
38 商店	46 汉语	54 下雨
39 看见	47 这儿	55 没关系
40 前面	48 椅子	56 那儿
41 火车站	49 桌子	57 饭馆
42 中午	50 对不起	58 不客气
43 睡觉	51 米饭	
44 哪儿	52 杯子	

Non-HSK Vocabulary

59 作出	68 没有什么	77 那样的
60 做出	69 电视机	78 八十
61 女子	70 医学院	79 五四
62 那里	71 商机	80 北京人
63 北大	72 叫做	81 出面
64 高中	73 日本人	82 再说
65 十五	74 生前	83 上前
66 再现	75 有的是	
67 看出	76 天上	

Lesson 6

Glossary

1 对 [duì] couple; pair; to be opposite; to oppose; to face; versus; for; to; correct (answer); to answer; to reply; to direct (towards sth); right

2 看 [kān] to look after; to take care of; to watch; to guard ◆ [kàn] to see; to look at; to read; to watch; to consider; to regard as; to view as; to treat as; to judge; (after repeated verb) to give it a try; depending on (how you're judging); to visit; to call on; to treat (an illness); to look after; Watch out! (for a danger)

3 出 [chū] to go out; to come out; to occur; to produce; to go beyond; to rise; to put forth; to happen; classifier for dramas, plays, operas etc

4 起 [qǐ] to rise; to raise; to get up; to set out; to start; to appear; to launch; to initiate (action); to draft; to establish; to get (from a depot or counter); verb suffix, to start; (before place or time) starting from; classifier for occurrences or unpredictable events: case, instance; classifier for groups: batch, group

5 车 [chē] surname Che ◇ car; vehicle; CL: 辆 [liàng]; machine; to shape with a lathe ◆ [jū] war chariot (archaic); rook (in Chinese chess); rook (in chess)

6 前 [qián] front; forward; ahead; ago; before; first; former; formerly; future; BC (e.g. 前 293 年)

7 再 [zài] again; once more; re-; second; another; then (after sth, and not until then)

8 站 [zhàn] station; to stand; to halt; to stop; branch of a company or organization; website

9 期 [qī] a period of time; phase; stage; (used for issue of a periodical, courses of study); time; term; period; to hope; Taiwan pr. [qí]

10 米 [mǐ] surname Mi ◇ rice; CL: 粒 [lì]; meter (classifier)

11 店 [diàn] inn; shop; store; CL: 家 [jiā]

12 商 [shāng] the Shang dynasty, 16th to 11th century BC ◇ commerce; to consult; quotient; 2nd note in pentatonic scale

13 馆 [guǎn] building; shop; term for certain service establishments; embassy or consulate; schoolroom (old); CL: 家 [jiā]

14 面 [miàn] face; side; surface; aspect; top; classifier for flat surfaces such as drums, mirrors, flags etc ◇ flour; noodles

15 见 [jiàn] to see; to meet; to appear (to be sth); to interview ◆ [xiàn] to appear

16 系 [jì] to tie; to fasten; to button up ◆ [xì] to connect; to relate to; to tie up; to bind; to be (literary) ◇ system; department; faculty ◇ to connect; to arrest; to worry

17 客 [kè] customer; visitor; guest

18 火 [huǒ] surname Huo ◇ fire; urgent; ammunition; fiery or flaming; internal heat (Chinese medicine); hot (popular); classifier for military units (old)

19 星 [xīng] star; satellite; small amount

20 关 [guān] surname Guan ◇ mountain pass; to close; to shut; to turn off; to concern; to involve

21 雨 [yǔ] rain; CL: 阵 [zhèn], 场 [cháng]

22 汉 [hàn] Han ethnic group; Chinese (language); the Han dynasty (206 BC–220 AD) ◇ man

23 杯 [bēi] cup; classifier for certain containers of liquids: glass, cup

24 租 [zū] to hire; to rent; to charter; to rent out; to lease out; rent; land tax

25 语 [yǔ] dialect; language; speech ◆ [yù] to tell to

26 饭 [fàn] food; cuisine; cooked rice; meal; CL: 碗 [wǎn], 顿 [dùn]

27 睡 [shuì] to sleep

28 觉 [jiào] a nap; a sleep; CL: 场 [cháng] ◆ [jué] feel; find that; thinking; awake; aware

29 桌 [zhuō] table

Lesson 6

30 耶 (*) [yē] (phonetic ye) ◆ [yé] interrogative particle (classical) ◆ [ye] final particle indicating enthusiasm etc

31 淇 (*) [qí] name of a river

32 彬 (*) [bīn] ornamental; refined

33 椅 [yǐ] chair

34 喂 (†) [wèi] hello (interj., esp. on telephone); hey; to feed (sb or some animal) ◇ to feed

35 骆 (*) [luò] surname Luo ◇ camel; white horse with a black mane (archaic)

36 粪 (*) [fèn] manure; dung

37 出租车 [chūzūchē] taxi; (Taiwan) rental car

38 商店 [shāngdiàn] store; shop; CL: 家 [jiā], 个 [gè]

39 看见 [kànjiàn] to see; to catch sight of

40 前面 [qiánmiàn] ahead; in front; preceding; above

41 火车站 [huǒchēzhàn] train station

42 中午 [zhōngwǔ] noon; midday; CL: 个 [gè]

43 睡觉 [shuìjiào] to go to bed; to sleep

44 哪儿 [nǎr] where?; wherever; anywhere

45 星期 [xīngqī] week; CL: 个 [gè]; day of the week; Sunday

46 汉语 [hànyǔ] Chinese language; CL: 门 [mén]

47 这儿 [zhèr] here

48 椅子 [yǐzi] chair; CL: 把 [bǎ], 套 [tào]

49 桌子 [zhuōzi] table; desk; CL: 张 [zhāng], 套 [tào]

50 对不起 [duìbuqǐ] unworthy; to let down; I'm sorry; excuse me; pardon me; if you please; sorry? (please repeat)

51 米饭 [mǐfàn] (cooked) rice

52 杯子 [bēizi] cup; glass; CL: 个 [gè], 支 [zhī], 枝 [zhī]

53 再见 [zàijiàn] goodbye; see you again later

54 下雨 [xiàyǔ] to rain; rainy

55 没关系 [méiguānxi] it doesn't matter

56 那儿 [nàr] there

57 饭馆 [fànguǎn] restaurant; CL: 家 [jiā]

58 不客气 [bùkèqi] you're welcome; impolite; rude; blunt; don't mention it

59 作出 [zuòchū] to put out; to come up with; to make (a choice, decision, proposal, response, comment etc); to issue (a permit, statement, explanation, apology, reassurance to the public etc); to draw (conclusion); to deliver (speech, judgment); to devise (explanation); to extract

60 做出 [zuòchū] to put out; to issue

61 女子 [nǚzǐ] woman; female

62 那里 [nàli] there; that place

63 北大 [běidà] Beijing University (abbr. for 北京大学)

64 高中 [gāozhōng] senior high school; abbr. for 高级中学 [gāojí zhōngxué]

65 十五 [shíwǔ] fifteen; 15

66 再现 [zàixiàn] to recreate; to reconstruct (a historical relic)

67 看出 [kànchū] to make out; to see

68 没有什么 [méiyǒushénme] it is nothing; there's nothing ... about it

69 电视机 [diànshìjī] television set; CL: 台 [tái]

70 医学院 [yīxuéyuàn] medical school

71 商机 [shāngjī] business opportunity; commercial opportunity

72 叫做 [jiàozuò] to be called; to be known as

73 日本人 [rìběnrén] Japanese person or people

74 生前 [shēngqián] (of a deceased) during one's life; while living

75 有的是 [yǒudeshì] have plenty of; there's no lack of

76 天上 [tiānshàng] celestial; heavenly

Lesson 6

77 那样的 [nàyàngde] that kind of; that sort of

78 八十 [bāshí] eighty; 80

79 五四 [wǔsì] fourth of May, cf 五四运动, national renewal movement that started with 4th May 1919 protest against the Treaty of Versailles

80 北京人 [běijīngrén] Beijing resident; Peking ape-man, Homo erectus pekinensis (c. 600,000 BC), discovered in 1921 at Zhoukoudian 周口店 [Zhōukǒudiàn], Beijing

81 出面 [chūmiàn] to appear personally; to step in; to step forth; to show up

82 再说 [zàishuō] to say again; to put off a discussion until later; moreover; what's more; besides

83 上前 [shàngqián] to go forward; front upper

Part 2
HSK II (A2) ELEMENTARY
Lessons 7-12

Lesson 7

New Characters

1	2 †	3 †	4 †	5 †	6 †
为	也	等	到	就	新

7	8 †	9 †	10 †	11 †	12 †
以	还	最	两	让	着

13	14 †	15 †	16	17 †	18 †
已	给	张	可	次	过

19 †	20 †	21	22	23	24
得	比	因	经	第	公

25	26	27	28	29	30
问	间	游	题	司	旅

31
始

Lesson 7

HSK Vocabulary

32 问题

33 可以

34 公司

35 已经

36 因为

37 旅游

38 开始

39 第一

40 时间

Lesson 7

Glossary

1 为 [wéi] as (in the capacity of); to take sth as; to act as; to serve as; to behave as; to become; to be; to do ◇ as (i.e. in the capacity of); to take sth as; to act as; to serve as; to behave as; to become; to be; to do ◆ [wèi] because of; for; to

2 也 (†) [yě] surname Ye ◇ also; too; (in Classical Chinese) final particle implying affirmation

3 等 (†) [děng] class; rank; grade; equal to; same as; to wait for; to await; et cetera; and so on; et al. (and other authors); after; as soon as; once

4 到 (†) [dào] to (a place); until (a time); up to; to go; to arrive

5 就 (†) [jiù] at once; right away; only; just (emphasis); as early as; already; as soon as; then; in that case; as many as; even if; to approach; to move towards; to undertake; to engage in; to suffer; subjected to; to accomplish; to take advantage of; to go with (of foods); with regard to; concerning

6 新 (†) [xīn] abbr. for Xinjiang 新疆 [Xīnjiāng] or Singapore 新加坡 [Xīnjiāpō] ◇ new; newly; meso- (chemistry)

7 以 [yǐ] abbr. for Israel 以色列 [Yǐsèliè] ◇ to use; according to; so as to; by means of; in order to; by; with; because

8 还 (†) [hái] still; still in progress; still more; yet; even more; in addition; fairly; passably (good); as early as; even; also; else ◆ [huán] surname Huan ◇ to pay back; to return

9 最 (†) [zuì] most; the most; -est (superlative suffix)

10 两 (†) [liǎng] both; two; ounce; some; a few; tael; weight equal to 50 grams

11 让 (†) [ràng] to yield; to permit; to let sb do sth; to have sb do sth

12 着 (†) [zhāo] catch; receive; suffer ◆ [zháo] to touch; to come in contact with; to feel; to be affected by; to catch fire; to fall asleep; to burn ◆ [zhe] particle attached after verb to indicate action in progress, like -ing ending ◆ [zhuó] to wear (clothes); to contact; to use; to apply

13 已 [yǐ] already; to stop; then; afterwards

14 给 (†) [gěi] to; for; for the benefit of; to give; to allow; to do sth (for sb); (passive particle) ◆ [jǐ] to supply; to provide

15 张 (†) [zhāng] surname Zhang ◇ to open up; to spread; sheet of paper; classifier for flat objects, sheet; classifier for votes

16 可 [kě] can; may; able to; to approve; to permit; certain(ly); to suit; very (particle used for emphasis)

17 次 (†) [cì] next in sequence; second; the second (day, time etc); secondary; vice-; sub-; infra-; inferior quality; substandard; order; sequence; hypo- (chemistry); classifier for enumerated events: time

18 过 (†) [guò] surname Guo ◇ (experienced action marker); to cross; to go over; to pass (time); to celebrate (a holiday); to live; to get along; excessively; too-

19 得 (†) [dé] to obtain; to get; to gain; to catch (a disease); proper; suitable; proud; contented; to allow; to permit; ready; finished ◆ [de] structural particle: used after a verb (or adjective as main verb), linking it to following phrase indicating effect, degree, possibility etc ◆ [děi] to have to; must; ought to; to need to

20 比 (†) [bǐ] Belgium; Belgian; abbr. for 比利时 [Bǐlìshí] ◇ (particle used for comparison and "-er than"); to compare; to contrast; to gesture (with hands); ratio ◆ [bì] to associate with; to be near

21 因 [yīn] cause; reason; because

Lesson 7

22 经 [jīng] surname Jing ◇ classics; sacred book; scripture; to pass through; to undergo; warp; longitude; abbr. for economics 经济 [jīngjì]

23 第 [dì] (prefix indicating ordinal number, e.g. first, number two etc)

24 公 [gōng] public; collectively owned; common; international (e.g. high seas, metric system, calendar); make public; fair; just; Duke, highest of five orders of nobility 五等爵位 [wǔděngjuéwèi]; honorable (gentlemen); father-in-law; male (animal)

25 问 [wèn] to ask

26 间 [jiān] between; among; within a definite time or space; room; section of a room or lateral space between two pairs of pillars; classifier for rooms ♦ [jiàn] gap; to separate; to thin out (seedlings); to sow discontent

27 游 [yóu] surname You ◇ to swim; to walk; to tour; to roam; to travel ◇ to walk; to tour; to roam; to travel

28 题 [tí] surname Ti ◇ topic; problem for discussion; exam question; subject; to inscribe; to mention; CL: 个 [gè], 道 [dào]

29 司 [sī] surname Si ◇ to take charge of; to manage; department (under a ministry)

30 旅 [lǚ] trip; travel; to travel

31 始 [shǐ] to begin; to start; then; only then

32 问题 [wèntí] question; problem; issue; topic; CL: 个 [gè]

33 可以 [kěyǐ] can; may; possible; able to

34 公司 [gōngsī] (business) company; company; firm; corporation; incorporated; CL: 家 [jiā]

35 已经 [yǐjīng] already

36 因为 [yīnwèi] because; owing to; on account of

37 旅游 [lǚyóu] trip; journey; tourism; travel; tour

38 开始 [kāishǐ] to begin; beginning; to start; initial; CL: 个 [gè]

39 第一 [dìyī] first; number one

40 时间 [shíjiān] time; period; CL: 段 [duàn]

Lesson 8

New Characters

1	2	3 †	4 †	5 †	6 †
但	所	它	长	路	每

7 †	8 †	9	10 †	11 †	12 †
走	红	正	外	快	号

13 †	14 †	15 †	16	17 †	18 †
进	件	您	非	百	真

19	20	21	22	23	24
手	常	望	希	绍	介

25
孩

Lesson 8

HSK Vocabulary

26 但是
27 可能
28 介绍
29 希望
30 大家
31 非常

32 所以
33 手机
34 正在
35 去年
36 孩子

Non-HSK Vocabulary

37 就是
38 一些
39 这样

40 有关
41 以上
42 不同

Lesson 8

Glossary

1 但 [dàn] but; yet; however; only; merely; still

2 所 [suǒ] actually; place; classifier for houses, small buildings, institutions etc; that which; particle introducing a relative clause or passive; CL: 个 [gè]

3 它 (†) [tā] it

4 长 (†) [cháng] length; long; forever; always; constantly ◆ [zhǎng] chief; head; elder; to grow; to develop; to increase; to enhance

5 路 (†) [lù] surname Lu ◇ road; path; way; CL: 条 [tiáo]

6 每 (†) [měi] each; every

7 走 (†) [zǒu] to walk; to go; to run; to move (of vehicle); to visit; to leave; to go away; to die (euph.); from; through; away (in compound verbs, such as 撤走); to change (shape, form, meaning)

8 红 (†) [hóng] bonus; popular; red; revolutionary

9 正 [zhēng] first month of the lunar year ◆ [zhèng] just (right); main; upright; straight; correct; positive; greater than zero; principle

10 外 (†) [wài] outside; in addition; foreign; external

11 快 (†) [kuài] rapid; quick; speed; rate; soon; almost; to make haste; clever; sharp (of knives or wits); forthright; plain-spoken; gratified; pleased; pleasant

12 号 (†) [háo] roar; cry; CL: 个 [gè] ◆ [hào] ordinal number; day of a month; mark; sign; business establishment; size; ship suffix; horn (wind instrument); bugle call; assumed name; to take a pulse; classifier used to indicate number of people

13 进 (†) [jìn] to advance; to enter; to come (or go) into; to receive or admit; to eat or drink; to submit or present; (used after a verb) into, in; to score a goal

14 件 (†) [jiàn] item; component; classifier for events, things, clothes etc

15 您 (†) [nín] you (courteous, as opposed to informal 你 [nǐ])

16 非 [fēi] abbr. for 非洲 [Fēizhōu], Africa ◇ to not be; not; wrong; incorrect; non-; un-; in-; to reproach or blame; (colloquial) to insist on; simply must

17 百 (†) [bǎi] surname Bai ◇ hundred; numerous; all kinds of

18 真 (†) [zhēn] really; truly; indeed; real; true; genuine

19 手 [shǒu] hand; (formal) to hold; person engaged in certain types of work; person skilled in certain types of work; personal(ly); convenient; CL: 双 [shuāng], 只 [zhī]

20 常 [cháng] surname Chang ◇ always; ever; often; frequently; common; general; constant

21 望 [wàng] full moon; to hope; to expect; to visit; to gaze (into the distance); to look towards; towards

22 希 [xī] rare; infrequent

23 绍 [shào] surname Shao ◇ to continue; to carry on

24 介 [jiè] to introduce; to lie between; between

25 孩 [hái] child

26 但是 [dànshì] but; however

27 可能 [kěnéng] might (happen); possible; probable; possibility; probability; maybe; perhaps; CL: 个 [gè]

28 介绍 [jièshào] to present; to introduce; to recommend; to suggest; to let know; to brief

29 希望 [xīwàng] to wish for; to desire; hope CL: 个 [gè]

30 大家 [dàjiā] everyone; influential family; great expert

31 非常 [fēicháng] unusual; extraordinary; extreme; very; exceptional

Lesson 8

32 所以 [suǒyǐ] therefore; as a result; so

33 手机 [shǒujī] cell phone; mobile phone; CL: 部 [bù], 支 [zhī]

34 正在 [zhèngzài] in the process of (doing something or happening); while (doing)

35 去年 [qùnián] last year

36 孩子 [háizi] child

37 就是 [jiùshì] (emphasizes that sth is precisely or exactly as stated); precisely; exactly; even; if; just like; in the same way as

38 一些 [yīxiē] some; a few; a little

39 这样 [zhèyàng] this kind of; so; this way; like this; such

40 有关 [yǒuguān] to have sth to do with; to relate to; related to; to concern; concerning

41 以上 [yǐshàng] more than; above; over; the above-mentioned

42 不同 [bùtóng] different; distinct; not the same; not alike

Lesson 9

New Characters

1	2 †	3 †	4 †	5 *	6 †
场	门	送	药	赵	千

7 †	8 †	9	10 *	11 †	12 †
卖	白	动	罗	远	找

13 †	14 †	15	16 †	17	18
票	吧	体	黑	身	帮

19	20 †	21 †	22	23	24
运	完	玩	迎	考	试

25	26	27	28	29
助	准	备	告	诉

Lesson 9

HSK Vocabulary

30 告诉	34 一起	38 身体
31 帮助	35 准备	39 运动
32 觉得	36 为什么	40 欢迎
33 小时	37 考试	41 机场

Non-HSK Vocabulary

42 还有	47 两国	52 公路
43 得到	48 每年	53 每天
44 第二	49 第三	54 出来
45 一次	50 长期	55 游客
46 到了	51 以下	56 来到

Lesson 9

Glossary

1 场 [cháng] threshing floor; classifier for events and happenings: spell, episode, bout ◆ [chǎng] large place used for a specific purpose; stage; scene (of a play); classifier for sporting or recreational activities; classifier for number of exams

2 门 (†) [mén] gate; door; CL: 扇 [shàn]; gateway; doorway; CL: 个 [gè]; opening; valve; switch; way to do something; knack; family; house; (religious) sect; school (of thought); class; category; phylum or division (taxonomy); classifier for large guns; classifier for lessons, subjects, branches of technology

3 送 (†) [sòng] to deliver; to carry; to give (as a present); to present (with); to see off; to send

4 药 (†) [yào] leaf of the iris ◇ medicine; drug; cure; CL: 种 [zhǒng], 服 [fù]

5 赵 (*) [zhào] surname Zhao; one of the seven states during the Warring States Period (476-220 BC); the Former Zhao 前赵 (304-329) and Later Zhao 後赵 (319-350), states of the Sixteen Kingdoms ◇ to surpass (old)

6 千 (†) [qiān] thousand ◇ a swing

7 卖 (†) [mài] to sell; to betray; to spare no effort; to show off or flaunt

8 白 (†) [bái] surname Bai ◇ white; snowy; pure; bright; empty; blank; plain; clear; to make clear; in vain; gratuitous; free of charge; reactionary; anti-communist; funeral; to stare coldly; to write wrong character; to state; to explain; vernacular; spoken lines in opera

9 动 [dòng] to use; to act; to move; to change; abbr. for verb 动词 [dòngcí]

10 罗 (*) [luó] surname Luo ◇ gauze; to collect; to gather; to catch; to sift

11 远 (†) [yuǎn] far; distant; remote ◆ [yuàn] to distance oneself from (classical)

12 找 (†) [zhǎo] to try to find; to look for; to call on sb; to find; to seek; to return; to give change

13 票 (†) [piào] ticket; ballot; bank note; CL: 张 [zhāng]; person held for ransom; amateur performance of Chinese opera; classifier for shipments and business transactions (topolect)

14 吧 (†) [bā] bar (serving drinks, or providing internet access etc); to puff (on a pipe etc); onomat. bang ◆ [ba] (modal particle indicating suggestion or surmise); ...right?; ...OK?; ...I presume.

15 体 [tǐ] body; form; style; system

16 黑 (†) [hēi] abbr. for Heilongjiang province 黑龙江 [Hēilóngjiāng] ◇ black; dark; (loanword) to hack

17 身 [shēn] body; life; oneself; personally; one's morality and conduct; the main part of a structure or body; pregnant; classifier for sets of clothes: suit, twinset; Kangxi radical 158

18 帮 [bāng] to help; to assist; to support; for sb (i.e. as a help); hired (as worker); side (of pail, boat etc); outer layer; group; gang; clique; party; secret society

19 运 [yùn] to move; to transport; to use; to apply; fortune; luck; fate

20 完 (†) [wán] to finish; to be over; whole; complete; entire

21 玩 (†) [wán] toy; sth used for amusement; curio or antique (Taiwan pr. [wàn]); to play; to have fun; to trifle with; to keep sth for entertainment

22 迎 [yíng] to welcome; to meet; to face; to forge ahead (esp. in the face of difficulties)

23 考 [kǎo] to check; to verify; to test; to examine; to take an exam; to take an entrance exam for

24 试 [shì] to test; to try; experiment; examination; test

25 助 [zhù] to help; to assist

Lesson 9

26 准 [zhǔn] to allow; to grant; in accordance with; in the light of ◊ horizontal (old); accurate; standard; definitely; certainly; about to become (bride, son-in-law etc); quasi-; para-

27 备 [bèi] to prepare; get ready; to provide or equip

28 告 [gào] to tell; to inform; to say

29 诉 [sù] to complain; to sue; to tell

30 告诉 [gàosu] to tell; to inform; to let know

31 帮助 [bāngzhù] assistance; aid; to help; to assist

32 觉得 [juéde] to think; to feel

33 小时 [xiǎoshí] hour; CL: 个 [gè]

34 一起 [yīqǐ] in the same place; together; with; altogether (in total)

35 准备 [zhǔnbèi] preparation; to prepare; to intend; to be about to; reserve (fund)

36 为什么 [wèishénme] why?; for what reason?

37 考试 [kǎoshì] to take an exam; exam; CL: 次 [cì]

38 身体 [shēntǐ] (human) body; health; CL: 个 [gè]

39 运动 [yùndòng] to move; to exercise; sports; exercise; motion; movement; campaign; CL: 场 [chǎng]

40 欢迎 [huānyíng] to welcome; welcome

41 机场 [jīchǎng] airport; airfield; CL: 家 [jiā], 处 [chù]

42 还有 [háiyǒu] furthermore; in addition; still; also

43 得到 [dédào] to get; to obtain; to receive

44 第二 [dì'èr] second; number two; next

45 一次 [yīcì] first; first time; once; (math.) linear (of degree one)

46 到了 [dàoliǎo] at last; finally; in the end

47 两国 [liǎngguó] both countries; two countries

48 每年 [měinián] every year; each year; yearly

49 第三 [dìsān] third; number three

50 长期 [chángqī] long term; long time; long range (of a forecast)

51 以下 [yǐxià] below; under; the following

52 公路 [gōnglù] public road; CL: 条 [tiáo]

53 每天 [měitiān] every day; everyday

54 出来 [chūlái] to come out; to emerge

55 游客 [yóukè] traveler; tourist

56 来到 [láidào] to come; to arrive

Lesson 10

New Characters

1	2	3	4	5	6
自	马	报	行	男	乐

7 *	8	9	10 †	11 †	12 †
宋	晚	色	离	贵	鱼

13 *	14 †	15	16	17 †	18 *
蒋	雪	夫	牛	笑	姜

19 *	20	21 †	22 *	23 †	24 †
孟	斤	别	凯	船	穿

25	26	27	28 †	29 †	30 †
奶	答	纸	姓	洗	课

31	32	33	34	35
息	颜	休	妻	丈

Lesson 10

HSK Vocabulary

36 男人	41 妻子	46 快乐
37 报纸	42 公斤	47 颜色
38 晚上	43 牛奶	48 休息
39 回答	44 丈夫	49 马上
40 女人	45 自行车	

Non-HSK Vocabulary

50 再次	59 有所	68 所在
51 本报	60 不再	69 那个
52 多次	61 最新	70 旅客
53 正是	62 会见	71 自我
54 第四	63 等等	72 面试
55 学会	64 找到	73 院长
56 工商	65 哪些	74 第六
57 年前	66 里面	
58 红十字	67 会长	

Lesson 10

Glossary

1 自 [zì] from; self; oneself; since

2 马 [mǎ] surname Ma; abbr. for Malaysia 马来西亚 [Mǎláixīyà] ◊ horse; CL: 匹 [pi]; horse or cavalry piece in Chinese chess; knight in Western chess

3 报 [bào] to announce; to inform; report; newspaper; recompense; revenge; CL: 份 [fèn], 张 [zhāng]

4 行 [háng] a row; series; age order (of brothers); profession; professional; relating to company ◆ [xíng] to walk; to go; to travel; a visit; temporary; makeshift; current; in circulation; to do; to perform; capable; competent; effective; all right; OK!; will do ◆ [xìng] behavior; conduct

5 男 [nán] male; Baron, lowest of five orders of nobility 五等爵位 [wǔ děng jué wèi]; CL: 个 [gè]

6 乐 [lè] surname Le ◊ happy; laugh; cheerful ◆ [yuè] surname Yue ◊ music

7 宋 (*) [sòng] surname Song; the Song dynasty (960-1279); also Song of the Southern dynasties 南朝宋 (420-479)

8 晚 [wǎn] evening; night; late

9 色 [sè] color; CL: 种 [zhǒng]; look; appearance; sex ◆ [shǎi] color; dice

10 离 (†) [lí] mythical beast (archaic) ◊ surname Li ◊ to leave; to part from; to be away from; (in giving distances) from; without (sth); independent of; one of the Eight Trigrams 八卦 [bāguà], symbolizing fire; ☲

11 贵 (†) [guì] expensive; noble; your (name); precious

12 鱼 (†) [yú] surname Yu ◊ fish; CL: 条 [tiáo], 尾 [wěi]

13 蒋 (*) [jiǎng] surname Jiang; refers to Chiang Kai-shek 蒋介石

14 雪 (†) [xuě] surname Xue ◊ snow; snowfall; CL: 场 [cháng]; to have the appearance of snow; to wipe away, off or out; to clean

15 夫 [fū] husband; man; manual worker; conscripted laborer (old) ◆ [fú] form word, grammar particle or demonstrative pronoun (classical)

16 牛 [niú] ox; cow; bull; CL: 条 [tiáo], 头 [tóu]; (slang) awesome

17 笑 (†) [xiào] laugh; smile; CL: 个 [gè]

18 姜 (*) [jiāng] surname Jiang ◊ surname Jiang ◊ ginger

19 孟 (*) [mèng] surname Meng ◊ first month of a season; eldest amongst brothers

20 斤 [jīn] catty; weight equal to 0.5 kg

21 别 (†) [bié] surname Bie ◊ to leave; to depart; to separate; to distinguish; to classify; other; another; do not; must not; to pin ◆ [biè] to make sb change their ways, opinions etc

22 凯 (*) [kǎi] surname Kai ◊ triumphant; victorious; chi (Greek letter Χχ)

23 船 (†) [chuán] a boat; vessel; ship; CL: 条 [tiáo], 艘 [sōu], 只 [zhī]

24 穿 (†) [chuān] to bore through; to pierce; to perforate; to penetrate; to pass through; to dress; to wear; to put on; to thread

25 奶 [nǎi] breast; lady; milk

26 答 [dā] to answer; to agree ◆ [dá] reply; answer; return; respond; echo

27 纸 [zhǐ] paper; CL: 张 [zhāng], 沓 [dá]; classifier for documents, letter etc

28 姓 (†) [xìng] family name; surname; name; CL: 个 [gè]

29 洗 (†) [xǐ] to wash; to bathe; to develop (photo)

30 课 (†) [kè] subject; course; class; lesson; CL: 堂 [táng], 节 [jié], 门 [mén]; to levy; tax

31 息 [xī] news; interest; breath; rest; Taiwan pr. [xí]

Lesson 10

32 颜 [yán] surname Yan ◇ color; face; countenance

33 休 [xiū] surname Xiu ◇ to rest; to stop doing sth for a period of time; to cease; (imperative) don't

34 妻 [qī] wife ◆ [qì] to marry off (a daughter)

35 丈 [zhàng] ten feet

36 男人 [nánrén] a man; a male; men; CL: 个 [gè]

37 报纸 [bàozhǐ] newspaper; newsprint; CL: 份 [fèn], 期 [qī], 张 [zhāng]

38 晚上 [wǎnshang] evening; night; CL: 个 [gè]; in the evening

39 回答 [huídá] to reply; to answer; the answer; CL: 个 [gè]

40 女人 [nǚrén] woman ◆ [nǚren] wife

41 妻子 [qīzǐ] wife and children ◆ [qīzi] wife; CL: 个 [gè]

42 公斤 [gōngjīn] kilogram (kg)

43 牛奶 [niúnǎi] cow's milk; CL: 瓶 [píng], 杯 [bēi]

44 丈夫 [zhàngfu] husband; CL: 个 [gè]

45 自行车 [zìxíngchē] bicycle; bike; CL: 辆 [liàng]

46 快乐 [kuàilè] happy; merry

47 颜色 [yánsè] color; CL: 个 [gè]

48 休息 [xiūxi] rest; to rest

49 马上 [mǎshàng] at once; right away; immediately; on horseback (i.e. by military force)

50 再次 [zàicì] one more time; again; one more; once again

51 本报 [běnbào] this newspaper

52 多次 [duōcì] many times; repeatedly

53 正是 [zhèngshì] (emphasizes that sth is precisely or exactly as stated); precisely; exactly; even; if; just like; in the same way as

54 第四 [dìsì] fourth; number four

55 学会 [xuéhuì] to learn; to master; institute; learned society; (scholarly) association

56 工商 [gōngshāng] industry and commerce

57 年前 [niánqián] ...years ago

58 红十字 [hóngshízì] Red Cross

59 有所 [yǒusuǒ] somewhat; to some extent

60 不再 [bùzài] no more; no longer

61 最新 [zuìxīn] latest; newest

62 会见 [huìjiàn] to meet with (sb who is paying a visit); CL: 次 [cì]

63 等等 [děngděng] etcetera; and so on ...; wait a minute!; hold on!

64 找到 [zhǎodào] to find

65 哪些 [nǎxiē] which ones?; who?; what?

66 里面 [lǐmiàn] inside; interior

67 会长 [huìzhǎng] president of a club, committee etc

68 所在 [suǒzài] place; location; whereabouts; domicile; to be located; to belong to (organization etc)

69 那个 [nàge] that one; also pr. [nèi ge]

70 旅客 [lǚkè] traveler; tourist

71 自我 [zìwǒ] self-; ego (psychology)

72 面试 [miànshì] to interview; to audition; interview; audition

73 院长 [yuànzhǎng] chair of board; president (of a university etc); department head; dean; CL: 个 [gè]

74 第六 [dìliù] sixth

Lesson 11

New Characters

1	2	3	4	5	6
房	员	便	早	务	班

7	8	9	10	11	12
边	表	眼	思	意	鸡

13 *	14 *	15 *	16	17 †	18 †
艾	楠	潘	宜	错	阴

19 †	20 †	21 *	22	23 *	24 †
圆	慢	棚	旁	坤	忙

25	26 †	27	28 †	29	30
蛋	懂	瓜	晴	泳	妹

31	32	33	34
弟	睛	咖	啡

Lesson 11

HSK Vocabulary

35	眼睛	41	意思	47	鸡蛋
36	便宜	42	上班	48	姐姐
37	水果	43	早上	49	弟弟
38	生日	44	咖啡	50	服务员
39	西瓜	45	游泳	51	妹妹
40	房间	46	旁边	52	手表

Non-HSK Vocabulary

53	工作人员	62	到来	71	做大
54	员工	63	出问题	72	生长
55	所得	64	作家	73	见到
56	早在	65	慢慢	74	第二次
57	亮点	66	名为	75	长期以来
58	三星	67	第八	76	宜兴
59	医师	68	得很	77	中非
60	明年	69	想到		
61	北京大学	70	公车		

Lesson 11

Glossary

1 房 [fáng] surname Fang ◊ house; room; CL: 间 [jiān]

2 员 [yuán] person; employee; member

3 便 [biàn] ordinary; plain; convenient; as convenient; when the chance arises; handy; easy; informal; simple; so; thus; to relieve oneself; to urinate; to defecate; equivalent to 就 [jiù]: then; in that case; even if; soon afterwards ◆ [pián] advantageous; cheap

4 早 [zǎo] early; morning; Good morning!

5 务 [wù] affair; business; matter

6 班 [bān] surname Ban ◊ team; class; squad; work shift; ranking; CL: 个 [gè]; classifier for groups

7 边 [biān] side; edge; margin; border; boundary; CL: 个 [gè]; simultaneously ◆ [bian] suffix of a noun of locality

8 表 [biǎo] exterior surface; family relationship via females; to show (one's opinion); a model; a table (listing information); a form; a meter (measuring sth) ◊ wrist or pocket watch

9 眼 [yǎn] eye; small hole; crux (of a matter); CL: 只 [zhī], 双 [shuāng]; classifier for big hollow things (wells, stoves, pots etc)

10 思 [sī] to think; to consider

11 意 [yì] Italy; Italian; abbr. for 意大利 [Yìdàlì] ◊ idea; meaning; thought; to think; wish; desire; intention; to expect; to anticipate

12 鸡 [jī] fowl; chicken; CL: 只 [zhī]

13 艾 (*) [ài] surname Ai ◊ Chinese mugwort or wormwood; to stop or cut short; phonetic "ai" or "i"; abbr. for 艾滋病 [àizībìng], AIDS ◆ [yì] to mow; to cut; to reap; to redress

14 楠 (*) [nán] Machilus nanmu; Chinese cedar; Chinese giant redwood

15 潘 (*) [pān] surname Pan; Pan, faun in Greek mythology, son of Hermes

16 宜 [yí] surname Yi ◊ proper; should; suitable; appropriate

17 错 (†) [cuò] surname Cuo ◊ mistake; wrong; bad; interlocking; complex; to grind; to polish; to alternate; to stagger; to miss; to let slip; to evade; to inlay with gold or silver

18 阴 (†) [yīn] surname Yin ◊ overcast (weather); cloudy; shady; Yin (the negative principle of Yin and Yang); negative (electric.); feminine; moon; implicit; hidden; genitalia

19 圆 (†) [yuán] circle; round; circular; spherical; (of the moon) full; unit of Chinese currency (Yuan); tactful; to justify

20 慢 (†) [màn] slow

21 棚 (*) [péng] shed; canopy; shack

22 旁 [páng] beside; one side; other; side; self; the right-hand side of split Chinese character, often the phonetic

23 坤 (*) [kūn] one of the Eight Trigrams 八卦 [bāguà], symbolizing earth; female principle; ☷

24 忙 (†) [máng] busy; hurriedly; to hurry; to rush

25 蛋 [dàn] egg; oval shaped; CL: 个 [gè], 打 [dá]

26 懂 (†) [dǒng] to understand; to know

27 瓜 [guā] melon; gourd; squash

28 晴 (†) [qíng] clear; fine (weather)

29 泳 [yǒng] swimming; to swim

30 妹 [mèi] younger sister

31 弟 [dì] younger brother; junior male; I (modest word in letter) ◆ [tì] variant of 悌 [tì]

32 睛 [jīng] eye; eyeball

33 咖 [kā] coffee; class; grade

34 啡 [fēi] coffee

35 眼睛 [yǎnjing] eye; CL: 只 [zhī], 双 [shuāng]

Lesson 11

36 便宜 [biànyí] convenient ◆ [piányi] small advantages; to let sb off lightly; cheap; inexpensive

37 水果 [shuǐguǒ] fruit; CL: 个 [gè]

38 生日 [shēngrì] birthday; CL: 个 [gè]

39 西瓜 [xīguā] watermelon; CL: 条 [tiáo]

40 房间 [fángjiān] room; CL: 间 [jiān]

41 意思 [yìsi] idea; opinion; meaning; wish; desire; CL: 个 [gè]

42 上班 [shàngbān] to go to work; to be on duty; to start work; to go to the office

43 早上 [zǎoshang] early morning; CL: 个 [gè]

44 咖啡 [kāfēi] coffee; CL:杯 [bēi]

45 游泳 [yóuyǒng] swimming; to swim

46 旁边 [pángbiān] lateral; side; to the side; beside

47 鸡蛋 [jīdàn] (chicken) egg; hen's egg; CL: 个 [gè], 打 [dá]

48 姐姐 [jiějie] older sister; CL: 个 [gè]

49 弟弟 [dìdi] younger brother; CL: 个 [gè], 位 [wèi]

50 服务员 [fúwùyuán] waiter; waitress; attendant; customer service personnel; CL: 个 [gè]

51 妹妹 [mèimei] younger sister; fig. younger woman (esp. girl friend or rival); CL: 个 [gè]

52 手表 [shǒubiǎo] wrist watch; CL: 块 [kuài], 只 [zhī], 个 [gè]

53 工作人员 [gōngzuòrényuán] staff member

54 员工 [yuángōng] staff; personnel; employee

55 所得 [suǒdé] what one acquires; one's gains

56 早在 [zǎozài] as early as

57 亮点 [liàngdiǎn] highlight; bright spot

58 三星 [sānxīng] Sanxing or Sanhsing township in Yilan county 宜兰县 [Yílánxiàn], Taiwan; Samsung (South Korean electronics company) ◇ three major stars of the Three Stars 参宿 [Shēnxiù] Chinese constellation; the belt of Orion; three spirits 福 [fú], 禄 [lù], and 寿 [shòu] associated with the Three Stars 参宿 [Shēnxiù] Chinese constellation

59 医师 [yīshī] doctor

60 明年 [míngnián] next year

61 北京大学 [běijīngdàxué] Beijing university

62 到来 [dàolái] arrival; advent

63 出问题 [chūwèntí] to give problems

64 作家 [zuòjiā] author; CL: 个 [gè], 位 [wèi]

65 慢慢 [mànmàn] slowly

66 名为 [míngwéi] named as

67 第八 [dìbā] eighth

68 得很 [dehěn] very (much, good etc)

69 想到 [xiǎngdào] to think of; to call to mind; to anticipate

70 公车 [gōngchē] bus

71 做大 [zuòdà] arrogant; putting on airs

72 生长 [shēngzhǎng] to grow

73 见到 [jiàndào] to see

74 第二次 [dì'èrcì] the second time; second; number two

75 长期以来 [chángqīyǐlái] ever since a long time ago

76 宜兴 [yíxīng] Yixing county level city in Wuxi 无锡 [Wúxī], Jiangsu

77 中非 [zhōngfēi] China-Africa (relations); Central Africa; Central African Republic

Lesson 12

New Characters

1	2	3	4	5	6
共	室	病	歌	唱	教

7	8	9	10	11	12
肉	球	跑	足	步	左

13	14	15	16	17	18
床	舞	羊	籃	跳	右

19	20	21	22 *	23 *	24 *
汽	哥	踢	皖	磷	狄

25 *	26 *
瑾	欒

Lesson 12

HSK Vocabulary

27 教室	32 跳舞	37 左边
28 哥哥	33 好吃	38 右边
29 生病	34 羊肉	39 打篮球
30 唱歌	35 跑步	40 踢足球
31 起床	36 公共汽车	

Non-HSK Vocabulary

41 进京	50 工期	59 最牛
42 进去	51 上车	60 看得见
43 新生	52 点钟	61 自学
44 离子	53 这边	62 本题
45 游人	54 电能	63 早前
46 打动	55 开学	64 不着
47 老字号	56 汉字	65 水路
48 试题	57 没问题	
49 中和	58 来得	

Lesson 12

Glossary

1 共 [gòng] common; general; to share; together; total; altogether; abbr. for 共产党 [gòngchǎndǎng], Communist party

2 室 [shì] surname Shi ◊ room; work unit; grave; scabbard; family or clan; one of the 28 constellations of Chinese astronomy

3 病 [bìng] ailment; sickness; illness; disease; fall ill; sick; defect; CL: 场 [cháng]

4 歌 [gē] song; CL: 支 [zhī], 首 [shǒu]; to sing

5 唱 [chàng] sing; to call loudly; to chant

6 教 [jiāo] to teach ◆ [jiào] surname Jiao ◊ religion; teaching; to make; to cause; to tell

7 肉 [ròu] meat; flesh; pulp (of a fruit)

8 球 [qiú] ball; sphere; globe; CL: 个 [gè]; ball game; match; CL: 场 [chǎng]

9 跑 [pǎo] to run; to escape; race

10 足 [jù] excessive ◆ [zú] foot; to be sufficient; ample

11 步 [bù] a step; a pace; walk; march; stages in a process

12 左 [zuǒ] surname Zuo ◊ left; the Left (politics); east; unorthodox; queer; wrong; differing; opposite; variant of 佐 [zuǒ]

13 床 [chuáng] bed; couch; classifier for beds; CL: 张 [zhāng]

14 舞 [wǔ] to dance; to wield; to brandish

15 羊 [yáng] surname Yang ◊ sheep; CL: 头 [tóu], 只 [zhī]

16 篮 [lán] basket; goal

17 跳 [tiào] to jump; to hop; to skip over; to bounce; to palpitate

18 右 [yòu] right (-hand); the Right (politics); west (old)

19 汽 [qì] steam; vapor

20 哥 [gē] elder brother

21 踢 [tī] to kick; to play (e.g. soccer)

22 皖 (*) [wǎn] abbr. for Anhui 安徽 province

23 磷 (*) [lín] phosphorus (chemistry); water in rocks

24 狄 (*) [dí] surname Di; generic name for northern ethnic minorities during the Qin and Han Dynasties (221 BC-220 AD) ◊ low ranking public official (old)

25 瑾 (*) [jǐn] brilliancy (of gems)

26 栾 (*) [luán] surname Luan ◊ Koelreuteria paniculata

27 教室 [jiàoshì] classroom; CL: 间 [jiān]

28 哥哥 [gēge] older brother; CL: 个 [gè], 位 [wèi]

29 生病 [shēngbìng] to fall ill; to sicken

30 唱歌 [chànggē] to sing a song

31 起床 [qǐchuáng] to get out of bed; to get up

32 跳舞 [tiàowǔ] to dance

33 好吃 [hǎochī] tasty; delicious ◆ [hàochī] to be fond of eating; to be gluttonous

34 羊肉 [yángròu] mutton

35 跑步 [pǎobù] to walk quickly; to march; to run

36 公共汽车 [gōnggòngqìchē] bus; CL: 辆 [liàng], 班 [bān]

37 左边 [zuǒbian] left; the left side; to the left of

38 右边 [yòubian] right side; right, to the right

39 打篮球

40 踢足球

41 进京 [jìnjīng] to enter the capital; to go to Beijing

42 进去 [jìnqù] to go in

43 新生 [xīnshēng] newborn; new student

44 离子 [lízǐ] ion

45 游人 [yóurén] a tourist

Lesson 12

46 打动 [dǎdòng] to move (to pity); arousing (sympathy); touching

47 老字号 [lǎozìhào] shop, firm, or brand of merchandise with a long-established reputation

48 试题 [shìtí] exam question; test topic

49 中和 [zhōnghé] Chungho city in Taipei county 台北县 [Táiběixiàn], Taiwan ◇ to neutralize; to counteract; neutralization (chemistry)

50 工期 [gōngqī] time allocated for a project; completion date

51 上车 [shàngchē] to get on or into (a bus, train, car etc)

52 点钟 [diǎnzhōng] (indicating time of day) o'clock

53 这边 [zhèbiān] this side; here

54 电能 [diànnéng] electrical energy

55 开学 [kāixué] foundation of a University or College; school opening; the start of a new term

56 汉字 [hànzì] Chinese character; CL: 个 [gè]; Japanese: kanji; Korean: hanja

57 没问题 [méiwèntí] no problem

58 来得 [láide] to emerge (from a comparison); to come out as; to be competent or equal to

59 最牛 [zuìniú] tough as nails

60 看得见 [kàndéjiàn] visible

61 自学 [zìxué] self-study; to study on one's own

62 本题 [běntí] the subject under discussion; the point at issue

63 早前 [zǎoqián] previously

64 不着 [bùzháo] no need; need not

65 水路 [shuǐlù] waterway

Part 3
HSK III (B1) INTERMEDIATE
Lessons 13-24

Lesson 13

New Characters

1 †	2 †	3 †	4 †	5 †	6 †
要	地	万	把	用	向

7 †	8	9 †	10 †	11 †	12
又	市	条	位	使	化

13	14	15	16	17	18
文	如	城	主	重	需

19	20	21	22	23	24
界	提	示	史	求	世

25	26
己	历

Lesson 13

HSK Vocabulary

27 国家
28 文化
29 自己
30 表示
31 重要
32 提高
33 要求
34 城市

35 认为
36 如果
37 需要
38 主要
39 历史
40 世界
41 关系

Non-HSK Vocabulary

42 服务

Lesson 13

Glossary

1 要 (†) [yāo] to demand; to request; to coerce ♦ [yào] important; vital; to want; will; going to (as future auxiliary); may; must; (used in a comparison) must be; probably

2 地 (†) [de] -ly; structural particle: used before a verb or adjective, linking it to preceding modifying adverbial adjunct ♦ [dì] earth; ground; field; place; land; CL: 片 [piàn]

3 万 (†) [mò] see 万俟 [Mòqí] ♦ [wàn] surname Wan ◇ ten thousand; a great number

4 把 (†) [bǎ] to hold; to contain; to grasp; to take hold of; handle; particle marking the following noun as a direct object; classifier for objects with handle; classifier for small objects: handful ♦ [bà] handle

5 用 (†) [yòng] to use; to employ; to have to; to eat or drink; expense or outlay; usefulness; hence; therefore

6 向 (†) [xiàng] surname Xiang ◇ towards; to face; to turn towards; direction; to support; to side with; shortly before; formerly; always; all along

7 又 (†) [yòu] (once) again; also; both... and...; again

8 市 [shì] market; city; CL: 个 [gè]

9 条 (†) [tiáo] strip; item; article; clause (of law or treaty); classifier for long thin things (ribbon, river, road, trousers etc)

10 位 (†) [wèi] position; location; place; seat; classifier for people (honorific); classifier for binary bits (e.g. 十六位 16-bit or 2 bytes)

11 使 (†) [shǐ] to make; to cause; to enable; to use; to employ; to send; to instruct sb to do sth; envoy; messenger

12 化 [huā] variant of 花 ♦ [huà] to make into; to change into; -ization; to ... -ize; to transform; abbr. for 化学 [huàxué]

13 文 [wén] surname Wen ◇ language; culture; writing; formal; literary; gentle; (old) classifier for coins; Kangxi radical 118

14 如 [rú] as; as if; such as

15 城 [chéng] city walls; city; town; CL: 座 [zuò], 道 [dào], 个 [gè]

16 主 [zhǔ] owner; master; host; individual or party concerned; God; Lord; main; to indicate or signify; trump card (in card games)

17 重 [chóng] to double; to repeat; repetition; iteration; again; a layer ♦ [zhòng] heavy; serious

18 需 [xū] to require; to need; to want; necessity; need

19 界 [jiè] boundary; scope; extent; circles; group; kingdom (taxonomy)

20 提 [tí] to carry (hanging down from the hand); to lift; to put forward; to mention; to raise (an issue); upwards character stroke; lifting brush stroke (in painting); scoop for measuring liquid

21 示 [shì] to show; reveal

22 史 [shǐ] surname Shi ◇ history; annals; title of an official historian in ancient China

23 求 [qiú] to seek; to look for; to request; to demand; to beseech

24 世 [shì] surname Shi ◇ life; age; generation; era; world; lifetime; epoch; descendant; noble

25 己 [jǐ] self; oneself; sixth of 10 heavenly stems 十天干; sixth in order; letter "F" or roman "VI" in list "A, B, C", or "I, II, III" etc; hexa

26 历 [lì] calendar ◇ to experience; to undergo; to pass through; all; each; every; history

27 国家 [guójiā] country; nation; state; CL: 个 [gè]

28 文化 [wénhuà] culture; civilization; cultural; CL: 个 [gè], 种 [zhǒng]

29 自己 [zìjǐ] oneself; one's own

Lesson 13

30 表示 [biǎoshì] to express; to show; to say; to state; to indicate; to mean

31 重要 [zhòngyào] important; significant; major

32 提高 [tígāo] to raise; to increase

33 要求 [yāoqiú] to request; to require; to stake a claim; to ask; to demand; CL: 点 [diǎn]

34 城市 [chéngshì] city; town; CL: 座 [zuò]

35 认为 [rènwéi] to believe; to think; to consider; to feel

36 如果 [rúguǒ] if; in case; in the event that

37 需要 [xūyào] to need; to want; to demand; to require; requirement; need

38 主要 [zhǔyào] main; principal; major; primary

39 历史 [lìshǐ] history; CL: 门 [mén], 段 [duàn]

40 世界 [shìjiè] world; CL: 个 [gè]

41 关系 [guānxì] relation; relationship; to concern; to affect; to have to do with; guanxi; CL: 个 [gè]

42 服务 [fúwù] to serve; service; CL: 项 [xiàng]

Lesson 14

New Characters

1	2	3	4	5 †	6
其	该	据	成	才	应

7	8 †	9 †	10 †	11	12
发	只	低	近	方	力

13	14	15	16	17	18
平	加	特	环	根	参

19	20	21	22	23	24
康	健	解	响	议	闻

25	26	27
境	决	努

Lesson 14

HSK Vocabulary

28 地方
29 会议
30 环境
31 了解
32 还是
33 影响
34 发现
35 出现
36 解决
37 参加
38 新闻

39 应该
40 作用
41 根据
42 特别
43 其他
44 水平
45 健康
46 为了
47 完成
48 努力

Non-HSK Vocabulary

49 进一步
50 提出

Lesson 14

Glossary

1 其 [qí] his; her; its; theirs; that; such; it (refers to sth preceding it)

2 该 [gāi] should; ought to; probably; must be; to deserve; to owe; to be sb's turn to do sth; that; the above-mentioned

3 据 [jū] see 拮据 [jiéjū] ◆ [jù] according to; to act in accordance with; to depend on; to seize; to occupy

4 成 [chéng] surname Cheng ◇ to succeed; to finish; to complete; to accomplish; to become; to turn into; to be all right; OK!; one tenth

5 才 (†) [cái] ability; talent; sb of a certain type; a capable individual; only; only then; just now ◇ a moment ago; just now; (preceded by a clause of condition or reason) not until; (followed by a numerical clause) only

6 应 [yīng] to answer; to respond; to agree (to do sth); should; ought to ◆ [yìng] surname Ying ◇ to answer; to respond; to comply with; to deal or cope with

7 发 [fā] to send out; to show (one's feeling); to issue; to develop; classifier for gunshots (rounds) ◆ [fà] hair; Taiwan pr. [fǎ]

8 只 (†) [zhī] classifier for birds and certain animals, one of a pair, some utensils, vessels etc ◆ [zhǐ] only; merely; just; but; but; only

9 低 (†) [dī] low; beneath; to lower (one's head); to let droop; to hang down; to incline

10 近 (†) [jìn] near; close to; approximately

11 方 [fāng] surname Fang ◇ square; power or involution (mathematics); upright; honest; fair and square; direction; side; party (to a contract, dispute etc); place; method; prescription (medicine); upright or honest; just when; only or just; classifier for square things; abbr. for square or cubic meter

12 力 [lì] surname Li ◇ power; force; strength; ability; strenuously

13 平 [píng] surname Ping ◇ flat; level; equal; to tie (make the same score); to draw (score); calm; peaceful; see also 平声 [píngshēng]

14 加 [jiā] abbr. for Canada 加拿大 [Jiānádà] ◇ to add; plus

15 特 [tè] special; unique; distinguished; especially; unusual; very

16 环 [huán] surname Huan ◇ ring; hoop; loop; (chain) link; classifier for scores in archery etc; to surround; to encircle; to hem in

17 根 [gēn] root; basis; classifier for long slender objects, e.g. cigarettes, guitar strings; CL: 条 [tiáo]; radical (chemistry)

18 参 [cān] take part in; participate; join; attend; to join; unequal; varied; irregular; to counsel; uneven; not uniform; abbr. for 参议院 Senate, Upper House ◆ [shēn] ginseng

19 康 [kāng] surname Kang ◇ healthy; peaceful; abundant

20 健 [jiàn] healthy; to invigorate; to strengthen; to be good at; to be strong in

21 解 [jiě] to divide; to break up; to split; to separate; to dissolve; to solve; to melt; to remove; to untie; to loosen; to open; to emancipate; to explain; to understand; to know; a solution; a dissection ◆ [jiè] to transport under guard ◆ [xiè] surname Xie ◇ acrobatic display (esp. on horseback) (old); variant of 懈 [xiè] and 邂 [xiè] (old)

22 响 [xiǎng] echo; sound; noise; to make a sound; to sound; to ring; loud; classifier for noises

23 议 [yì] to comment on; to discuss; to suggest

24 闻 [wén] surname Wen ◇ to hear; news; well-known; famous; reputation; fame; to smell; to sniff at

Lesson 14

25 境 [jìng] border; place; condition; boundary; circumstances; territory

26 决 [jué] to decide; to determine; to execute (sb); (of a dam etc) to breach or burst; definitely; certainly

27 努 [nǔ] to exert; to strive

28 地方 [dìfāng] region; regional (away from the central administration); local ◆ [dìfang] area; place; space; room; territory; CL: 处 [chù], 个 [gè], 块 [kuài]

29 会议 [huìyì] meeting; conference; CL: 场 [chǎng], 届 [jiè]

30 环境 [huánjìng] environment; circumstances; surroundings; CL: 个 [gè]; ambient

31 了解 [liǎojiě] to understand; to realize; to find out ◇ to understand; to realize; to find out

32 还是 [háishi] or; still; nevertheless; had better

33 影响 [yǐngxiǎng] an influence; an effect; to influence; to affect (usually adversely); to disturb; CL:股 [gǔ]

34 发现 [fāxiàn] to find; to discover

35 出现 [chūxiàn] to appear; to arise; to emerge; to show up

36 解决 [jiějué] to settle (a dispute); to resolve; to solve

37 参加 [cānjiā] to participate; to take part; to join

38 新闻 [xīnwén] news; CL: 条 [tiáo], 个 [gè]

39 应该 [yīnggāi] ought to; should; must

40 作用 [zuòyòng] to act on; to affect; action; function; activity; impact; result; effect; purpose; intent; to play a role; corresponds to English –ity, –ism, –ization; CL: 个 [gè]

41 根据 [gēnjù] according to; based on; basis; foundation; CL: 个 [gè]

42 特别 [tèbié] especially; special; particular; unusual

43 其他 [qítā] other; the others; else; other than (that person); in addition to the person mentioned above

44 水平 [shuǐpíng] level (of achievement etc); standard; horizontal

45 健康 [jiànkāng] health; healthy

46 为了 [wèile] in order to; for the purpose of; so as to

47 完成 [wánchéng] to complete; to accomplish

48 努力 [nǔlì] great effort; to strive; to try hard

49 进一步 [jìnyībù] one step further; to move forward a step; further onwards

50 提出 [tíchū] to raise (an issue); to propose; to put forward; to suggest; to post (on a website); to withdraw (cash)

Lesson 15

New Characters

1	2	3	4	5 †	6 †
而	于	或	者	种	段

7 †	8	9 †	10 †	11 †	12 †
黄	较	难	带	南	几

13 †	14 †	15	16	17	18
口	放	选	实	定	且

19	20	21	22	23	24
直	查	戏	举	检	必

25	26	27	28
然	虽	须	择

Lesson 15

HSK Vocabulary

29 关于
30 或者
31 选择
32 必须
33 而且
34 举行
35 一直
36 决定
37 比较
38 虽然
39 检查
40 一定
41 经过
42 认真
43 其实
44 游戏

Non-HSK Vocabulary

45 这种
46 一种
47 加快
48 重大
49 只有

Lesson 15

Glossary

1 而 [ér] and; as well as; and so; but (not); yet (not); (indicates causal relation); (indicates change of state); (indicates contrast)

2 于 [yú] surname Yu ◇ to go; to take; sentence-final interrogative particle ◇ surname Yu ◇ in; at; to; from; by; than; out of

3 或 [huò] maybe; perhaps; might; possibly; or

4 者 [zhě] (after a verb or adjective) one who (is) ...; (after a noun) person involved in ...; -er; -ist; (used after a number or 后 [hòu] or 前 [qián] to refer to sth mentioned previously); (used after a term, to mark a pause before defining the term); (old) (used at the end of a command); (old) this

5 种 (†) [zhǒng] abbr. for 物种, genus; race; seed; breed; species; strain; kind; type; has guts (i.e. courage); nerve; classifier for types: kind, sort; classifier for languages ♦ [zhòng] to plant; to grow; to cultivate

6 段 (†) [duàn] surname Duan ◇ paragraph; section; segment; stage (of a process); classifier for stories, periods of time, lengths of thread etc

7 黄 (†) [huáng] surname Huang or Hwang ◇ yellow; pornographic; to fall through

8 较 [jiào] comparatively; (preposition comparing difference in degree); to contrast; to compare; rather; fairly; clearly (different); markedly; to haggle over; to quibble

9 难 (†) [nán] difficult (to...); problem; difficulty; difficult; not good ♦ [nàn] disaster; distress; to scold

10 带 (†) [dài] band; belt; girdle; ribbon; tire; area; zone; region; CL: 条 [tiáo]; to wear; to carry; to take along; to bear (i.e. to have); to lead; to bring; to look after; to raise

11 南 (†) [nán] surname Nan ◇ south

12 几 (†) [jī] small table ◇ almost ♦ [jǐ] how much; how many; several; a few

13 口 (†) [kǒu] mouth; classifier for things with mouths (people, domestic animals, cannons, wells etc); classifier for bites or mouthfuls

14 放 (†) [fàng] to release; to free; to let go; to put; to place; to let out; to set off (fireworks)

15 选 [xuǎn] to choose; to pick; to select; to elect

16 实 [shí] real; true; honest; really; solid; fruit; seed; definitely

17 定 [dìng] to set; to fix; to determine; to decide; to order

18 且 [qiě] and; moreover; yet; for the time being; to be about to; both (... and...)

19 直 [zhí] surname Zhi; Zhi (c. 2000 BC), fifth of the legendary Flame Emperors 炎帝 [Yándì] descended from Shennong 神农 [Shénnóng] Farmer God ◇ straight; to straighten; fair and reasonable; frank; straightforward; (indicates continuing motion or action); vertical; vertical downward stroke in Chinese characters

20 查 [chá] to research; to check; to investigate; to examine; to refer to; to search ♦ [zhā] surname Zha

21 戏 [xì] trick; drama; play; show; CL:出 [chū], 场 [chǎng], 台 [tái]

22 举 [jǔ] to lift; to hold up; to cite; to enumerate; to act; to raise; to choose; to elect

23 检 [jiǎn] to check; to examine; to inspect; to exercise restraint

24 必 [bì] certainly; must; will; necessarily

25 然 [rán] correct; right; so; thus; like this; -ly

26 虽 [suī] although; even though

27 须 [xū] must; to have to; to wait ◇ beard; mustache; feeler (of an insect etc); tassel

Lesson 15

28 择 [zé] to select; to choose; to pick over; to pick out; to differentiate; to eliminate; also pr. [zhái]

29 关于 [guānyú] pertaining to; concerning; regarding; with regards to; about; a matter of ◇ pertaining to; concerning; regarding; with regards to; about; a matter of

30 或者 [huòzhě] or; possibly; maybe; perhaps

31 选择 [xuǎnzé] to select; to pick; choice; option; alternative

32 必须 [bìxū] to have to; must; compulsory; necessarily

33 而且 [érqiě] (not only ...) but also; moreover; in addition; furthermore

34 举行 [jǔxíng] to hold (a meeting, ceremony etc)

35 一直 [yīzhí] straight (in a straight line); continuously; always; from the beginning of ... up to ...; all along

36 决定 [juédìng] to decide (to do something); to resolve; decision; CL: 个 [gè], 项 [xiàng]; certainly

37 比较 [bǐjiào] to compare; to contrast; comparatively; relatively; quite; comparison

38 虽然 [suīrán] although; even though; even if

39 检查 [jiǎnchá] inspection; to examine; to inspect; CL:次 [cì]

40 一定 [yīdìng] surely; certainly; necessarily; fixed; a certain (extent etc); given; particular; must

41 经过 [jīngguò] to pass; to go through; process; course; CL: 个 [gè]

42 认真 [rènzhēn] conscientious; earnest; serious; to take seriously; to take to heart

43 其实 [qíshí] actually; in fact; really

44 游戏 [yóuxì] game; CL: 场 [chǎng]; to play

45 这种 [zhèzhǒng] this; this kind of; this sort of; this type of

46 一种 [yīzhǒng] one kind of; one type of

47 加快 [jiākuài] to accelerate; to speed up

48 重大 [zhòngdà] great; important; major; significant

49 只有 [zhǐyǒu] only

Lesson 16

New Characters

1	2	3	4	5 †	6
后	当	法	办	春	赛

7 †	8 †	9 †	10 †	11 †	12 †
双	越	跟	河	讲	花

13 †	14 †	15 †	16 †	17 †	18
云	拿	楼	信	换	除

19	20	21	22	23	24
变	结	银	般	绩	束

Lesson 16

HSK Vocabulary

25 变化
26 办法
27 以后
28 过去
29 一般
30 除了
31 一样

32 办公室
33 比赛
34 银行
35 成绩
36 结束
37 当然

Non-HSK Vocabulary

38 北京市
39 带来
40 汽车
41 应当
42 才能

43 加大
44 公务员
45 公共
46 只是
47 越来越

Lesson 16

Glossary

1 后 [hòu] surname Hou ◇ empress; queen ◇ back; behind; rear; afterwards; after; later

2 当 [dāng] to be; to act as; manage; withstand; when; during; ought; should; match equally; equal; same; obstruct; just at (a time or place); on the spot; right; just at ◆ [dàng] at or in the very same...; suitable; adequate; fitting; proper; to replace; to regard as; to think; to pawn

3 法 [fǎ] France; French; abbr. for 法国 [Fǎguó] ◇ law; method; way; Buddhist teaching; Legalist

4 办 [bàn] to do; to manage; to handle; to go about; to run; to set up; to deal with

5 春 (†) [chūn] spring (time); gay; joyful; youthful; love; lust; life

6 赛 [sài] to compete; competition; match; to surpass; better than; superior to; to excel

7 双 (†) [shuāng] surname Shuang ◇ two; double; pair; both

8 越 (†) [yuè] generic word for peoples or states of south China or south Asia at different historical periods; abbr. for Vietnam 越南 ◇ to exceed; to climb over; to surpass; the more... the more

9 跟 (†) [gēn] heel; to follow closely; to go with; to marry sb (of woman); with; towards; as (compared to); from (different from); and (in addition to)

10 河 (†) [hé] river; CL: 条 [tiáo], 道 [dào]

11 讲 (†) [jiǎng] to speak; to explain; to negotiate; to emphasise; to be particular about; as far as sth is concerned; speech; lecture

12 花 (†) [huā] surname Hua ◇ flower; blossom; CL: 朵 [duǒ], 支 [zhī], 束 [shù], 把 [bǎ], 盆 [pén], 簇 [cù]; fancy pattern; florid; to spend (money, time)

13 云 (†) [yún] (classical) to say ◇ surname Yun; abbr. for Yunnan Province 云南省 [Yúnnán Shěng] ◇ cloud; CL: 朵 [duǒ]

14 拿 (†) [ná] to hold; to seize; to catch; to apprehend; to take

15 楼 (†) [lóu] house with more than 1 story; storied building; floor; CL: 层 [céng], 座 [zuò], 栋 [dòng]

16 信 (†) [xìn] letter; mail; CL: 封 [fēng]; to trust; to believe; to profess faith in; truthful; confidence; trust; at will; at random

17 换 (†) [huàn] to change; to exchange

18 除 [chú] to get rid of; to remove; to exclude; to eliminate; to wipe out; to divide; except; not including

19 变 [biàn] to change; to become different; to transform; to vary; rebellion

20 结 [jiē] to bear fruit; to produce; firm; solid ◆ [jié] knot; sturdy; bond; to tie; to bind; to check out (of a hotel)

21 银 [yín] silver; silver-colored; relating to money or currency

22 般 [bān] sort; kind; class; way; manner ◆ [pán] see 般乐 [pánlè]

23 绩 [jì] merit; accomplishment; grade; Taiwan pr. [jī]

24 束 [shù] surname Shu ◇ to bind; bunch; bundle; classifier for bunches, bundles, beams of light etc; to control

25 变化 [biànhuà] change; variation; to change; to vary; CL: 个 [gè]

26 办法 [bànfǎ] means; method; way (of doing sth); CL: 条 [tiáo], 个 [gè]

27 以后 [yǐhòu] after; later; afterwards; following; later on; in the future

28 过去 [guòqu] (in the) past; former; previous; to go over; to pass by

29 一般 [yībān] same; ordinary; common; general; generally; in general

30 除了 [chúle] besides; apart from (... also...); in addition to; except (for)

Lesson 16

31 一样 [yīyàng] same; like; equal to; the same as; just like

32 办公室 [bàngōngshì] office; business premises; bureau; CL: 间 [jiān]

33 比赛 [bǐsài] competition (sports etc); match; CL: 场 [chǎng], 次 [cì]

34 银行 [yínháng] bank; CL: 家 [jiā], 个 [gè]

35 成绩 [chéngjì] achievement; performance records; grades; CL: 项 [xiàng], 个 [gè]

36 结束 [jiéshù] termination; to finish; to end; to conclude; to close

37 当然 [dāngrán] only natural; as it should be; certainly; of course; without doubt

38 北京市 [běijīngshì] Beijing; capital of People's Republic of China; one of the four municipalities 直辖市 [zhíxiáshì]

39 带来 [dàilái] to bring; to bring about; to produce

40 汽车 [qìchē] car; automobile; bus; CL: 辆 [liàng]

41 应当 [yīngdāng] should; ought to

42 才能 [cáinéng] talent; ability; capacity

43 加大 [jiādà] to increase (e.g. one's effort)

44 公务员 [gōngwùyuán] functionary; office-bearer

45 公共 [gōnggòng] public; common (use)

46 只是 [zhǐshì] merely; simply; only; but

47 越来越 [yuèláiyuè] more and more

Lesson 17

New Characters

1	2	3	4	5	6 †
园	心	相	片	单	短

7 *	8 *	9 †	10	11 †	12 †
邓	韩	画	注	辆	接

13	14 †	15 †	16 †	17 †	18 †
易	极	包	夏	树	灯

19	20	21	22	23	24
轻	照	育	容	音	乎

25
简

Lesson 17

HSK Vocabulary

26 经常
27 容易
28 注意
29 体育
30 关心
31 最近
32 机会
33 然后
34 年轻
35 简单
36 几乎
37 相信
38 公园
39 音乐
40 照片
41 以前

Non-HSK Vocabulary

42 关注
43 近日
44 红色
45 讲话
46 大力
47 先后
48 住房
49 平方米
50 近年来
51 不要
52 而是
53 上市
54 中共
55 人大
56 中医
57 中方
58 手段
59 今后
60 不到
61 那些
62 为主
63 应对
64 对外
65 来看
66 用于

Lesson 17

Glossary

1 园 [yuán] surname Yuan ◇ land used for growing plants; site used for public recreation

2 心 [xīn] heart; mind; intention; centre; core; CL: 颗 [kē], 个 [gè]

3 相 [xiāng] each other; one another; mutually ◆ [xiàng] appearance; portrait; picture

4 片 [piān] disc; sheet ◆ [piàn] thin piece; flake; a slice; film; TV play; to slice; to carve thin; partial; incomplete; one-sided; classifier for slices, tablets, tract of land, area of water; classifier for CDs, movies, DVDs etc; used with numeral 一 [yī]: classifier for scenario, scene, feeling, atmosphere, sound etc

5 单 [chán] see 单于 [Chányú] ◆ [dān] bill; list; form; single; only; sole; odd number; CL: 个 [gè] ◆ [shàn] surname Shan

6 短 (†) [duǎn] short or brief; to lack; weak point; fault

7 邓 (*) [dèng] surname Deng

8 韩 (*) [hán] Han, one of the Seven Hero States of the Warring States 战国七雄; Korea from the fall of the Joseon dynasty in 1897; Korea, esp. South Korea 大韩民国; surname Han

9 画 (†) [huà] to draw; picture; painting; CL: 幅 [fú], 张 [zhāng]

10 注 [zhù] to inject; to pour into; to concentrate; to pay attention; stake (gambling); classifier for sums of money ◇ to register; to annotate; note; comment

11 辆 (†) [liàng] classifier for vehicles

12 接 (†) [jiē] to receive; to answer (the phone); to meet or welcome sb; to connect; to catch; to join; to extend; to take one's turn on duty; to take over for sb

13 易 [yì] surname Yi ◇ easy; amiable; to change; to exchange

14 极 (†) [jí] extremely; pole (geography, physics); utmost; top

15 包 (†) [bāo] surname Bao ◇ to cover; to wrap; to hold; to include; to take charge of; to contract (to or for); package; wrapper; container; bag; to hold or embrace; bundle; packet; CL: 个 [gè], 只 [zhī]

16 夏 (†) [xià] the Xia or Hsia dynasty c. 2000 BC; Xia of the Sixteen Kingdoms (407–432); surname Xia ◇ summer

17 树 (†) [shù] tree; CL:棵 [kē]

18 灯 (†) [dēng] lamp; light; lantern; CL: 盏 [zhǎn]

19 轻 [qīng] light; easy; gentle; soft; reckless; unimportant; frivolous; small in number; unstressed; neutral

20 照 [zhào] according to; in accordance with; to shine; to illuminate; to reflect; to look at (one's reflection); to take (a photo); photo

21 育 [yù] to have children; to raise or bring up; to educate

22 容 [róng] to hold; to contain; to allow; appearance; look; countenance

23 音 [yīn] sound; noise; note (of musical scale); tone; news; syllable; reading (phonetic value of a character)

24 乎 [hū] (classical particle similar to 于 [yú]) in; at; from; because; than; (classical final particle similar to 吗 [ma], 吧 [ba], 呢 [ne], expressing question, doubt or astonishment)

25 简 [jiǎn] simple; uncomplicated; letter; to choose; to select; bamboo strips used for writing (old)

26 经常 [jīngcháng] day to day; everyday; daily; frequently; constantly; regularly; often

27 容易 [róngyì] easy; likely; liable (to)

28 注意 [zhùyì] to take note of; to pay attention to

29 体育 [tǐyù] sports; physical education

Lesson 17

30 关心 [guānxīn] to care for sth; caring; concerned

31 最近 [zuìjìn] recent; recently; these days; latest; soon; nearest (of locations); shortest (of routes)

32 机会 [jīhuì] opportunity; chance; occasion; CL: 个 [gè]

33 然后 [ránhòu] after; then (afterwards); after that; afterwards

34 年轻 [niánqīng] young

35 简单 [jiǎndān] simple; not complicated

36 几乎 [jīhū] almost; nearly; practically

37 相信 [xiāngxìn] to be convinced (that sth is true); to believe; to accept sth as true

38 公园 [gōngyuán] public park; CL: 场 [chǎng]

39 音乐 [yīnyuè] music; CL: 张 [zhāng], 曲 [qǔ], 段 [duàn]

40 照片 [zhàopiàn] photograph; picture; CL: 张 [zhāng], 套 [tào], 幅 [fú]

41 以前 [yǐqián] before; formerly; previous; ago

42 关注 [guānzhù] to pay attention to; to follow sth closely; concern; interest; attention

43 近日 [jìnrì] in the past few days; recently; in the last few days

44 红色 [hóngsè] red (color); revolutionary

45 讲话 [jiǎnghuà] a speech; to speak; to talk; to address; CL: 个 [gè]

46 大力 [dàlì] energetically; vigorously

47 先后 [xiānhòu] early or late; priority; in succession; one after another

48 住房 [zhùfáng] housing

49 平方米 [píngfāngmǐ] square meter

50 近年来 [jìnniánlái] for the past few years

51 不要 [bùyào] don't!; must not

52 而是 [érshì] rather

53 上市 [shàngshì] to hit the market (of a new product); to float (a company on the stock market)

54 中共 [zhōnggòng] abbr. for Chinese Communist (party, regime etc)

55 人大 [réndà] (Chinese) National People's Congress; abbr. for 全国人民代表大会 [Quánguó Rénmín Dàibiǎo Dàhuì]

56 中医 [zhōngyī] traditional Chinese medical science; a doctor trained in Chinese medicine

57 中方 [zhōngfāng] the Chinese side (in an international venture)

58 手段 [shǒuduàn] method; means (of doing sth); strategy; trick; CL: 个 [gè]

59 今后 [jīnhòu] hereafter; henceforth; in the future; from now on

60 不到 [bùdào] not to arrive; not reaching; insufficient; less than

61 那些 [nàxiē] those

62 为主 [wéizhǔ] to rely mainly on; to attach most importance to

63 应对 [yìngduì] response; to answer; to reply

64 对外 [duìwài] external; foreign; pertaining to external or foreign (affairs)

65 来看 [láikàn] to come and see; to see a topic from a certain point of view

66 用于 [yòngyú] use in; use on; use for

Lesson 18

New Characters

1	2	3	4	5	6
总	网	道	超	节	物

7	8 *	9	10 *	11 †	12 *
街	冯	满	瑞	层	兰

13 †	14 *	15 †	16 †	17	18 *
久	梅	啊	旧	愿	秦

19	20 †	21 †	22 †	23 †	24
演	半	借	差	绿	突

25	26	27	28	29
附	遇	目	终	惯

Lesson 18

HSK Vocabulary

30 节目	36 附近	42 上网
31 方便	37 街道	43 突然
32 习惯	38 终于	44 愿意
33 满意	39 离开	45 总是
34 表演	40 同意	46 超市
35 动物	41 遇到	

Non-HSK Vocabulary

47 网友	56 习近平	65 走向
48 在于	57 这位	66 当中
49 节能	58 商务	67 信息化
50 车辆	59 河南	68 电信
51 法国	60 使得	69 影响力
52 教师	61 近期	70 举报
53 总体	62 主体	71 发出
54 电力	63 南京	
55 一定要	64 加上	

Lesson 18

Glossary

1 总 [zǒng] always; to assemble; gather; total; overall; head; chief; general; in every case

2 网 [wǎng] net; network

3 道 [dào] direction; way; road; path; principle; truth; morality; reason; skill; method; Dao (of Daoism); to say; to speak; to talk; classifier for long thin stretches, rivers, roads etc; province (of Korea do 도, and formerly Japan dō); CL: 条 [tiáo], 股 [gǔ]

4 超 [chāo] to exceed; to overtake; to surpass; to transcend; to pass; to cross; ultra-; super-

5 节 [jié] festival; holiday; node; joint; section; segment; part; to economize; to save; to abridge; moral integrity; classifier for segments, e.g. lessons, train wagons, biblical verses; CL: 个 [gè]

6 物 [wù] thing; object; matter; abbr. for physics 物理

7 街 [jiē] street; CL: 条 [tiáo]

8 冯 (*) [féng] surname Feng ♦ [píng] to gallop; to assist; to attack; to wade; great; old variant of 凭 [píng]

9 满 [mǎn] full; filled; packed; fully; completely; quite; to reach the limit; to satisfy; satisfied; contented; to fill; abbr. for Manchurian

10 瑞 (*) [ruì] lucky; auspicious; propitious; rayl (acoustical unit)

11 层 (†) [céng] layer; stratum; laminated; floor (of a building); storey; classifier for layers; repeated; sheaf (math.)

12 兰 (*) [lán] surname Lan; abbr. for Lanzhou 兰州 [Lánzhōu], Gansu ◇ orchid (兰花 Cymbidium goeringii); fragrant thoroughwort (兰草 Eupatorium fortunei); lily magnolia (木兰)

13 久 (†) [jiǔ] (long) time; (long) duration of time

14 梅 (*) [méi] surname Mei ◇ plum; plum flower; Japanese apricot (Prunus mume)

15 啊 (†) [ā] interjection of surprise; Ah!; Oh! ♦ [á] interjection expressing doubt or requiring answer; Eh?; what?; to show realization; to stress ♦ [ǎ] interjection of surprise or doubt; Eh?; My!; what's up? ♦ [à] interjection or grunt of agreement; uhm; Ah, OK; expression of recognition; Oh, it's you! ♦ [a] modal particle ending sentence, showing affirmation, approval, or consent

16 旧 (†) [jiù] old; opposite: new 新; former; worn (with age)

17 愿 [yuàn] to hope; to wish; to desire; hoped-for; ready; willing; sincere

18 秦 (*) [qín] surname Qin; Qin dynasty (221-207 BC) of the first emperor 秦始皇 [Qín Shǐhuáng]; abbr. for 陕西 [Shǎnxī]

19 演 [yǎn] to develop; to evolve; to practice; to perform; to play; to act

20 半 (†) [bàn] half; semi-; incomplete; (after a number) and a half

21 借 (†) [jiè] to lend; to borrow; excuse; pretext; by means of; to seize (an opportunity); to take (an opportunity)

22 差 (†) [chā] difference; discrepancy; to differ; error; to err; to make a mistake ♦ [chà] to differ from; to fall short of; lacking; wrong; inferior ♦ [chāi] to send; to commission; messenger; mission ♦ [cī] uneven

23 绿 (†) [lǜ] green

24 突 [tū] to dash; to move forward quickly; to bulge; to protrude; to break through; to rush out; sudden; Taiwan pr. [tú]

25 附 [fù] to add; to attach; to be close to; to be attached

26 遇 [yù] surname Yu ◇ to meet; to encounter; to treat; to receive; opportunity; chance

27 目 [mù] eye; item; section; list; catalogue; table of contents; order (taxonomy); goal; name; title

Lesson 18

28 终 [zhōng] end; finish

29 惯 [guàn] accustomed to; used to; indulge; to spoil (a child)

30 节目 [jiémù] program; item (on a program); CL: 台 [tái], 个 [gè], 套 [tào]

31 方便 [fāngbiàn] convenient; to help out; to make things easy for people; convenience; suitable; having money to spare; (euphemism) to go to the toilet

32 习惯 [xíguàn] habit; custom; usual practice; to be used to; CL: 个 [gè]

33 满意 [mǎnyì] satisfied; pleased; to one's satisfaction

34 表演 [biǎoyǎn] play; show; performance; exhibition; to perform; to act; to demonstrate; CL: 场 [chǎng]

35 动物 [dòngwù] animal; CL: 只 [zhī], 群 [qún], 个 [gè]

36 附近 [fùjìn] (in the) vicinity; nearby; neighboring; next to

37 街道 [jiēdào] street; CL: 条 [tiáo]; subdistrict; residential district

38 终于 [zhōngyú] at last; in the end; finally; eventually

39 离开 [líkāi] to depart; to leave

40 同意 [tóngyì] to agree; to consent; to approve

41 遇到 [yùdào] to meet; to run into; to come across

42 上网 [shàngwǎng] to be on the internet; to stretch a net (in a sports game or for covering sth); to be netted (of fish)

43 突然 [tūrán] sudden; abrupt; unexpected

44 愿意 [yuànyì] to wish; to want; ready; willing (to do sth)

45 总是 [zǒngshì] always

46 超市 [chāoshì] supermarket (abbr.); CL: 家 [jiā]

47 网友 [wǎngyǒu] online friend; Internet user

48 在于 [zàiyú] to be in; to lie in; to consist in; to depend on; to rest with

49 节能 [jiénéng] to save energy; energy-saving

50 车辆 [chēliàng] vehicle

51 法国 [fǎguó] France; French; Taiwan pr. [Fà guó]

52 教师 [jiàoshī] teacher; CL: 个 [gè]

53 总体 [zǒngtǐ] completely; totally; total; entire; overall; population (statistics)

54 电力 [diànlì] electrical power; electricity

55 一定要 [yīdìngyào] must

56 习近平 [xíjìnpíng] Xi Jinping (1953-), PRC politician, PRC vice-chair from 2008

57 这位 [zhèwèi] this (person)

58 商务 [shāngwù] commercial affairs; commercial; commerce; business

59 河南 [hénán] Henan province (Honan) in central China, abbr. 豫, capital Zhengzhou 郑州

60 使得 [shǐde] usable; workable; feasible; doable; to make; to cause

61 近期 [jìnqī] near in time; in the near future; very soon; recent

62 主体 [zhǔtǐ] main part; subject; agent

63 南京 [nánjīng] Nanjing subprovincial city on the Changjiang, capital of Jiangsu province 江苏; capital of China at different historical periods

64 加上 [jiāshàng] plus; to put in; to add; to add on; to add into; in addition; on top of that

65 走向 [zǒuxiàng] direction; strike (i.e. angle of inclination in geology); inclination; trend; to move towards; to head for

66 当中 [dāngzhōng] among; in the middle; in the center

67 信息化 [xìnxīhuà] informatization (the Information Age analog of industrialization)

68 电信 [diànxìn] telecommunications

Lesson 18

69 影响力 [yǐngxiǎnglì] influence; impact

70 举报 [jǔbào] to report (malefactors to the police); to denounce

71 发出 [fāchū] to issue (an order, decree etc); to send out; to dispatch; to produce a sound; to let out (a laugh)

Lesson 19

New Characters

1	2	3	4	5	6
酒	清	声	调	空	理

7 *	8 †	9 *	10 *	11 †	12 †
斌	冬	伊	芳	脸	糖

13 *	14 †	15 *	16 †	17 †	18
彭	背	吕	秋	脚	婚

19 †	20 †	21 †	22 †	23	24
草	角	蓝	敢	楚	炼

25	26	27
担	锻	啤

Lesson 19

HSK Vocabulary

28	担心	33	一边	38	结婚
29	空调	34	经理	39	锻炼
30	声音	35	校长	40	节日
31	啤酒	36	司机	41	相同
32	以为	37	清楚	42	中间

Non-HSK Vocabulary

43	韩国	52	房子	61	晚会
44	东方	53	天下	62	影片
45	绿化	54	读者	63	候选人
46	名单	55	药物	64	要有
47	酒店	56	家人	65	化工
48	不错	57	面向	66	现有
49	背后	58	新城	67	最为
50	日照	59	第二十		
51	年轻人	60	共识		

Lesson 19

Glossary

1 酒 [jiǔ] wine (esp. rice wine); liquor; spirits; alcoholic beverage; CL: 杯 [bēi], 瓶 [píng], 罐 [guàn], 桶 [tǒng], 缸 [gāng]

2 清 [qīng] Qing or Ch'ing dynasty of Imperial China (1644-1911); surname Qing ◇ clear; distinct; quiet; just and honest; pure; to settle or clear up; to clean up or purge

3 声 [shēng] sound; voice; tone; noise; classifier for sounds

4 调 [diào] to transfer; to move (troops or cadres); to investigate; to enquire into; accent; view; argument; key (in music); mode (music); tune; tone; melody ◆ [tiáo] to harmonize; to reconcile; to blend; to suit well; to season (food); to provoke; to incite

5 空 [kōng] empty; air; sky; in vain ◆ [kòng] to empty; vacant; unoccupied; space; leisure; free time

6 理 [lǐ] texture; grain (of wood); inner essence; intrinsic order; reason; logic; truth; science; natural science (esp. physics); to manage; to pay attention to; to run (affairs); to handle; to put in order; to tidy up

7 斌 (*) [bīn] variant of 彬 [bīn]

8 冬 (†) [dōng] winter ◇ surname Dong ◇ sound of beating a drum; onomatopoeia for rat-a-tat etc

9 伊 (*) [yī] surname Yi; abbr. for Iraq or Iran ◇ he; she

10 芳 (*) [fāng] fragrant

11 脸 (†) [liǎn] face; CL: 张 [zhāng], 个 [gè]

12 糖 (†) [táng] sugar; sweets; candy; CL: 颗 [kē], 块 [kuài]

13 彭 (*) [péng] surname Peng

14 背 (†) [bēi] to be burdened; to carry on the back or shoulder ◆ [bèi] the back of a body or object; to turn one's back; to hide something from; to learn by heart; to recite from memory; unlucky (slang); hard of hearing

15 吕 (*) [lǚ] surname Lü ◇ pitchpipe, pitch standard, one of the twelve semitones in the traditional tone system

16 秋 (†) [qiū] surname Qiu ◇ autumn; fall; harvest time; a swing ◇ a swing

17 脚 (†) [jiǎo] foot; leg; base; kick; CL: 双 [shuāng], 只 [zhī] ◆ [jué] role

18 婚 [hūn] to marry; marriage; wedding; to take a wife

19 草 (†) [cǎo] grass; straw; manuscript; draft (of a document); careless; rough; CL: 棵 [kē], 撮 [zuǒ], 株 [zhū], 根 [gēn]

20 角 (†) [jiǎo] angle; corner; horn; horn-shaped; unit of money equal to 0.1 yuan; CL: 个 [gè] ◆ [jué] surname Jue ◇ role (theater); to compete; ancient three legged wine vessel; third note of pentatonic scale

21 蓝 (†) [lán] surname Lan ◇ blue; indigo plant

22 敢 (†) [gǎn] to dare; daring; (polite) may I venture

23 楚 [chǔ] surname Chu; abbr. for Hubei 湖北省 [Húběi Shěng] and Hunan 湖南省 [Húnán Shěng] provinces together; Chinese kingdom during the Spring and Autumn and Warring States Periods (722-221 BC) ◇ distinct; clear; orderly; pain; suffering; deciduous bush used in Chinese medicine (genus Vitex); punishment cane (old)

24 炼 [liàn] to refine; to smelt

25 担 [dān] to undertake; to carry; to shoulder; to take responsibility ◆ [dàn] picul (100 catties, 50 kg); two buckets full; carrying pole and its load; classifier for loads carried on a shoulder pole

26 锻 [duàn] forge; wrought; to discipline

27 啤 [pí] beer

Lesson 19

28 担心 [dānxīn] anxious; worried; uneasy; to worry; to be anxious

29 空调 [kōngtiáo] air conditioning

30 声音 [shēngyīn] voice; sound; CL: 个 [gè]

31 啤酒 [píjiǔ] beer; CL: 杯 [bēi], 瓶 [píng], 罐 [guàn], 桶 [tǒng], 缸 [gāng]

32 以为 [yǐwéi] to believe; to think; to consider; to be under the impression

33 一边 [yībiān] one side; either side; on the one hand; on the other hand; doing while

34 经理 [jīnglǐ] manager; director; CL: 个 [gè], 位 [wèi], 名 [míng]

35 校长 [xiàozhǎng] (college, university) president; headmaster; CL: 个 [gè], 位 [wèi], 名 [míng]

36 司机 [sījī] chauffeur; driver; CL: 个 [gè]

37 清楚 [qīngchu] clear; distinct; to understand thoroughly; to be clear about

38 结婚 [jiéhūn] to marry; to get married; CL: 次 [cì]

39 锻炼 [duànliàn] to engage in physical exercise; to work out; to toughen; to temper

40 节日 [jiérì] holiday; festival; CL: 个 [gè]

41 相同 [xiāngtóng] identical; same

42 中间 [zhōngjiān] between; intermediate; mid; middle

43 韩国 [hánguó] Han, one of the Seven Hero States of the Warring States 战国七雄 [zhànguó qīxióng]; Korea from the fall of the Joseon dynasty in 1897; Korea, esp. Republic of Korea (South Korea) 大韩民国 [Dàhán mínguó]

44 东方 [dōngfāng] the East; eastern countries; the orient

45 绿化 [lǜhuà] to make green with plants; to reforest

46 名单 [míngdān] list (of names)

47 酒店 [jiǔdiàn] wine shop; pub (public house); hotel; restaurant

48 不错 [bùcuò] correct; right; not bad; pretty good

49 背后 [bèihòu] behind; at the back; in the rear; behind sb's back

50 日照 [rìzhào] Rizhao prefecture level city in Shandong ◇ sunshine

51 年轻人 [niánqīngrén] young people

52 房子 [fángzi] house; building (single- or two-story); apartment; room; CL: 栋 [dòng], 幢 [zhuàng], 座 [zuò], 套 [tào]

53 天下 [tiānxià] land under heaven; the whole world; the whole of China; realm; rule; domination

54 读者 [dúzhě] reader; CL: 个 [gè]

55 药物 [yàowù] medicaments; pharmaceuticals; medication; medicine; drug

56 家人 [jiārén] household; (one's) family

57 面向 [miànxiàng] to face; to turn towards; to incline to; geared towards; catering for; -oriented; facial feature; appearance; aspect; facet

58 新城 [xīnchéng] Xincheng or Hsincheng township in Hualien county 花莲县 [Huāliánxiàn], east Taiwan

59 第二十 [dì'èrshí] twentieth

60 共识 [gòngshí] common understanding; consensus

61 晚会 [wǎnhuì] evening party; CL: 个 [gè]

62 影片 [yǐngpiàn] film; movie; CL: 部 [bù]

63 候选人 [hòuxuǎnrén] candidate; CL: 名 [míng]

64 要有 [yàoyǒu] to need; to require; must have

65 化工 [huàgōng] chemical industry, abbr. of 化学工业 [huàxué gōngyè]; chemical engineering, abbr. of 化学工程 [huàxué gōngchéng]

66 现有 [xiànyǒu] currently existing; currently available

67 最为 [zuìwéi] the most

Lesson 20

New Characters

1	2	3	4	5	6
事	业	图	刚	铁	算

7	8	9	10 *	11	12
记	冰	鲜	萨	顾	箱

13 *	14 †	15 †	16 *	17 *	18 *
寨	刻	腿	姚	曼	贾

19 †	20 †	21	22 †	23 †	24 †
骑	甜	忘	搬	祝	坏

25	26	27
宾	趣	梯

Lesson 20

HSK Vocabulary

28	照顾	34	地铁	40	兴趣
29	同事	35	记得	41	宾馆
30	新鲜	36	刚才	42	作业
31	放心	37	北方	43	图书馆
32	冰箱	38	客人	44	忘记
33	打算	39	见面	45	电梯

Non-HSK Vocabulary

46	铁路	55	较为	64	西南
47	服务业	56	旅游业	65	主角
48	事实上	57	其它	66	办事
49	病人	58	天然	67	工业化
50	难题	59	百万	68	法定
51	画面	60	理事长	69	种种
52	白酒	61	下一步	70	一步
53	发电	62	拿出		
54	起点	63	一半		

Lesson 20

Glossary

1 事 [shì] matter; thing; item; work; affair; CL: 件 [jiàn], 桩 [zhuāng]

2 业 [yè] business; occupation; study; estate; property

3 图 [tú] diagram; picture; drawing; chart; map; CL: 张 [zhāng]; to plan; to scheme; to attempt; to pursue; to seek

4 刚 [gāng] hard; firm; strong; just; barely; exactly

5 铁 [tiě] surname Tie ◇ iron (metal); arms; weapons; hard; strong; violent; unshakeable; determined; close; tight (slang)

6 算 [suàn] to regard as; to figure; to calculate; to compute

7 记 [jì] to remember; to note; mark; sign; to record

8 冰 [bīng] ice; CL: 块 [kuài]; methamphetamine (slang)

9 鲜 [xiān] fresh; bright (in color); delicious; tasty; delicacy; aquatic foods; seldom ◆ [xiǎn] few; rare

10 萨 (*) [sà] Bodhisattva; surname Sa

11 顾 [gù] surname Gu ◇ to look after; to take into consideration; to attend to

12 箱 [xiāng] box; trunk; chest

13 寨 (*) [zhài] stronghold; stockade; camp; village

14 刻 (†) [kè] quarter (hour); moment; to carve; to engrave; to cut; oppressive; classifier for short time intervals

15 腿 (†) [tuǐ] leg; CL: 条 [tiáo]

16 姚 (*) [yáo] surname Yao ◇ handsome; good-looking

17 曼 (*) [màn] handsome; large; long

18 贾 (*) [gǔ] merchant; to buy ◆ [jiǎ] surname Jia

19 骑 (†) [jì] (Taiwan) saddle horse; mounted soldier ◆ [qí] to ride (an animal or bike); to sit astride

20 甜 (†) [tián] sweet

21 忘 [wàng] to forget; to overlook; to neglect

22 搬 (†) [bān] to move; to shift; to remove; to transport; to apply indiscriminately; to copy mechanically

23 祝 (†) [zhù] surname Zhu ◇ to wish; to express good wishes; to pray; (old) wizard

24 坏 (†) [huài] bad; spoiled; broken; to break down

25 宾 [bīn] visitor; guest; object (in grammar)

26 趣 [qù] interesting; to interest

27 梯 [tī] ladder; stairs

28 照顾 [zhàogu] to take care of; to show consideration; to attend to; to look after

29 同事 [tóngshì] colleague; co-worker; CL: 个 [gè], 位 [wèi]

30 新鲜 [xīnxiān] fresh (experience, food etc); freshness

31 放心 [fàngxīn] to feel relieved; to feel reassured; to be at ease

32 冰箱 [bīngxiāng] icebox; freezer cabinet; refrigerator; CL: 台 [tái], 个 [gè]

33 打算 [dǎsuàn] to plan; to intend; to calculate; plan; intention; calculation; CL: 个 [gè]

34 地铁 [dìtiě] subway; metro

35 记得 [jìde] to remember

36 刚才 [gāngcái] just now; a moment ago ◇ (just) a moment ago

37 北方 [běifāng] north; the northern part a country; China north of the Yellow River

38 客人 [kèrén] visitor; guest; customer; client; CL: 位 [wèi]

39 见面 [jiànmiàn] to meet; to see sb; CL: 次 [cì]

Lesson 20

40 兴趣 [xìngqù] interest (desire to know about sth); interest (thing in which one is interested); hobby; CL: 个 [gè]

41 宾馆 [bīnguǎn] guesthouse; CL: 个 [gè], 家 [jiā]

42 作业 [zuòyè] school assignment; homework; work; task; operation; CL: 个 [gè]; to operate

43 图书馆 [túshūguǎn] library; CL: 家 [jiā], 个 [gè]

44 忘记 [wàngjì] to forget

45 电梯 [diàntī] elevator; escalator; CL: 台 [tái], 部 [bù]

46 铁路 [tiělù] railroad; railway; CL: 条 [tiáo]

47 服务业 [fúwùyè] service industry

48 事实上 [shìshíshàng] in fact; in reality; actually; as a matter of fact; de facto; ipso facto

49 病人 [bìngrén] sick person; patient; invalid; CL: 个 [gè]

50 难题 [nántí] difficult problem

51 画面 [huàmiàn] scene; tableau; picture; image; screen (displayed by a computer); (motion picture) frame; field of view

52 白酒 [báijiǔ] spirit usually distilled from sorghum or maize; white spirit

53 发电 [fādiàn] to generate electricity; to send a telegram

54 起点 [qǐdiǎn] starting point

55 较为 [jiàowéi] comparatively; relatively; fairly

56 旅游业 [lǚyóuyè] tourism industry

57 其它 [qítā] other; the others; else; other than it; in addition to the thing mentioned above

58 天然 [tiānrán] natural

59 百万 [bǎiwàn] million; millions

60 理事长 [lǐshìzhǎng] director general

61 下一步 [xiàyībù] the next step

62 拿出 [náchū] to take out; to put out; to provide; to put forward (a proposal); to come up with (evidence)

63 一半 [yībàn] half

64 西南 [xīnán] southwest

65 主角 [zhǔjué] leading role; lead

66 办事 [bànshì] to handle (affairs); to work; to run an errand (outside the office); to go on a business trip

67 工业化 [gōngyèhuà] to industrialize; industrialization

68 法定 [fǎdìng] legal; statutory; rightful

69 种种 [zhǒngzhǒng] all kinds of

70 一步 [yībù] (single) step

Lesson 21

New Characters

1	2	3	4	5	6
萄	级	周	头	感	干

7	8	9	10	11	12
阳	礼	季	护	净	末

13 *	14	15 †	16 *	17 †	18 *
萍	熊	鞋	琪	哭	淑

19 *	20	21 *	22 †	23	24 †
遂	厨	邵	瘦	聪	饱

25	26 †	27
冒	鸟	葡

Lesson 21

HSK Vocabulary

28 季节	35 年级	42 护照
29 厨房	36 可爱	43 小心
30 太阳	37 周末	44 帮忙
31 明白	38 花园	45 多么
32 干净	39 礼物	46 感冒
33 葡萄	40 熊猫	47 聪明
34 地图	41 头发	

Non-HSK Vocabulary

48 太阳能	57 一方	66 出国
49 一周	58 机动车	67 实体
50 半年	59 二次	68 同年
51 当日	60 不易	69 当晚
52 下调	61 门口	70 网店
53 决算	62 哪个	71 旅行
54 大城市	63 九十	72 多样
55 不满	64 演唱	
56 发起	65 健身	

Lesson 21

Glossary

1 萄 [táo] grapes

2 级 [jí] level; grade; rank; step; CL: 个 [gè]

3 周 [zhōu] surname Zhou; Zhou Dynasty (1046-256 BC) ◊ to make a circuit; to circle; circle; circumference; lap; cycle; complete; all; all over; thorough; to help financially ◊ week; weekly

4 头 [tóu] head; hair style; the top; end; beginning or end; a stub; remnant; chief; boss; side; aspect; first; leading; classifier for pigs or livestock; CL: 个 [gè] ◆ [tou] suff. for nouns

5 感 [gǎn] to feel; to move; to touch; to affect

6 干 [gān] surname Gan ◊ dry; clean; in vain; dried food; foster; adoptive; to ignore ◊ to concern; to interfere; shield; stem ◆ [gàn] to work; to do; to manage ◊ tree trunk; main part of sth; to manage; to work; to do; capable; cadre; to kill (slang); to fuck (vulgar)

7 阳 [yáng] positive (electric.); sun; male principle (Taoism); Yang, opposite: 阴 [yīn] ☯

8 礼 [lǐ] surname Li ◊ gift; rite; ceremony; CL: 份 [fèn]; propriety; etiquette; courtesy

9 季 [jì] surname Ji ◊ season; the last month of a season; fourth or youngest amongst brothers; classifier for seasonal crop yields

10 护 [hù] to protect

11 净 [jìng] clean; completely; only

12 末 [mò] tip; end; final stage; latter part; inessential detail; powder; dust; opera role of old man

13 萍 (*) [píng] duckweed

14 熊 [xióng] surname Xiong ◊ bear; to scold; to rebuke; brilliant light; to shine brightly

15 鞋 (†) [xié] shoe; CL: 双 [shuāng], 只 [zhī]

16 琪 (*) [qí] fine jade

17 哭 (†) [kū] to cry; to weep

18 淑 (*) [shū] warm and virtuous; used in given names; Taiwan pr. [shú]

19 遂 (*) [suì] to satisfy; to succeed; then; thereupon; finally; unexpectedly; to proceed; to reach

20 厨 [chú] kitchen

21 邵 (*) [shào] surname Shao; place name

22 瘦 (†) [shòu] thin; to lose weight; (of clothing) tight; (of meat) lean; (of land) unproductive

23 聪 [cōng] quick at hearing; wise; clever; sharp-witted; intelligent; acute

24 饱 (†) [bǎo] to eat till full; satisfied

25 冒 [mào] to emit; to give off; to send out (or up, forth); brave; bold; to cover

26 鸟 (†) [niǎo] bird; CL: 只 [zhī], 群 [qún]

27 葡 [pú] Portugal; Portuguese; abbr. for 葡萄牙 [Pútáoyá] ◊ grapes

28 季节 [jìjié] time; season; period; CL: 个 [gè]

29 厨房 [chúfáng] kitchen; CL: 间 [jiān]

30 太阳 [tàiyáng] sun; CL: 个 [gè]

31 明白 [míngbai] clear; obvious; unequivocal; to understand; to realize

32 干净 [gānjìng] clean; neat

33 葡萄 [pútao] grape

34 地图 [dìtú] map; CL: 张 [zhāng], 本 [běn]

35 年级 [niánjí] grade; CL: 个 [gè]

36 可爱 [kě'ài] adorable; cute; lovely

37 周末 [zhōumò] weekend

38 花园 [huāyuán] garden; CL: 座 [zuò], 个 [gè]

39 礼物 [lǐwù] gift; present; CL: 件 [jiàn], 个 [gè], 份 [fèn]

40 熊猫 [xióngmāo] panda; CL: 只 [zhī]

41 头发 [tóufa] hair (on the head)

Lesson 21

42 护照 [hùzhào] passport; CL: 本 [běn], 个 [gè]

43 小心 [xiǎoxīn] to be careful; to take care

44 帮忙 [bāngmáng] to help; to lend a hand; to do a favor; to do a good turn

45 多么 [duōme] how (wonderful etc); what (a great idea etc); however (difficult it may be etc)

46 感冒 [gǎnmào] to catch cold; (common) cold; CL: 场 [cháng], 次 [cì]

47 聪明 [cōngming] acute (of sight and hearing); clever; intelligent; bright; smart

48 太阳能 [tàiyángnéng] solar energy

49 一周 [yīzhōu] one week; all the way around; a whole cycle

50 半年 [bànnián] half a year

51 当日 [dàngrì] that very day; the same day

52 下调 [xiàdiào] to demote; to pass down to a lower unit ◆ [xiàtiáo] to adjust downwards; to lower (prices, wages etc)

53 决算 [juésuàn] final account; to calculate the final bill; fig. to draw up plans to deal with sth

54 大城市 [dàchéngshì] major city; big city; metropolis; large city

55 不满 [bùmǎn] resentful; discontented; dissatisfied

56 发起 [fāqǐ] to originate; to initiate; to launch (an attack, an initiative etc); to start; to propose sth (for the first time)

57 一方 [yīfāng] a party (in a contract or legal case); one side; area; region

58 机动车 [jīdòngchē] motor vehicle

59 二次 [èrcì] second (i.e. number two); second time; twice; (math.) quadratic (of degree two)

60 不易 [bùyì] not easy to do sth; difficult; unchanging

61 门口 [ménkǒu] doorway; gate; CL: 个 [gè]

62 哪个 [nǎge] which; who

63 九十 [jiǔshí] ninety

64 演唱 [yǎnchàng] sung performance; to sing for an audience

65 健身 [jiànshēn] physical exercise; gymnastics for fitness

66 出国 [chūguó] to go abroad; to leave the country; emigration

67 实体 [shítǐ] entity; substance; thing that has a material existence (as opposed to a conceptual, virtual or online existence); the real thing (as opposed to an image or model of it)

68 同年 [tóngnián] the same year

69 当晚 [dàngwǎn] that evening; the same evening

70 网店 [wǎngdiàn] online shop

71 旅行 [lǚxíng] to travel; journey; trip; CL: 趟 [tàng], 次 [cì], 个 [gè]

72 多样 [duōyàng] diverse; diversity; manifold

Lesson 22

New Characters

1	2	3	4	5	6
数	安	阿	奇	居	静

7	8	9	10	11	12 *
怕	练	镜	怪	汁	晖

13	14	15 *	16 †	17 *	18
害	邻	徽	碗	逆	帽

19	20 †	21 *	22 *	23 †	24 †
鼻	胖	烨	禄	疼	渴

25	26	27	28
爷	糕	澡	姨

Lesson 22

HSK Vocabulary

29 邻居	36 爷爷	43 爱好
30 有名	37 生气	44 一会儿
31 蛋糕	38 帽子	45 奶奶
32 一共	39 奇怪	46 安静
33 害怕	40 眼镜	47 面包
34 数学	41 果汁	48 阿姨
35 练习	42 洗澡	49 鼻子

Non-HSK Vocabulary

50 工地	59 定点	68 如期
51 意愿	60 有一次	69 使馆
52 不怕	61 服用	70 万里
53 祝愿	62 高低	71 万物
54 几个月	63 大业	72 选定
55 讲解	64 脚步	73 前方
56 当作	65 选用	74 蓝月亮
57 一号	66 有影响	
58 就算	67 同等	

Lesson 22

Glossary

1 数 [shǔ] to count; to enumerate; to criticize (i.e. enumerate shortcomings) ♦ [shù] number; figure; several; CL: 个 [gè] ♦ [shuò] frequently; repeatedly

2 安 [ān] surname An ◇ content; calm; still; quiet; safe; secure; in good health; to find a place for; to install; to fix; to fit; to bring (a charge against sb); to pacify; security; safety; peace; ampere

3 阿 [ā] abbr. for Afghanistan 阿富汗 [Āfùhàn] ◇ prefix used before monosyllabic names, kinship terms etc to indicate familiarity; used in transliteration; also pr. [à] ♦ [ē] flatter

4 奇 [jī] odd (number) ♦ [qí] strange; odd; weird; wonderful

5 居 [jī] (archaic) sentence-final particle expressing a doubting attitude ♦ [jū] surname Ju ◇ to reside; to be (in a certain position); to store up; to be at a standstill; residence; house; restaurant; classifier for bedrooms

6 静 [jìng] still; calm; quiet; not moving

7 怕 [pà] surname Pa ◇ to be afraid; to fear; to dread; to be unable to endure; perhaps

8 练 [liàn] to practice; to train; to drill; to perfect (one's skill); exercise

9 镜 [jìng] mirror

10 怪 [guài] bewildering; odd; strange; uncanny; devil; monster; to wonder at; to blame; quite; rather

11 汁 [zhī] juice

12 晖 (*) [huī] sunshine; to shine upon; variant of 辉 [huī]

13 害 [hài] to do harm to; to cause trouble to; harm; evil; calamity

14 邻 [lín] neighbor; adjacent; close to

15 徽 (*) [huī] badge; emblem; insignia; crest; logo; coat of arms

16 碗 (†) [wǎn] bowl; cup; CL: 只 [zhī], 个 [gè]

17 逆 (*) [nì] contrary; opposite; backwards; to go against; to oppose; to betray; to rebel

18 帽 [mào] hat; cap

19 鼻 [bí] nose

20 胖 (†) [pàng] fat; plump

21 烨 (*) [yè] blaze of fire; glorious

22 禄 (*) [lù] good fortune; official salary

23 疼 (†) [téng] (it) hurts; sore; to love dearly

24 渴 (†) [kě] thirsty

25 爷 [yé] grandpa; old gentleman

26 糕 [gāo] cake

27 澡 [zǎo] bath

28 姨 [yí] mother's sister; aunt

29 邻居 [línjū] neighbor; next door; CL: 个 [gè]

30 有名 [yǒumíng] famous; well-known

31 蛋糕 [dàngāo] cake; CL: 块 [kuài], 个 [gè]

32 一共 [yīgòng] altogether

33 害怕 [hàipà] to be afraid; to be scared

34 数学 [shùxué] mathematics; mathematical

35 练习 [liànxí] exercise; drill; practice; CL: 个 [gè]

36 爷爷 [yéye] (informal) father's father; paternal grandfather; CL: 个 [gè]

37 生气 [shēngqì] angry; mad; offended; animated; to get angry; to be enraged; to take offense; animation

38 帽子 [màozi] hat; cap; CL: 顶 [dǐng]

39 奇怪 [qíguài] strange; odd; to marvel; to be baffled

40 眼镜 [yǎnjìng] spectacles; eyeglasses; CL: 副 [fù]

41 果汁 [guǒzhī] fruit juice

42 洗澡 [xǐzǎo] to bathe; to take a shower

Lesson 22

43 爱好 [àihào] to like; to take pleasure in; keen on; fond of; interest; hobby; appetite for; CL: 个 [gè]

44 一会儿 [yīhuìr] a while; also pr. [yī huǐ r]

45 奶奶 [nǎinai] (informal) father's mother; paternal grandmother; CL: 位 [wèi]

46 安静 [ānjìng] quiet; peaceful; calm

47 面包 [miànbāo] bread; CL: 片 [piàn], 袋 [dài], 块 [kuài]

48 阿姨 [āyí] maternal aunt; step-mother; childcare worker; nursemaid; woman of similar age to one's parents (term of address used by child); CL: 个 [gè]

49 鼻子 [bízi] nose; CL: 个 [gè], 只 [zhī]

50 工地 [gōngdì] construction site

51 意愿 [yìyuàn] aspiration; wish (for); desire

52 不怕 [bùpà] fearless; not worried (by setbacks or difficulties)

53 祝愿 [zhùyuàn] to wish

54 几个月 [jǐgeyuè] several months; the last few months

55 讲解 [jiǎngjiě] to explain

56 当作 [dàngzuò] to treat as; to regard as

57 一号 [yīhào] first day of the month

58 就算 [jiùsuàn] granted that; even if

59 定点 [dìngdiǎn] fixed point or location; point of reference; (math.) fixed point; to determine a location

60 有一次 [yǒuyīcì] once; once upon a time

61 服用 [fúyòng] to take (medicine)

62 高低 [gāodī] height; altitude (aviation); pitch (music); ups and downs (success or failure); whether sth is right or wrong; comparative strength, weight, depth, stature; (spoken interjection) anyway, whatever; eventually, in the end

63 大业 [dàyè] great cause; great undertaking

64 脚步 [jiǎobù] footstep; step

65 选用 [xuǎnyòng] to choose for some purpose; to select and use

66 有影响 [yǒuyǐngxiǎng] influential

67 同等 [tóngděng] equal to; having the same social class or status

68 如期 [rúqī] as scheduled; on time; punctual

69 使馆 [shǐguǎn] consulate; diplomatic mission

70 万里 [wànlǐ] Wan Li (1916-), PRC politician ◇ Wanli township in Taipei county 台北县 [Táiběixiàn], Taiwan ◇ far away; thousands of miles; 10000 li

71 万物 [wànwù] all living things

72 选定 [xuǎndìng] to pick out; to select; chosen and fixed

73 前方 [qiánfāng] ahead; the front

74 蓝月亮 [lányuèliang] Blue Moon, a hypothetical planet

Lesson 23

New Characters

1	2	3	4	5	6
通	香	盘	普	词	复

7	8	9	10	11	12
急	烧	耳	舒	刷	牙

13	14	15	16	17 *	18
朵	扫	裙	迟	贞	邮

19 *	20	21	22 *	23 *	24 †
闽	衫	叔	阁	婧	伞

25 *	26 †	27	28 †	29	30
葱	饿	裤	矮	衬	蕉

31
筷

Lesson 23

HSK Vocabulary

32 复习	40 着急	48 筷子
33 香蕉	41 普通话	49 月亮
34 耳朵	42 打扫	50 盘子
35 刷牙	43 迟到	51 词语
36 电子邮件	44 难过	52 面条
37 叔叔	45 发烧	53 裙子
38 舒服	46 裤子	
39 菜单	47 衬衫	

Non-HSK Vocabulary

54 回复	63 新春	72 南越
55 西班牙	64 天使	73 口水
56 较长	65 头上	74 环境影响
57 想办法	66 马力	75 自带
58 香水	67 超前	76 就地
59 家用	68 学业	77 过错
60 高发	69 花样	78 国务院新闻办公室
61 考查	70 名城	
62 必备	71 高楼	

Lesson 23

Glossary

1 通 [tōng] to go through; to know well; to connect; to communicate; open; to clear; classifier for letters, telegrams, phone calls etc ◆ [tòng] classifier for sections of music playing; classifier for bouts of unpleasant language

2 香 [xiāng] fragrant; sweet smelling; aromatic; savory or appetizing; (to eat) with relish; (of sleep) sound; perfume or spice; joss or incense stick; CL: 根 [gēn]

3 盘 [pán] plate; dish; tray; board; to build; to coil; to check; to examine; to transfer (property); to make over; classifier for food: dish, helping; to coil; classifier for coils of wire; classifier for games of chess

4 普 [pǔ] general; popular; everywhere; universal

5 词 [cí] word; statement; speech; lyrics; CL: 组 [zǔ], 个 [gè]; classical Chinese poem; CL: 首 [shǒu]

6 复 [fù] to go and return; to return; to resume; to return to a normal or original state; to repeat; again; to recover; to restore; to turn over; to reply; to answer; to reply to a letter; to retaliate; to carry out ◇ to repeat; to double; to overlap; complex (not simple); compound; composite; double; diplo-; duplicate; overlapping; to duplicate

7 急 [jí] urgent; pressing; rapid; hurried; worried

8 烧 [shāo] to burn; to cook; to stew; to bake; to roast; fever

9 耳 [ěr] ear; handle (archaeology); and that is all (classical Chinese)

10 舒 [shū] surname Shu ◇ to stretch; to unfold; to relax; leisurely

11 刷 [shuā] to brush; to paint; to daub; to paste up; to skip class (of students); to fire from a job ◆ [shuà] to select

12 牙 [yá] tooth; ivory; CL: 颗 [kē]

13 朵 [duǒ] flower; earlobe; fig. item on both sides; classifier for flowers, clouds etc

14 扫 [sǎo] to sweep ◆ [sào] broom

15 裙 [qún] skirt

16 迟 [chí] surname Chi ◇ late; delayed; slow

17 贞 (*) [zhēn] chaste

18 邮 [yóu] post (office); mail

19 闽 (*) [mǐn] abbr. for Fujian 福建 province

20 衫 [shān] garment; jacket with open slits in place of sleeves

21 叔 [shū] uncle; father's younger brother; husband's younger brother; Taiwan pr. [shú]

22 阎 (*) [yán] Yama; gate of village; surname Yan

23 婧 (*) [jìng] modest; supple

24 伞 (†) [sǎn] umbrella; parasol; CL: 把 [bǎ]

25 葱 (*) [cōng] scallion; green onion

26 饿 (†) [è] to be hungry; hungry

27 裤 [kù] drawers; trousers; pants

28 矮 (†) [ǎi] low; short (in length)

29 衬 [chèn] (of garments) against the skin; to line; lining; to contrast with; to assist financially

30 蕉 [jiāo] banana

31 筷 [kuài] chopstick

32 复习 [fùxí] to revise; to review; revision; CL: 次 [cì]

33 香蕉 [xiāngjiāo] banana; CL: 枝 [zhī], 根 [gēn], 个 [gè], 把 [bǎ]

34 耳朵 [ěrduo] ear; CL: 只 [zhī], 个 [gè], 对 [duì]

35 刷牙 [shuāyá] to brush teeth

36 电子邮件 [diànzǐyóujiàn] electronic mail; email; CL: 封 [fēng]

37 叔叔 [shūshu] father's younger brother; uncle; Taiwan pr. [shú shu]; CL: 个 [gè]

Lesson 23

38 舒服 [shūfu] comfortable; feeling well

39 菜单 [càidān] menu; CL: 份 [fèn], 张 [zhāng]

40 着急 [zháojí] to worry; to feel anxious; Taiwan pron. [zhāo jí]

41 普通话 [pǔtōnghuà] Mandarin (common language); Putonghua (common speech of the Chinese language); ordinary speech

42 打扫 [dǎsǎo] to clean; to sweep

43 迟到 [chídào] to arrive late

44 难过 [nánguò] to feel sad; to feel unwell; (of life) to be difficult

45 发烧 [fāshāo] to have a high temperature (from illness); to have a fever

46 裤子 [kùzi] trousers; pants; CL: 条 [tiáo]

47 衬衫 [chènshān] shirt; blouse; CL: 件 [jiàn]

48 筷子 [kuàizi] chopsticks; CL: 对 [duì], 根 [gēn], 把 [bǎ], 双 [shuāng]

49 月亮 [yuèliang] moon

50 盘子 [pánzi] tray; plate; dish; CL: 个 [gè]

51 词语 [cíyǔ] word (general term including monosyllables through to short phrases); term (e.g. technical term); expression

52 面条 [miàntiáo] noodles

53 裙子 [qúnzi] skirt; CL: 条 [tiáo]

54 回复 [huífù] to reply; to recover; to return (to a previous condition); Re: in reply to (email)

55 西班牙 [xībānyá] Spain

56 较长 [jiàocháng] comparatively long

57 想办法 [xiǎngbànfǎ] to think of a method

58 香水 [xiāngshuǐ] perfume; cologne

59 家用 [jiāyòng] home-use; domestic; family expenses; housekeeping money

60 高发 [gāofā] to score highly in imperial exams (and obtain a post); widespread

61 考查 [kǎochá] investigate; study

62 必备 [bìbèi] essential

63 新春 [xīnchūn] Chinese New Year

64 天使 [tiānshǐ] angel

65 头上 [tóushàng] overhead; above

66 马力 [mǎlì] horsepower

67 超前 [chāoqián] to be ahead of one's time; to surpass or outdo one's predecessors; to be ahead of the pack; to take the lead; advanced

68 学业 [xuéyè] studies; schoolwork

69 花样 [huāyàng] pattern; type; trick

70 名城 [míngchéng] famous city

71 高楼 [gāolóu] high building; multistory building; skyscraper; CL: 座 [zuò]

72 南越 [nányuè] South Vietnam; South Vietnamese

73 口水 [kǒushuǐ] saliva

74 环境影响 [huánjìngyǐngxiǎng] environmental impact

75 自带 [zìdài] to bring one's own; BYO

76 就地 [jiùdì] locally; on the spot

77 过错 [guòcuò] mistake

78 国务院新闻办公室 [guówùyuàn xīnwén bàngōngshì] State Council Information Office of the People's Republic of China

Lesson 24

New Characters

1	2	3	4	5	6
李	山	风	情	笔	板

7	8	9	10	11	12*
句	刮	典	爬	铅	镛

13*	14*	15*	16*
骓	瞿	酣	垛

Lesson 24

HSK Vocabulary

17 照相机	21 黑板	25 行李箱
18 句子	22 爬山	26 热情
19 铅笔	23 字典	
20 洗手间	24 刮风	

Non-HSK Vocabulary

27 笔者	36 纸条	45 调查人员
28 乐山	37 买东西	46 问好
29 大风	38 放学	47 两下
30 笔钱	39 黑山	48 右上
31 问道	40 红外	49 检定
32 前人	41 泳衣	50 热病
33 水汽	42 起重机	51 水道
34 跑道	43 过世	
35 国家开发银行	44 通向	

Lesson 24

Glossary

1 李 [lǐ] surname Li ◇ plum

2 山 [shān] surname Shan ◇ mountain; hill; anything that resembles a mountain; CL: 座 [zuò]; bundled straw in which silkworms spin cocoons; gable

3 风 [fēng] wind; news; style; custom; manner; CL: 阵 [zhèn], 丝 [sī]

4 情 [qíng] feeling; emotion; passion; situation

5 笔 [bǐ] pen; pencil; writing brush; to write or compose; the strokes of Chinese characters; classifier for sums of money, deals; CL: 支 [zhī], 枝 [zhī]

6 板 [bǎn] board; plank; plate; shutter; table tennis bat; clappers (music); CL: 块 [kuài]; accented beat in Chinese music; hard; stiff; to stop smiling or look serious ◇ see 老板, boss ◆ [pàn] to catch sight of in a doorway (old)

7 句 [gōu] variant of 勾 [gōu] ◆ [jù] sentence; clause; phrase; classifier for phrases or lines of verse

8 刮 [guā] to scrape; to blow; to shave; to plunder; to extort ◇ to blow (of the wind)

9 典 [diǎn] canon; law; standard work of scholarship; literary quotation or allusion; ceremony; to be in charge of; to mortgage or pawn

10 爬 [pá] to crawl; to climb; to get up or sit up

11 铅 [qiān] lead (chemistry)

12 镛 (*) [yōng] large bell

13 骓 (*) [zhuī] surname Zhui ◇ piebald

14 瞿 (*) [jù] startled ◆ [qú] surname Qu

15 酣 (*) [hān] intoxicated

16 垛 (*) [duǒ] battlement; target ◆ [duò] pile

17 照相机 [zhàoxiàngjī] camera; CL: 个 [gè], 架 [jià], 部 [bù], 台 [tái], 只 [zhī]

18 句子 [jùzi] sentence; CL: 个 [gè]

19 铅笔 [qiānbǐ] (lead) pencil; CL: 支 [zhī], 枝 [zhī], 杆 [gǎn]

20 洗手间 [xǐshǒujiān] toilet; lavatory; washroom

21 黑板 [hēibǎn] blackboard; CL: 块 [kuài], 个 [gè]

22 爬山 [páshān] to climb a mountain; to mountaineer; hiking; mountaineering

23 字典 [zìdiǎn] dictionary; character dictionary; CL: 本 [běn]

24 刮风 [guāfēng] to be windy

25 行李箱 [xínglixiāng] suitcase

26 热情 [rèqíng] cordial; enthusiastic; passion; passionate; passionately

27 笔者 [bǐzhě] the author; the writer

28 乐山 [lèshān] Leshan prefecture level city in Sichuan

29 大风 [dàfēng] gale; CL: 场 [cháng]

30 笔钱 [bǐqián] fund; sum of money

31 问道 [wèndào] to ask the way; to ask

32 前人 [qiánrén] predecessor; forebears; the person facing you

33 水汽 [shuǐqì] water vapor; steam; moisture

34 跑道 [pǎodào] athletic track; track; runway (i.e. airstrip)

35 国家开发银行 [guójiākāifāyínháng] China Development Bank

36 纸条 [zhǐtiáo] slip of paper

37 买东西 [mǎidōngxi] to go shopping

38 放学 [fàngxué] to dismiss students at the end of the school day

39 黑山 [hēishān] Montenegro, former Yugoslavia; Heishan county in Jinzhou 锦州, Liaoning ◇ black mountain

40 红外 [hóngwài] infrared (ray)

41 泳衣 [yǒngyī] swimsuit; bathing suit

42 起重机 [qǐzhòngjī] crane

43 过世 [guòshì] to die; to pass away

Lesson 24

44 通向 [tōngxiàng] lead to

45 调查人员 [diàochárényuán] investigator

46 问好 [wènhǎo] to say hello to; to send one's regards to

47 两下 [liǎngxià] twice; for a little while

48 右上 [yòushàng] upper right

49 检定 [jiǎndìng] a test; determination; to check up on; to examine; to assay

50 热病 [rèbìng] fever; pyrexia

51 水道 [shuǐdào] aqueduct; sewer

Part 4
HSK IV (B2) INTERMEDIATE
Lessons 25-47

Lesson 25

New Characters

1 †	2 †	3 †	4 †	5 †	6 †
元	被	之	各	由	亿

7 †	8 †	9	10	11	12
内	省	组	展	管	社

13	14	15	16	17	18
活	济	术	技	际	阅

19	20
织	况

Lesson 25

HSK Vocabulary

21 发展	27 活动	33 组织
22 记者	28 通过	34 技术
23 社会	29 市场	35 方面
24 进行	30 阅读	36 情况
25 经济	31 成为	37 教育
26 管理	32 国际	

Lesson 25

Glossary

1 元 (†) [yuán] surname Yuan; the Yuan or Mongol dynasty (1279-1368) ◊ Chinese monetary unit; dollar; primary; first

2 被 (†) [bèi] quilt; by; (indicates passive-voice clauses); (literary) to cover; to meet with

3 之 (†) [zhī] (possessive particle, literary equivalent of 的); him; her; it

4 各 (†) [gè] each; every

5 由 (†) [yóu] to follow; from; it is for...to; reason; cause; because of; due to; to; to leave it (to sb); by (introduces passive verb)

6 亿 (†) [yì] 100 million

7 内 (†) [nèi] inside; inner; internal; within; interior

8 省 (†) [shěng] to save; to economize; to do without; to omit; to leave out; province; CL: 个 [gè] ♦ [xǐng] introspection; to examine oneself critically; awareness; to visit (an elderly relative)

9 组 [zǔ] surname Zu ◊ to form; to organize; group; team; classifier for sets, series, groups of people, batteries

10 展 [zhǎn] surname Zhan ◊ to spread out; to open up; to exhibit; to put into effect; to postpone; to prolong; exhibition

11 管 [guǎn] surname Guan ◊ to take care (of); to control; to manage; to be in charge of; to look after; to run; to care about; tube; pipe; (spoken) to; towards

12 社 [shè] society; group; club; agency; god of the soil (old)

13 活 [huó] to live; alive; living; work; workmanship

14 济 [jì] to cross a river; to aid or relieve; to be of help

15 术 [shù] method; technique ♦ [zhú] various genera of flowers of Asteracea family (daisies and chrysanthemums), including Atractylis lancea

16 技 [jì] skill

17 际 [jì] border; edge; boundary; interval; between; inter-; to meet; time; occasion; to meet with (circumstances)

18 阅 [yuè] to inspect; ro review; to read; to peruse; to go through; to experience

19 织 [zhī] to weave; to knit

20 况 [kuàng] moreover; situation

21 发展 [fāzhǎn] development; growth; to develop; to grow; to expand

22 记者 [jìzhě] reporter; journalist; CL: 个 [gè]

23 社会 [shèhuì] society; CL: 个 [gè]

24 进行 [jìnxíng] to advance; to conduct; underway; in progress; to do; to carry out; to carry on; to execute

25 经济 [jīngjì] economy; economic

26 管理 [guǎnlǐ] to supervise; to manage; to administer; management; administration; CL: 个 [gè]

27 活动 [huódòng] to exercise; to move about; to operate; activity; loose; shaky; active; movable; maneuver; to use connections; CL: 项 [xiàng], 个 [gè]

28 通过 [tōngguò] by means of; through; via; to pass through; to get through; to adopt; to pass (a bill or inspection etc); to switch over

29 市场 [shìchǎng] market place; market (also in abstract); abbr. for 超级市场 supermarket; CL: 个 [gè]

30 阅读 [yuèdú] to read; reading

31 成为 [chéngwéi] to become; to turn into

32 国际 [guójì] international

33 组织 [zǔzhī] to organize; organization; organized system; nerve; tissue; CL: 个 [gè]

34 技术 [jìshù] technology; technique; skill; CL: 门 [mén], 种 [zhǒng], 项 [xiàng]

35 方面 [fāngmiàn] respect; aspect; field; side; CL: 个 [gè]

Lesson 25

36 情况 [qíngkuàng] circumstances; state of affairs; situation; CL: 个 [gè], 种 [zhǒng]

37 教育 [jiàoyù] to educate; to teach; education

Lesson 26

New Characters

1	2	3	4 †	5	6
村	科	全	却	入	农

7	8	9	10	11	12
增	收	供	价	支	代

13	14	15	16	17	18
格	基	神	持	精	程

19	20	21	22	23	24
标	坚	规	积	础	括

Lesson 26

HSK Vocabulary

25	提供	33	科学	41	基础
26	安全	34	标准	42	能力
27	生活	35	价格	43	增长
28	其中	36	支持	44	发生
29	积极	37	精神	45	过程
30	代表	38	重点	46	收入
31	规定	39	坚持	47	由于
32	使用	40	包括	48	农村

Non-HSK Vocabulary

49	全国	50	工程	51	科技

Lesson 26

Glossary

1 村 [cūn] village

2 科 [kē] branch of study; administrative section; division; field; branch; stage directions; family (taxonomy); rules; laws; to mete out (punishment); to levy (taxes etc); to fine sb; CL: 个 [gè]

3 全 [quán] surname Quan ◇ all; whole; entire; every; complete

4 却 (卻) [què] but; yet; however; while; to go back; to decline; to retreat; nevertheless; even though

5 入 [rù] to enter; to go into; to join; to become a member of; to confirm or agree with; abbr. for 入声 [rùshēng]

6 农 [nóng] surname Nong ◇ peasant; to farm; agriculture; diligent (old); government field official (old)

7 增 [zēng] to increase; to expand; to add

8 收 [shōu] to receive; to accept; to collect; in care of (used on address line after name)

9 供 [gōng] to provide; to supply ◆ [gòng] sacrificial offering; to confess

10 价 [jià] price; value; valence (on an atom) ◆ [jie] great; good; middleman; servant

11 支 [zhī] surname Zhi ◇ to support; to sustain; to erect; to raise; branch; division; to draw money; classifier for rods such as pens and guns, for army divisions and for songs or compositions

12 代 [dài] to substitute; to act on behalf of others; to replace; generation; dynasty; age; period; (historical) era; (geological) eon

13 格 [gé] square; frame; rule; (legal) case; style; character; standard; pattern; (classical) to obstruct; to hinder; (classical) to arrive; to come; (classical) to investigate; to study exhaustively

14 基 [jī] base; foundation; basic; radical (chemistry)

15 神 [shén] God; unusual; mysterious; soul; spirit; divine essence; lively; spiritual being; CL: 个 [gè]; abbr. for 神舟 [Shénzhōu]

16 持 [chí] to hold; to grasp; to support; to maintain; to persevere; to manage; to run (i.e. administer); to control

17 精 [jīng] essence; extract; vitality; energy; semen; sperm; mythical goblin spirit; highly perfected; elite; the pick of sth; proficient (refined ability); extremely (fine); selected rice (archaic)

18 程 [chéng] surname Cheng ◇ rule; order; regulations; formula; journey; procedure; sequence

19 标 [biāo] the topmost branches of a tree; surface; sign; to mark; (outward) sign; indication; prize; award; bid

20 坚 [jiān] strong; solid; firm; unyielding; resolute

21 规 [guī] compass; a rule; regulation; to admonish; to plan; to scheme

22 积 [jī] to amass; to accumulate; to store; measured quantity (such as area of volume); product (the result of multiplication); to integrate (math.); to solve (or integrate) an ordinary differential equation (math.); old; long-standing

23 础 [chǔ] foundation; base

24 括 [kuò] to enclose; to include; also pr. [guā]

25 提供 [tígōng] to offer; to supply; to provide; to furnish

26 安全 [ānquán] safe; secure; safety; security

27 生活 [shēnghuó] life; activity; to live; livelihood

28 其中 [qízhōng] among; in; included among these

29 积极 [jījí] active; energetic; vigorous; positive (outlook); proactive

Lesson 26

30 代表 [dàibiǎo] representative; delegate; CL: 位 [wèi], 个 [gè], 名 [míng]; to represent; to stand for; on behalf of; in the name of

31 规定 [guīdìng] provision; to fix; to set; to formulate; to stipulate; to provide; regulation; rule; CL: 个 [gè]

32 使用 [shǐyòng] to use; to employ; to apply; to make use of

33 科学 [kēxué] science; scientific knowledge; scientific; CL: 门 [mén], 个 [gè], 种 [zhǒng]

34 标准 [biāozhǔn] (an official) standard; norm; criterion; CL: 个 [gè]

35 价格 [jiàgé] price; CL: 个 [gè]

36 支持 [zhīchí] to be in favor of; to support; to back; support; backing; to stand by; CL: 个 [gè]

37 精神 [jīngshén] spirit; mind; consciousness; thought; mental; psychological; essence; gist; CL: 个 [gè] ◆ [jīngshen] vigor; vitality; drive; spiritual

38 重点 [chóngdiǎn] to recount (e.g. results of election); to re-evaluate ◆ [zhòngdiǎn] emphasis; focal point; priority; key; with the emphasis on; focusing on

39 坚持 [jiānchí] to persevere with; to persist in; to insist on

40 包括 [bāokuò] to comprise; to include; to involve; to incorporate; to consist of

41 基础 [jīchǔ] base; foundation; basis; underlying; CL: 个 [gè]

42 能力 [nénglì] capability; capable; able; ability; CL: 个 [gè]

43 增长 [zēngzhǎng] to grow; to increase

44 发生 [fāshēng] to happen; to occur; to take place; to break out

45 过程 [guòchéng] course of events; process; CL: 个 [gè]

46 收入 [shōurù] to take in; income; revenue; CL: 笔 [bǐ], 个 [gè]

47 由于 [yóuyú] due to; as a result of; thanks to; owing to; since; because

48 农村 [nóngcūn] rural area; village; CL: 个 [gè]

49 全国 [quánguó] entire country; nationwide

50 工程 [gōngchéng] engineering; an engineering project; project; undertaking; CL: 个 [gè], 项 [xiàng]

51 科技 [kējì] science and technology

Lesson 27

New Characters

1	2	3	4 †	5	6
至	此	任	无	受	仅

7	8	9	10	11	12
保	按	品	交	流	继

13	14	15	16	17	18
专	食	计	艺	责	甚

19	20	21
划	续	律

Lesson 27

HSK Vocabulary

22	食品	30	增加	38	计划
23	内容	31	因此	39	不仅
24	按照	32	责任	40	超过
25	交流	33	艺术	41	专业
26	继续	34	意见	42	接受
27	保护	35	调查	43	甚至
28	共同	36	条件	44	网站
29	报道	37	法律	45	任务

Non-HSK Vocabulary

46	国内	47	进入

Lesson 27

Glossary

1 至 [zhì] to arrive; most; to; until

2 此 [cǐ] this; these

3 任 [rèn] surname Ren ◊ to assign; to appoint; to take up a post; office; responsibility; to let; to allow; to give free rein to; no matter (how, what etc)

4 无 (亡) [wú] -less; not to have; no; none; not; to lack; un-

5 受 [shòu] to receive; to accept; to suffer; subjected to; to bear; to stand; pleasant; (passive marker)

6 仅 [jǐn] barely; only; merely

7 保 [bǎo] Bulgaria; Bulgarian; abbr. for 保加利亚 [Bǎojiālìyà] ◊ to defend; to protect; to insure or guarantee; to maintain; hold or keep; to guard

8 按 [àn] to press; to push; to leave aside or shelve; to control; to restrain; to keep one's hand on; to check or refer to; according to; in the light of; (of an editor or author) to make a comment

9 品 [pǐn] article; commodity; product; goods; kind; grade; rank; character; disposition; nature; temperament; variety; to taste sth; to sample; to criticize; to comment; to judge; to size up

10 交 [jiāo] to hand over; to deliver; to pay (money); to turn over; to make friends; to intersect (lines)

11 流 [liú] to flow; to disseminate; to circulate or spread; to move or drift; to degenerate; to banish or send into exile; stream of water or sth resembling one; class, rate or grade

12 继 [jì] to continue; to follow after; to go on with; to succeed; to inherit; then; afterwards

13 专 [zhuān] for a particular person, occasion, purpose; focused on one thing; special; expert; particular (to sth); concentrated; specialized

14 食 [shí] to eat; food; animal feed; eclipse ◆ [sì] to feed

15 计 [jì] surname Ji ◊ to calculate; to compute; to count; to regard as important; to plan; ruse; meter; gauge

16 艺 [yì] skill; art

17 责 [zé] duty; responsibility; to reproach; to blame

18 甚 [shèn] what; very; extremely; any

19 划 [huá] to row; to paddle; to scratch a surface; profitable; worth (the effort); it pays (to do sth) ◊ to scratch ◆ [huà] to delimit; to transfer; to assign; to differentiate; to mark off; to draw (a line); to delete; stroke of a Chinese character

20 续 [xù] to continue; to replenish

21 律 [lǜ] law

22 食品 [shípǐn] foodstuff; food; provisions; CL: 种 [zhǒng]

23 内容 [nèiróng] content; substance; details; CL: 个 [gè], 项 [xiàng]

24 按照 [ànzhào] according to; in accordance with; in the light of; on the basis of

25 交流 [jiāoliú] exchange; give-and-take; to exchange; to alternate; communication; alternating current (electricity)

26 继续 [jìxù] to continue; to proceed with; to go on with

27 保护 [bǎohù] to protect; to defend; to safeguard; protection; CL: 种 [zhǒng]

28 共同 [gòngtóng] common; joint; jointly; together; collaborative

29 报道 [bàodào] report; CL: 篇 [piān], 份 [fèn]

30 增加 [zēngjiā] to raise; to increase

31 因此 [yīncǐ] thus; consequently; as a result

32 责任 [zérèn] responsibility; blame; duty; CL: 个 [gè]

33 艺术 [yìshù] art

Lesson 27

34 意见 [yìjiàn] idea; opinion; suggestion; objection; complaint; CL: 点 [diǎn], 条 [tiáo]

35 调查 [diàochá] investigation; inquiry; to investigate; to survey; survey; (opinion) poll; CL: 项 [xiàng], 个 [gè]

36 条件 [tiáojiàn] condition; circumstances; term; factor; requirement; prerequisite; qualification; CL: 个 [gè]

37 法律 [fǎlǜ] law; CL: 条 [tiáo], 套 [tào], 个 [gè]

38 计划 [jìhuà] plan; project; program; to plan; to map out; CL: 个 [gè], 项 [xiàng]

39 不仅 [bùjǐn] not only (this one); not just (...) but also

40 超过 [chāoguò] to surpass; to exceed; to outstrip

41 专业 [zhuānyè] specialty; specialized field; main field of study (at university); major; CL: 门 [mén], 个 [gè]; professional

42 接受 [jiēshòu] to accept; to receive

43 甚至 [shènzhì] even; so much so that

44 网站 [wǎngzhàn] website; network station; node

45 任务 [rènwu] mission; assignment; task; duty; role; CL: 项 [xiàng], 个 [gè]

46 国内 [guónèi] domestic; internal (to a country); civil

47 进入 [jìnrù] to enter; to join; to go into

Lesson 28

New Characters

1	2 †	3 †	4 †	5	6
量	台	拉	座	原	式

7	8	9	10	11	12
优	质	许	获	秀	随

13	14	15	16	17	18
范	负	功	扩	围	验

Lesson 28

HSK Vocabulary

19	成功		27	实际		35	不过
20	交通		28	直接		36	重视
21	所有		29	经验		37	范围
22	质量		30	随着		38	现代
23	当时		31	负责		39	原因
24	正式		32	优秀		40	举办
25	获得		33	扩大			
26	公里		34	许多			

Non-HSK Vocabulary

41	基层		44	主任		47	之间
42	之后		45	负责人		48	全球
43	各种		46	平台		49	之一

Lesson 28

Glossary

1 量 [liáng] to measure ◆ [liàng] capacity; quantity; amount; to estimate; abbr. for 量词 [liàng cí], classifier (in Chinese grammar); measure word

2 台 (†) [tái] Taiwan (abbr.); surname Tai ◊ (classical) you (in letters); platform ◊ desk; platform ◊ Taiwan (abbr.) ◊ platform; stage; terrace; stand; support; desk; station; broadcasting station; classifier for vehicles or machines ◊ typhoon

3 拉 (†) [lā] to pull; to play (string instruments); to drag; to draw; to chat

4 座 (†) [zuò] seat; base; stand; CL: 个 [gè]; classifier for buildings, mountains and similar immovable objects

5 原 [yuán] former; original; primary; raw; level; cause; source

6 式 [shì] type; form; pattern; style

7 优 [yōu] excellent; superior

8 质 [zhì] character; nature; quality; plain; to pawn; pledge; hostage; to question; Taiwan pr. [zhí]

9 许 [xǔ] surname Xu ◊ to allow; to permit; to praise; somewhat; perhaps

10 获 [huò] to catch; to obtain; to capture ◊ to reap; to harvest

11 秀 [xiù] handsome; refined; elegant; graceful; performance; ear of grain; show (loanword); CL: 场 [cháng]

12 随 [suí] surname Sui ◊ to follow; to comply with; varying according to...; to allow

13 范 [fàn] pattern; model; example ◊ surname Fan

14 负 [fù] to bear; to carry (on one's back); to turn one's back on; to be defeated; negative (math. etc)

15 功 [gōng] meritorious deed or service; achievement; result; service; accomplishment; work (physics)

16 扩 [kuò] enlarge

17 围 [wéi] surname Wei ◊ to encircle; to surround; all around; to wear by wrapping around (scarf, shawl)

18 验 [yàn] to examine; to test; to check

19 成功 [chénggōng] Chenggong or Chengkung town in Taitung county 台东县 [Táidōngxiàn], southeast Taiwan ◊ success; to succeed; CL: 次 [cì], 个 [gè]

20 交通 [jiāotōng] to be connected; traffic; communications; liaison

21 所有 [suǒyǒu] all; to have; to possess; to own

22 质量 [zhìliàng] quality; mass (in physics); CL: 个 [gè]

23 当时 [dāngshí] then; at that time; while

24 正式 [zhèngshì] formal; official

25 获得 [huòdé] to obtain; to receive; to get

26 公里 [gōnglǐ] kilometer

27 实际 [shíjì] actual; reality; practice

28 直接 [zhíjiē] direct; opposite: indirect 间接; immediate; directly; straightforward

29 经验 [jīngyàn] to experience; experience

30 随着 [suízhe] along with; in the wake of; following

31 负责 [fùzé] to be in charge of; to take responsibility for; to be to blame; conscientious

32 优秀 [yōuxiù] outstanding; excellent

33 扩大 [kuòdà] to expand; to enlarge; to broaden one's scope

34 许多 [xǔduō] many; a lot of; much

35 不过 [bùguò] only; merely; no more than; but; however; anyway (to get back to a previous topic)

36 重视 [zhòngshì] to attach importance to sth; to value

37 范围 [fànwéi] range; scope; limit; extent; CL: 个 [gè]

Lesson 28

38 现代 [xiàndài] Hyundai, South Korean company ◇ modern times; modern age; modern era

39 原因 [yuányīn] cause; origin; root cause; reason; CL: 个 [gè]

40 举办 [jǔbàn] to conduct; to hold

41 基层 [jīcéng] basic level; grass-roots unit; basement layer

42 之后 [zhīhòu] afterwards; following; later; after

43 各种 [gèzhǒng] every kind of; all kinds of; various kinds

44 主任 [zhǔrèn] director; head; CL: 个 [gè]

45 负责人 [fùzérén] person in charge of sth

46 平台 [píngtái] platform; terrace; flat-roofed building

47 之间 [zhījiān] between; among; inter-

48 全球 [quánqiú] entire; total; global; the (whole) world; worldwide

49 之一 [zhīyī] one of (sth); one out of a multitude; one (third, quarter, percent etc)

Lesson 29

New Characters

1	2	3	4	5	6 †
及	部	民	首	联	连

7 †	8 †	9	10	11	12
份	光	何	富	证	引

13	14	15	16	17	18
效	反	严	族	丰	困

19	20	21
消	映	键

Lesson 29

HSK Vocabulary

22 当地	30 真正	38 自然
23 反映	31 最后	39 效果
24 困难	32 关键	40 方法
25 严重	33 及时	41 首先
26 联系	34 丰富	42 引起
27 全部	35 完全	43 保证
28 任何	36 十分	
29 民族	37 消息	

Non-HSK Vocabulary

44 干部	48 居民	52 大量
45 人民	49 各级	53 经济发展
46 人民网	50 此次	
47 有效	51 全市	

Lesson 29

Glossary

1 及 [jí] and; to reach; up to; in time for

2 部 [bù] ministry; department; section; part; division; troops; board; classifier for works of literature, films, machines etc

3 民 [mín] the people; nationality; citizen

4 首 [shǒu] head; chief; first (occasion, thing etc); classifier for poems, songs etc

5 联 [lián] to ally; to unite; to join

6 连 (†) [lián] surname Lian ◊ to link; to join; to connect; continuously; in succession; including; (used with 也, 都 etc) even; company (military)

7 份 (†) [fèn] classifier for gifts, newspaper, magazine, papers, reports, contracts etc; variant of 分 [fèn]

8 光 (†) [guāng] light; ray; CL: 道 [dào]; bright; only; merely; to use up

9 何 [hé] surname He ◊ what; how; why; which; carry

10 富 [fù] surname Fu ◊ rich; abundant; wealthy

11 证 [zhèng] certificate; proof; to prove; to demonstrate; to confirm

12 引 [yǐn] to draw (e.g. a bow); to pull; to stretch sth; to extend; to lengthen; to involve or implicate in; to attract; to lead; to guide; to leave; to provide evidence or justification for; old unit of distance equal to 10 丈 [zhāng], one-thirtieth of a km or 33.33 meters

13 效 [xiào] to imitate ◊ effect; efficacy; to imitate

14 反 [fǎn] contrary; in reverse; inside-out or upside-down; to reverse; to return; to oppose; opposite; against; anti-; to rebel; to use analogy; instead; abbr. for 反切 phonetic system

15 严 [yán] surname Yan ◊ tight (closely sealed); stern; strict; rigorous; severe; father

16 族 [zú] race; nationality; ethnicity; clan; by extension, social group (e.g. office workers 上班族)

17 丰 [fēng] luxuriant; buxom; appearance; charm ◊ surname Feng ◊ abundant; plentiful; fertile; plump; great

18 困 [kùn] to trap; to surround; hard-pressed; stranded; destitute ◊ sleepy; tired

19 消 [xiāo] to disappear; to vanish; to eliminate; to spend (time); have to; need

20 映 [yìng] reflect; shine

21 键 [jiàn] (door lock) key; key (on piano or keyboard)

22 当地 [dāngdì] local

23 反映 [fǎnyìng] to mirror; to reflect; mirror image; reflection; fig. to report; to make known; to render; used erroneously for 反应, response or reaction

24 困难 [kùnnan] (financial etc) difficulty; problem; issue; CL: 个 [gè]

25 严重 [yánzhòng] grave; serious; severe; critical

26 联系 [liánxì] connection; contact; relation; to get in touch with; to integrate; to link; to touch

27 全部 [quánbù] whole; entire; complete

28 任何 [rènhé] any; whatever; whichever; whatsoever

29 民族 [mínzú] nationality; ethnic group; CL: 个 [gè]

30 真正 [zhēnzhèng] genuine; real; true; genuinely

31 最后 [zuìhòu] final; last; finally; ultimate

32 关键 [guānjiàn] crucial point; crux; CL: 个 [gè]; key; crucial; pivotal

33 及时 [jíshí] in time; promptly; without delay; timely

34 丰富 [fēngfù] to enrich; rich; plentiful; abundant

35 完全 [wánquán] complete; whole; totally; entirely

Lesson 29

36 十分 [shífēn] to divide into ten equal parts; very; hundred percent; completely; extremely; utterly; absolutely

37 消息 [xiāoxi] news; information; CL: 条 [tiáo]

38 自然 [zìrán] nature; natural; naturally

39 效果 [xiàoguǒ] result; effect; quality; CL: 个 [gè]

40 方法 [fāngfǎ] method; way; means; CL: 个 [gè]

41 首先 [shǒuxiān] first (of all); in the first place

42 引起 [yǐnqǐ] to give rise to; to lead to; to cause; to arouse

43 保证 [bǎozhèng] guarantee; to guarantee; to ensure; to safeguard; to pledge; CL: 个 [gè]

44 干部 [gànbù] personnel; employees; cadre (in communist party); CL: 个 [gè]

45 人民 [rénmín] the people; CL: 个 [gè]

46 人民网 [rénmínwǎng] online version of the People's Daily 人民日报

47 有效 [yǒuxiào] effective; in effect; valid

48 居民 [jūmín] resident; inhabitant

49 各级 [gèjí] all levels

50 此次 [cǐcì] this time

51 全市 [quánshì] whole city

52 大量 [dàliàng] great amount; large quantity; bulk; numerous; generous; magnanimous

53 经济发展 [jīngjìfāzhǎn] economic development

Lesson 30

New Characters

1 †	2	3	4	5 †	6
群	争	广	观	指	改

7	8	9	10	11	12
降	资	排	合	知	减

13	14	15	16	17	18
众	压	另	申	材	料

19	20	21	22	23	24
竞	著	鼓	肯	授	符

25	26
励	虑

Lesson 30

HSK Vocabulary

27 广告	35 严格	43 通知
28 另外	36 方向	44 特点
29 安排	37 竞争	45 符合
30 考虑	38 教授	46 观众
31 减少	39 压力	47 材料
32 工资	40 著名	48 降低
33 改变	41 肯定	49 鼓励
34 申请	42 知识	

Non-HSK Vocabulary

50 指出	54 道路	58 公众
51 最终	55 公安	59 食品安全
52 民生	56 之前	60 全省
53 网上	57 无法	

Lesson 30

Glossary

1 群 (†) [qún] group; crowd; flock, herd, pack etc

2 争 [zhēng] to strive for; to vie for; to argue or debate; deficient or lacking (topolect); how or what (literary)

3 广 [guǎng] surname Guang ◇ wide; numerous; to spread

4 观 [guān] to look at; to watch; to observe; to behold; to advise; concept; point of view ◆ [guàn] surname Guan ◇ Taoist monastery; palace gate watchtower; platform

5 指 (†) [zhǐ] finger; to point at or to; to indicate or refer to; to depend on; to count on; (of hair) to stand on end

6 改 [gǎi] to change; to alter; to transform; to correct

7 降 [jiàng] to drop; to fall; to come down; to descend ◆ [xiáng] to surrender; to capitulate; to subdue; to tame

8 资 [zī] resources; capital; to provide; to supply; to support; money; expense

9 排 [pái] a row; a line; to set in order; to arrange; to line up; to eliminate; to drain; to push open; platoon; raft; classifier for lines, rows etc

10 合 [gě] 100 ml; one-tenth of a peck; measure for dry grain equal to one-tenth of sheng 升 or liter, or one-hundredth dou 斗 ◆ [hé] to close; to join; to fit; to be equal to; whole; together; round (in battle); conjunction (astronomy); 1st note of pentatonic scale; old variant of 盒 [hé]

11 知 [zhī] to know; to be aware

12 减 [jiǎn] to lower; to decrease; to reduce; to subtract; to diminish

13 众 [zhòng] abbr. for 众议院 [Zhòng Yì Yuàn] House of Representatives ◇ many; numerous; crowd; multitude

14 压 [yā] to press; to push down; to keep under (control); pressure ◆ [yà] in the first place; to crush

15 另 [lìng] other; another; separate; separately

16 申 [shēn] surname Shen ◇ to extend; to state; to explain; 9th earthly branch: 3–5 p.m., 7th solar month (7th August–7th September), year of the Monkey

17 材 [cái] material; timber; ability; aptitude; a capable individual; coffin (old)

18 料 [liào] material; stuff; grain; feed; to expect; to anticipate; to guess

19 竞 [jìng] to compete; to contend; to struggle

20 著 [zhù] to make known; to show; to prove; to write; book; outstanding

21 鼓 [gǔ] convex; drum; to rouse; to beat; CL: 通 [tòng], 面 [miàn]

22 肯 [kěn] to agree; to consent; to be ready (to do sth); willing

23 授 [shòu] to teach; to instruct; to award; to give

24 符 [fú] surname Fu ◇ mark; sign; talisman; to seal; to correspond to; tally; symbol; written charm; to coincide

25 励 [lì] surname Li ◇ to encourage; to urge

26 虑 [lǜ] to think over; to consider; anxiety

27 广告 [guǎnggào] to advertise; a commercial; advertisement; CL: 项 [xiàng]

28 另外 [lìngwài] additional; in addition; besides; separate; other; moreover; furthermore

29 安排 [ānpái] to arrange; to plan; to set up

30 考虑 [kǎolǜ] to think over; to consider; consideration

31 减少 [jiǎnshǎo] to lessen; to decrease; to reduce; to lower

Lesson 30

32 工资 [gōngzī] wages; pay; CL: 个 [gè], 份 [fèn], 月 [yuè]

33 改变 [gǎibiàn] to change; to alter; to transform

34 申请 [shēnqǐng] to apply for sth; application (form etc); CL: 份 [fèn]

35 严格 [yángé] strict; stringent; tight; rigorous

36 方向 [fāngxiàng] direction; orientation; path to follow; CL: 个 [gè]

37 竞争 [jìngzhēng] to compete; competition

38 教授 [jiàoshòu] professor; to instruct; to lecture on; CL: 个 [gè], 位 [wèi]

39 压力 [yālì] pressure

40 著名 [zhùmíng] famous; noted; well-known; celebrated

41 肯定 [kěndìng] to be sure; to be certain; sure; certain; definite; to confirm; to affirm; affirmative; to approve; approval; recognition

42 知识 [zhīshi] intellectual; knowledge-related; knowledge; CL: 门 [mén]

43 通知 [tōngzhī] to notify; to inform; notice; notification; CL: 个 [gè]

44 特点 [tèdiǎn] characteristic (feature); trait; feature; CL: 个 [gè]

45 符合 [fúhé] in keeping with; in accordance with; tallying with; in line with; to agree with; to accord with; to conform to; to correspond with; to manage; to handle

46 观众 [guānzhòng] spectators; audience; visitors (to an exhibition etc)

47 材料 [cáiliào] material; data; makings; stuff; CL: 个 [gè], 种 [zhǒng]

48 降低 [jiàngdī] to reduce; to lower; to bring down

49 鼓励 [gǔlì] to encourage

50 指出 [zhǐchū] to indicate; to point out

51 最终 [zuìzhōng] final; ultimate

52 民生 [mínshēng] people's livelihood; people's welfare

53 网上 [wǎngshàng] on-line

54 道路 [dàolù] road; path; way; CL: 条 [tiáo]

55 公安 [gōng'ān] (Ministry of) Public Security; public safety; public security

56 之前 [zhīqián] before; prior to; ago; previously; beforehand

57 无法 [wúfǎ] unable; incapable

58 公众 [gōngzhòng] public

59 食品安全 [shípǐn'ānquán] food safety

60 全省 [quánshěng] the whole province

Lesson 31

New Characters

1	2	3 †	4 †	5	6 †
费	度	深	谈	福	桥

7 †	8	9	10	11	12
推	职	论	尽	免	速

13	14	15	16	17	18
切	童	吸	毕	讨	幸

Lesson 31

HSK Vocabulary

19 主动	26 职业	33 尽管
20 幸福	27 一切	34 友好
21 吸引	28 免费	35 数量
22 目的	29 讨论	36 后来
23 专门	30 儿童	37 感觉
24 无论	31 然而	38 毕业
25 经历	32 只要	39 速度

Non-HSK Vocabulary

40 推进	49 深化	58 环保
41 推动	50 高速	59 首次
42 深入	51 如此	60 普通
43 消费者	52 市民	61 村民
44 收费	53 各地	62 的话
45 高度	54 主持人	63 老人
46 推出	55 日前	64 公安部
47 职工	56 月份	
48 力度	57 自身	

Lesson 31

Glossary

1 费 [fèi] surname Fei ◇ to cost; to spend; fee; wasteful; expenses

2 度 [dù] to pass; to spend (time); measure; limit; extent; degree of intensity; degree (angles, temperature etc); kilowatt-hour; classifier for events and occurrences ♦ [duó] to estimate

3 深 (†) [shēn] close; deep; late; profound; dark (of color, water etc)

4 谈 (†) [tán] surname Tan ◇ to speak; to talk; to converse; to chat; to discuss

5 福 [fú] surname Fu; abbr. for Fujian province 福建省 [Fújiànshěng] ◇ good fortune; happiness; luck

6 桥 (†) [qiáo] bridge; CL: 座 [zuò]

7 推 (†) [tuī] to push; to cut; to refuse; to reject; to decline; to shirk (responsibility); to put off; to delay; to push forward; to nominate; to elect

8 职 [zhí] office; duty

9 论 [lún] the Analects (of Confucius) ♦ [lùn] by the; per; theory; to discuss; to talk (about); to discuss

10 尽 [jǐn] to the greatest extent; (when used before a noun of location) furthest or extreme; to be within the limits of; to give priority to ♦ [jìn] to use up; to exhaust; to end; to finish; to the utmost; exhausted; finished; to the limit (of sth)

11 免 [miǎn] to excuse sb; to exempt; to remove or dismiss from office; to avoid; to avert; to escape; to be prohibited

12 速 [sù] fast; rapid; quick; velocity

13 切 [qiē] to cut; to slice; tangent (math) ♦ [qiè] definitely; absolutely (not); (scoffing or dismissive interjection) Yeah, right.; Tut!; to grind; close to; eager; to correspond to; see also 反切 [fǎnqiè]

14 童 [tóng] surname Tong ◇ boy; child; children

15 吸 [xī] to breathe; to suck in; to absorb; to inhale

16 毕 [bì] surname Bi ◇ the whole of; to finish; to complete; complete; full; finished

17 讨 [tǎo] to invite; to provoke; to demand or ask for; to send armed forces to suppress; to denounce or condemn; to marry (a woman); to discuss or study

18 幸 [xìng] trusted; intimate; (of the emperor) to visit ◇ surname Xing ◇ fortunate; lucky

19 主动 [zhǔdòng] to take the initiative; to do sth of one's own accord; spontaneous; active; opposite: passive 被动 [bèidòng]; drive (of gears and shafts etc)

20 幸福 [xìngfú] happiness; happy; blessed

21 吸引 [xīyǐn] to attract (interest, investment etc); CL: 个 [gè]

22 目的 [mùdì] purpose; aim; goal; target; objective; CL: 个 [gè]

23 专门 [zhuānmén] specialist; specialized; customized

24 无论 [wúlùn] no matter what or how; regardless of whether...

25 经历 [jīnglì] experience; CL: 个 [gè], 次 [cì]; to experience; to go through

26 职业 [zhíyè] occupation; profession; vocation; professional

27 一切 [yīqiè] everything; every; all

28 免费 [miǎnfèi] free (of charge)

29 讨论 [tǎolùn] to discuss; to talk over; CL: 个 [gè]

30 儿童 [értóng] child; CL: 个 [gè]

31 然而 [rán'ér] however; yet; but

32 只要 [zhǐyào] if only; so long as

33 尽管 [jǐnguǎn] despite; although; even though; in spite of; unhesitatingly; do not hesitate (to ask, complain etc); (go ahead and do it) without hesitating

Lesson 31

34 友好 [yǒuhǎo] Youhao district of Yichun city 伊春市 [Yīchūnshì], Heilongjiang ◇ friendly; amicable; close friend

35 数量 [shùliàng] amount; quantity; CL: 个 [gè]; quantitative

36 后来 [hòulái] afterwards; later

37 感觉 [gǎnjué] to feel; to become aware of; feeling; sense; perception; CL: 个 [gè]

38 毕业 [bìyè] graduation; to graduate; to finish school

39 速度 [sùdù] speed; rate; velocity; CL: 个 [gè]

40 推进 [tuījìn] to impel; to carry forward; to push on; to advance; to drive forward

41 推动 [tuīdòng] to push (for acceptance of a plan); to push forward; to promote; to actuate; CL: 个 [gè]

42 深入 [shēnrù] to penetrate deeply; thorough

43 消费者 [xiāofèizhě] consumer

44 收费 [shōufèi] fee; charge

45 高度 [gāodù] height; altitude; elevation; high degree; highly; CL: 个 [gè]

46 推出 [tuīchū] to push out; to release; to launch; to publish; to recommend

47 职工 [zhígōng] workers; staff; CL: 个 [gè]

48 力度 [lìdu] strength; vigor; dynamism

49 深化 [shēnhuà] to deepen; to intensify

50 高速 [gāosù] high speed

51 如此 [rúcǐ] in this way; so

52 市民 [shìmín] city resident

53 各地 [gèdì] in all parts of (a country); various regions

54 主持人 [zhǔchírén] TV or radio presenter; host; anchor

55 日前 [rìqián] the other day; a few days ago

56 月份 [yuèfèn] month

57 自身 [zìshēn] itself; oneself; one's own

58 环保 [huánbǎo] environmental protection; environmentally friendly

59 首次 [shǒucì] first; first time; for the first time

60 普通 [pǔtōng] common; ordinary; general; average

61 村民 [cūnmín] villager

62 的话 [dehuà] if (coming after a conditional clause)

63 老人 [lǎorén] old man or woman; the elderly; one's aged parents or grandparents

64 公安部 [gōng'ānbù] Ministry of Public Security

Lesson 32

New Characters

1	2	3	4	5	6
并	达	仍	制	利	章

7 †	8 †	9 †	10	11	12
篇	往	猪	访	顺	纪

13	14	15	16	17	18
造	亲	命	父	尊	遍

19	20	21
确	邀	币

Lesson 32

HSK Vocabulary

22 正常	30 尊重	38 顺利
23 仍然	31 文章	39 生命
24 制造	32 表达	40 访问
25 并且	33 父亲	41 普遍
26 最好	34 说明	42 人民币
27 总结	35 确实	43 数字
28 正确	36 组成	
29 世纪	37 邀请	

Non-HSK Vocabulary

44 机制	53 广东	62 国外
45 打造	54 只能	63 网民
46 体制	55 加入	64 小组
47 改造	56 快速	65 学院
48 并不	57 绿色	66 都会
49 下降	58 出台	67 优化
50 做到	59 部长	68 引进
51 情况下	60 着力	
52 现代化	61 有着	

Lesson 32

Glossary

1 并 [bìng] and; furthermore; also; together with; (not) at all; simultaneously; to combine; to join; to merge ◇ to combine; to amalgamate

2 达 [dá] surname Da ◇ to attain; to reach; to amount to; to communicate; eminent

3 仍 [réng] still; yet; to remain

4 制 [zhì] system; to control; to regulate ◇ to manufacture; to make

5 利 [lì] surname Li ◇ sharp; favorable; advantage; benefit; profit; interest; to do good to; to benefit

6 章 [zhāng] surname Zhang ◇ chapter; section; clause; movement (of symphony); seal; badge; regulation; order

7 篇 (†) [piān] sheet; piece of writing; bound set of bamboo slips used for record keeping (old); classifier for written items: chapter, article

8 往 (†) [wǎng] to go (in a direction); to; towards; (of a train) bound for; past; previous

9 猪 (†) [zhū] hog; pig; swine; CL: 口 [kǒu], 头 [tóu]

10 访 [fǎng] to visit; to call on; to seek; to inquire; to investigate

11 顺 [shùn] to obey; to follow; to arrange; to make reasonable; along; favorable

12 纪 [jì] surname Ji ◇ discipline; age; era; period; order; record

13 造 [zào] to make; to build; to invent; to manufacture

14 亲 [qīn] parent; one's own (flesh and blood); relative; related; marriage; bride; close; intimate; in person; first-hand; in favor of; pro-; to kiss ♦ [qìng] parents-in-law of one's offspring

15 命 [mìng] life; fate; order or command; to assign a name, title etc

16 父 [fù] father

17 尊 [zūn] senior; of a senior generation; to honor; to respect; honorific; classifier for cannons and statues; ancient wine vessel

18 遍 [biàn] everywhere; all over; classifier for actions: one time

19 确 [què] authenticated; solid; firm ◇ authenticated; solid; firm; real; true

20 邀 [yāo] to invite; to request; to intercept; to solicit or seek

21 币 [bì] money; coins; currency; silk

22 正常 [zhèngcháng] regular; normal; ordinary

23 仍然 [réngrán] still; yet

24 制造 [zhìzào] to manufacture; to make

25 并且 [bìngqiě] and; besides; moreover; furthermore; in addition

26 最好 [zuìhǎo] best; (you) had better (do what we suggest)

27 总结 [zǒngjié] to sum up; to conclude; summary; résumé; CL: 个 [gè]

28 正确 [zhèngquè] correct; proper

29 世纪 [shìjì] century; CL: 个 [gè]

30 尊重 [zūnzhòng] to esteem; to respect; to honor; to value; eminent; serious; proper

31 文章 [wénzhāng] article; essay; literary works; writings; hidden meaning; CL: 篇 [piān], 段 [duàn], 页 [yè]

32 表达 [biǎodá] to voice (an opinion); to express; to convey

33 父亲 [fùqīn] father; also pr. with light tone [fù qin]; CL: 个 [gè]

34 说明 [shuōmíng] to explain; to illustrate; to indicate; to show; to prove; explanation; directions; caption; CL: 个 [gè]

35 确实 [quèshí] indeed; really; reliable; real; true

36 组成 [zǔchéng] to form; to make up; to constitute

37 邀请 [yāoqǐng] to invite; invitation; CL: 个 [gè]

Lesson 32

38 顺利 [shùnlì] smoothly; without a hitch

39 生命 [shēngmìng] life; living; biological; CL: 个 [gè]

40 访问 [fǎngwèn] to visit; to call on; to interview; CL: 次 [cì]

41 普遍 [pǔbiàn] universal; general; widespread; common

42 人民币 [rénmínbì] Renminbi (RMB); Chinese Yuan (CNY)

43 数字 [shùzì] numeral; digit; number; figure; amount; digital (electronics etc); CL: 个 [gè]

44 机制 [jīzhì] mechanism ◇ machine processed; machine made; mechanism

45 打造 [dǎzào] to create; to build; to develop; to forge (of metal)

46 体制 [tǐzhì] system; organization

47 改造 [gǎizào] to transform; to reform; to remodel; to remould

48 并不 [bìngbù] not at all; emphatically not

49 下降 [xiàjiàng] to decline; to drop; to fall; to go down; to decrease

50 做到 [zuòdào] to accomplish; to achieve

51 情况下 [qíngkuàngxià] under (these) circumstances

52 现代化 [xiàndàihuà] modernization; CL: 个 [gè]

53 广东 [guǎngdōng] Guangdong province (Kwangtung) in south China, abbr. 粤, capital Guangzhou 广州

54 只能 [zhǐnéng] can only; obliged to do sth; to have no other choice

55 加入 [jiārù] to become a member; to join; to mix into; to participate in; to add in

56 快速 [kuàisù] fast; high-speed; rapid

57 绿色 [lǜsè] green

58 出台 [chūtái] to officially launch (a policy, program etc); to appear on stage; to appear publicly; prostitution

59 部长 [bùzhǎng] head of a (government etc) department; section chief; section head; secretary; minister; CL: 个 [gè], 位 [wèi], 名 [míng]

60 着力 [zhuólì] to put effort into sth; to try really hard

61 有着 [yǒuzhe] have; possess

62 国外 [guówài] abroad; external (affairs); overseas; foreign

63 网民 [wǎngmín] web users; netizens

64 小组 [xiǎozǔ] group

65 学院 [xuéyuàn] college; educational institute; school; faculty; CL: 所 [suǒ]

66 都会 [dūhuì] society; community; city; metropolis

67 优化 [yōuhuà] optimization; to optimize; to make superior

68 引进 [yǐnjìn] to recommend; to introduce (from outside)

Lesson 33

New Characters

1	2	3	4 †	5 †	6
海	即	亚	留	修	底

7	8	9	10	11	12
洋	母	逐	洲	渐	污

13	14	15	16	17
适	杂	染	释	态

Lesson 33

HSK Vocabulary

18	演员	26	海洋	34	亚洲
19	解释	27	证明	35	到底
20	演出	28	态度	36	重新
21	往往	29	逐渐	37	作者
22	母亲	30	信心	38	复杂
23	感谢	31	适应	39	污染
24	原来	32	参观	40	即使
25	理解	33	于是		

Non-HSK Vocabulary

41	上海	50	感到	59	内部
42	随后	51	每一	60	实际上
43	父母	52	海外	61	第五
44	多种	53	总经理	62	职责
45	成了	54	做法	63	日至
46	物流	55	高铁	64	西部
47	引发	56	总书记	65	年以来
48	各个	57	带动		
49	第一次	58	难以		

Lesson 33

Glossary

1 海 [hǎi] ocean; sea; CL: 个 [gè], 片 [piàn]

2 即 [jí] namely; that is; i.e.; prompt; at once; at present; even if; prompted (by the occasion); to approach; to come into contact; to assume (office); to draw near

3 亚 [yà] Asia; Asian; second; next to; inferior; sub-; Taiwan pr. [yǎ]

4 留 (†) [liú] to leave (a message etc); to retain; to stay; to remain; to keep; to preserve

5 修 (†) [xiū] surname Xiu ◇ to decorate; to embellish; to repair; to build; to study; to write; to cultivate

6 底 [de] (equivalent to 的 as possessive particle) ◆ [dǐ] background; bottom; base; the end of a period of time; towards the end of (last month)

7 洋 [yáng] ocean; vast; foreign; silver dollar or coin

8 母 [mǔ] female; mother

9 逐 [zhú] to pursue; to chase; individually; one by one

10 洲 [zhōu] continent; island

11 渐 [jiān] to imbue ◆ [jiàn] gradual; gradually

12 污 [wū] dirty; filthy; foul; corrupt; to smear; to defile; dirt; filth

13 适 [shì] surname Shi ◇ to fit; suitable; proper; just (now); comfortable; well; to go; to follow or pursue

14 杂 [zá] mixed; miscellaneous; various; to mix

15 染 [rǎn] to dye; to catch (a disease); to acquire (bad habits etc); to contaminate; to add colour washes to a painting

16 释 [shì] to explain; to release

17 态 [tài] attitude

18 演员 [yǎnyuán] actor or actress; performer; CL: 个 [gè], 位 [wèi], 名 [míng]

19 解释 [jiěshì] explanation; to explain; to interpret; to resolve; CL: 个 [gè]

20 演出 [yǎnchū] to act (in a play); to perform; to put on (a performance); performance; concert; show; CL: 场 [cháng], 次 [cì]

21 往往 [wǎngwǎng] often; frequently

22 母亲 [mǔqīn] mother; also pr. with light tone [mǔ qin]; CL: 个 [gè]

23 感谢 [gǎnxiè] (express) thanks; gratitude; grateful; thankful; thanks

24 原来 [yuánlái] original; former; originally; formerly; at first; so... actually

25 理解 [lǐjiě] to comprehend; to understand; comprehension; understanding

26 海洋 [hǎiyáng] ocean; CL: 个 [gè]

27 证明 [zhèngmíng] proof; certificate; identification; testimonial; CL: 个 [gè]; to prove; to testify; to confirm the truth of

28 态度 [tàidu] manner; bearing; attitude; approach; CL: 个 [gè]

29 逐渐 [zhújiàn] gradually

30 信心 [xìnxīn] confidence; faith (in sb or sth); CL: 个 [gè]

31 适应 [shìyìng] to adapt; to fit; to suit

32 参观 [cānguān] to look around; to tour; to visit

33 于是 [yúshì] thereupon; as a result; consequently; thus; hence

34 亚洲 [yàzhōu] Asia; Asian

35 到底 [dàodǐ] finally; in the end; when all is said and done; after all; to the end; to the last

36 重新 [chóngxīn] again; once more; re-

37 作者 [zuòzhě] author; writer; CL: 个 [gè]

38 复杂 [fùzá] complicated; complex

39 污染 [wūrǎn] pollution; contamination; CL: 个 [gè]

40 即使 [jíshǐ] even if; even though; given that

Lesson 33

41 上海 [shànghǎi] Shanghai municipality, central east China, abbr. to 沪 [Hù]

42 随后 [suíhòu] soon after

43 父母 [fùmǔ] father and mother; parents

44 多种 [duōzhǒng] many kinds of; multiple; diverse; multi-

45 成了 [chéngle] to be done; to be ready; that's enough!; that will do!

46 物流 [wùliú] distribution (business); logistics

47 引发 [yǐnfā] to lead to; to trigger; to initiate; to cause; to evoke (emotions)

48 各个 [gègè] every; various; separately one-by-one

49 第一次 [dìyīcì] the first time; first; number one

50 感到 [gǎndào] to feel; to sense; to have the feeling that; to think that; to move; to affect

51 每一 [měiyī] every

52 海外 [hǎiwài] overseas; abroad

53 总经理 [zǒngjīnglǐ] general manager; CEO

54 做法 [zuòfǎ] way of handling sth; method for making; work method; recipe; practice; CL: 个 [gè]

55 高铁 [gāotiě] highspeed rail

56 总书记 [zǒngshūji] general-secretary (of Communist Party)

57 带动 [dàidòng] to spur; to provide impetus; to drive

58 难以 [nányǐ] hard to (predict, imagine etc)

59 内部 [nèibù] interior; inside (part, section); internal

60 实际上 [shíjìshàng] in fact; in reality; as a matter of fact; in practice

61 第五 [dìwǔ] fifth

62 职责 [zhízé] duty; responsibility; obligation

63 日至 [rìzhì] solstice; the winter solstice 冬至 and summer solstice 夏至

64 西部 [xībù] western part

65 年以来 [niányǐlái] since the year ...

Lesson 34

New Characters

1	2	3	4	5	6 †
永	彩	限	博	值	墙

7 †	8 †	9 †	10 †	11 †	12 †
死	汤	取	宽	挂	乱

13 †	14	15	16	17	18
破	细	士	险	紧	码

19	20	21
危	龄	详

Lesson 34

HSK Vocabulary

22 限制	28 高级	34 年龄
23 律师	29 理想	35 博士
24 值得	30 详细	36 至少
25 精彩	31 永远	37 报名
26 首都	32 适合	38 紧张
27 号码	33 危险	

Non-HSK Vocabulary

39 取得	48 听取	57 供应
40 有限公司	49 有力	58 人民日报
41 院士	50 回应	59 电动
42 访谈	51 图片	60 群体
43 开通	52 留下	61 市长
44 百姓	53 农民工	62 走进
45 另一	54 优质	63 共有
46 成都	55 班子	
47 知名	56 各界	

Lesson 34

Glossary

1 永 [yǒng] forever; always; perpetual

2 彩 [cǎi] (bright) color; variety; applause; applaud; lottery prize

3 限 [xiàn] limit; bound

4 博 [bó] extensive; ample; rich; obtain; aim; to win; to get; plentiful; to gamble

5 值 [zhí] value; (to be) worth; to happen to; to be on duty

6 墙 (†) [qiáng] wall; CL: 面 [miàn], 堵 [dǔ]

7 死 (†) [sǐ] to die; impassable; uncrossable; inflexible; rigid; extremely

8 汤 (†) [shāng] rushing current ◆ [tāng] surname Tang ◇ soup; hot or boiling water; decoction of medicinal herbs; water in which sth has been boiled

9 取 (†) [qǔ] to take; to get; to choose; to fetch

10 宽 (†) [kuān] surname Kuan ◇ lenient; wide; broad

11 挂 (†) [guà] to hang or suspend (from a hook etc); (of a telephone call) to hang up; to be worried or concerned; to make a phone call (topolect); to register or record; to hitch; classifier for sets or clusters of objects

12 乱 (†) [luàn] in confusion or disorder; in a confused state of mind; disorder; upheaval; riot; illicit sexual relations; to throw into disorder; to mix up; indiscriminate; random; arbitrary

13 破 (†) [pò] broken; damaged; worn out; to break, split or cleave; to get rid of; to destroy; to break with; to defeat; to capture (a city etc); to expose the truth of

14 细 [xì] thin or slender; finely particulate; thin and soft; fine; delicate; trifling; (of a sound) quiet; frugal

15 士 [shì] surname Shi ◇ member of the senior ministerial class (old); scholar (old); bachelor; honorific; first class military rank; specialist worker

16 险 [xiǎn] danger; dangerous; rugged

17 紧 [jǐn] tight; strict; close at hand; near; urgent; tense; hard up; short of money; to tighten

18 码 [mǎ] weight; number; code; to pile; to stack; classifier for length or distance (yard), happenings etc

19 危 [wēi] surname Wei ◇ danger; to endanger; Taiwan pr. [wéi]

20 龄 [líng] age

21 详 [xiáng] detailed; comprehensive

22 限制 [xiànzhì] to restrict; to limit; to confine; restriction; limit; CL: 个 [gè]

23 律师 [lǜshī] lawyer

24 值得 [zhíde] to be worth; to deserve

25 精彩 [jīngcǎi] brilliant; splendid

26 首都 [shǒudū] capital (city); CL: 个 [gè]

27 号码 [hàomǎ] number; CL: 堆 [duī], 个 [gè]

28 高级 [gāojí] high level; high grade; advanced; high-ranking

29 理想 [lǐxiǎng] a dream; an ideal; perfection; ideal; perfect; desirable; CL: 个 [gè]

30 详细 [xiángxì] detailed; in detail; minute

31 永远 [yǒngyuǎn] forever; eternal

32 适合 [shìhé] to fit; to suit

33 危险 [wēixiǎn] danger; dangerous

34 年龄 [niánlíng] (a person's) age; CL: 把 [bǎ], 个 [gè]

35 博士 [bóshì] doctor; court academician (in feudal China); Ph.D.

36 至少 [zhìshǎo] at least; (to say the) least

37 报名 [bàomíng] to sign up; to enter one's name; to apply; to register; to enroll; to enlist

38 紧张 [jǐnzhāng] nervous; keyed up; intense; tense; strained; in short supply; scarce; CL: 阵 [zhèn]

39 取得 [qǔdé] to acquire; to get; to obtain

Lesson 34

40 有限公司 [yǒuxiàngōngsī] limited company; corporation

41 院士 [yuànshì] scholar; academician; fellow (of an academy)

42 访谈 [fǎngtán] to visit and discuss; to interview

43 开通 [kāitong] to open up (windows for air, ideas for discussion, transport routes etc); open-minded

44 百姓 [bǎixìng] common people

45 另一 [lìngyī] another; the other

46 成都 [chéngdū] Chengdu subprovincial city and capital of Sichuan province 四川 in southwest China

47 知名 [zhīmíng] well known; famous

48 听取 [tīngqǔ] to hear (news); to listen to

49 有力 [yǒulì] powerful; forceful; vigorous

50 回应 [huíyìng] response; respond

51 图片 [túpiàn] image; picture; photograph; CL: 张 [zhāng]

52 留下 [liúxià] to leave behind; to stay behind; to remain; to keep; not to let go (sb)

53 农民工 [nóngmíngōng] migrant workers

54 优质 [yōuzhì] excellent quality

55 班子 [bānzi] organized group; theatrical troupe

56 各界 [gèjiè] all walks of life; all social circles

57 供应 [gōngyìng] to supply; to provide; to offer

58 人民日报 [rénmínrìbào] Renmin Ribao (People's Daily)

59 电动 [diàndòng] electric powered

60 群体 [qúntǐ] community; colony

61 市长 [shìzhǎng] mayor

62 走进 [zǒujìn] to enter

63 共有 [gòngyǒu] to have altogether; in all

Lesson 35

New Characters

1	2	3	4	5 *	6 †
志	江	具	停	蔡	血

7 †	8 †	9 †	10	11	12
戴	掉	假	播	研	距

13	14	15	16	17	18
禁	止	熟	饮	醒	谊

19
究

Lesson 35

HSK Vocabulary

20 友谊	27 广播	34 对话
21 出生	28 实在	35 可是
22 感情	29 停止	36 距离
23 反对	30 禁止	37 准确
24 研究生	31 阳光	38 成熟
25 提醒	32 工具	39 饮料
26 杂志	33 提前	40 长江

Non-HSK Vocabulary

41 研究	50 之外	59 大众
42 具有	51 广东省	60 在内
43 科研	52 工艺	61 收到
44 调研	53 有限	62 多元
45 各国	54 省长	63 新技术
46 应急	55 另一方面	64 民意
47 一部分	56 公安机关	65 国内外
48 法规	57 各位	
49 全力	58 世博会	

Lesson 35

Glossary

1 志 [zhì] aspiration; ambition; the will ◇ sign; mark; to record; to write a footnote

2 江 [jiāng] surname Jiang ◇ river; CL: 条 [tiáo], 道 [dào]

3 具 [jù] tool; device; utensil; equipment; instrument; talent; ability; to possess; to have; to provide; to furnish; to state; classifier for devices, coffins, dead bodies

4 停 [tíng] to stop; to halt; to park (a car)

5 蔡 (*) [cài] surname Cai

6 血 (†) [xuè] blood; informal colloquial and Taiwan pr. [xiě]; also pr. [xuě]; CL: 滴 [dī], 片 [piàn]

7 戴 (†) [dài] surname Dai ◇ to put on or wear (glasses, hat, gloves etc); to respect; to bear; to support

8 掉 (†) [diào] to fall; to drop; to lag behind; to lose; to go missing; to reduce; fall (in prices); to lose (value, weight etc); to wag; to swing; to turn; to change; to exchange; to swap; to show off; to shed (hair)

9 假 (†) [jiǎ] fake; false; artificial; to borrow; if; suppose ◆ [jià] vacation

10 播 [bō] to sow; to scatter; to spread; to broadcast; Taiwan pr. [bò]

11 研 [yán] to grind; study; research

12 距 [jù] at a distance of; distance; to be apart

13 禁 [jīn] to endure ◆ [jìn] to prohibit; to forbid

14 止 [zhǐ] to stop; to prohibit; until; only

15 熟 [shú] cooked (of food); ripe (of fruit); mature (of seeds); familiar; skilled; done; also [shóu] (coll.)

16 饮 [yǐn] to drink

17 醒 [xǐng] to wake up; to awaken; to be awake

18 谊 [yì] friendship; also pr. [yí]

19 究 [jiū] after all; to investigate; to study carefully; Taiwan pr. [jiù]

20 友谊 [yǒuyì] companionship; fellowship; friendship

21 出生 [chūshēng] to be born

22 感情 [gǎnqíng] feeling; emotion; sensation; likes and dislikes; deep affection for sb or sth; relationship (i.e. love affair); CL: 个 [gè], 种 [zhǒng]

23 反对 [fǎnduì] to fight against; to oppose; to be opposed to; opposition

24 研究生 [yánjiūshēng] graduate student; postgraduate student; research student

25 提醒 [tíxǐng] to remind; to call attention to; to warn of

26 杂志 [zázhì] magazine; CL: 本 [běn], 份 [fèn], 期 [qī]

27 广播 [guǎngbō] broadcast; CL: 个 [gè]; broadcasting; to broadcast; (formal) to propagate; to publicize

28 实在 [shízài] really; actually; indeed; true; real; honest; dependable; (philosophy) reality

29 停止 [tíngzhǐ] to stop; to halt; to cease

30 禁止 [jìnzhǐ] to prohibit; to forbid; to ban

31 阳光 [yángguāng] sunshine; CL: 线 [xiàn]

32 工具 [gōngjù] tool; instrument; utensil; means (to achieve a goal etc)

33 提前 [tíqián] to shift to an earlier date; to bring forward; to advance

34 对话 [duìhuà] dialog; CL: 个 [gè]

35 可是 [kěshì] but; however

36 距离 [jùlí] distance; to be apart; CL: 个 [gè]

37 准确 [zhǔnquè] accurate; exact; precise

38 成熟 [chéngshú] mature; ripe; to mature; to ripen; Taiwan pr. [chéng shóu]

39 饮料 [yǐnliào] drink; beverage

40 长江 [chángjiāng] Yangtze River, or Chang Jiang

Lesson 35

41 研究 [yánjiū] research; a study; CL: 项 [xiàng]

42 具有 [jùyǒu] to have; to possess

43 科研 [kēyán] (scientific) research

44 调研 [diàoyán] to investigate and research; research; investigation

45 各国 [gèguó] each country; every country; various countries

46 应急 [yìngjí] emergency; to respond to an emergency; to meet a contingency

47 一部分 [yībùfèn] portion; part of; subset

48 法规 [fǎguī] legislation; statute

49 全力 [quánlì] with all one's strength; full strength; all-out (effort); fully (support)

50 之外 [zhīwài] outside; excluding

51 广东省 [guǎngdōngshěng] Guangdong province (Kwangtung) in south China, abbr. 粤, capital Guangzhou 广州

52 工艺 [gōngyì] arts and crafts; industrial arts

53 有限 [yǒuxiàn] limited; finite

54 省长 [shěngzhǎng] governor of a province

55 另一方面 [lìngyīfāngmiàn] on the other hand; another aspect

56 公安机关 [gōng'ānjīguān] Public Security Bureau

57 各位 [gèwèi] everybody (a term of address)

58 世博会 [shìbóhuì] World Exposition

59 大众 [dàzhòng] Volkswagen (automobile manufacturer) ◇ the masses; the great bulk of the population; popular (of music, science etc)

60 在内 [zàinèi] including

61 收到 [shōudào] to receive

62 多元 [duōyuán] poly-; multi-; multielement; multivariant; multivariate (math.)

63 新技术 [xīnjìshù] new technology

64 民意 [mínyì] public opinion; popular will; public will

65 国内外 [guónèiwài] domestic and international; at home and abroad

Lesson 36

New Characters

1	2	3	4	5	6
金	美	奖	林	批	约

7	8	9	10	11	12 *
购	评	言	丽	森	鹏

13	14 *	15 *	16 *	17 †	18 †
皮	菲	剑	燕	帅	硬

19 †	20	21	22	23	24
苦	绝	断	累	判	例

25	26	27
拒	肤	允

Lesson 36

HSK Vocabulary

28 出发	36 奖金	44 其次
29 皮肤	37 语言	45 美丽
30 判断	38 购物	46 平时
31 不管	39 批评	47 动作
32 森林	40 感动	48 积累
33 不但	41 允许	49 例如
34 也许	42 节约	
35 千万	43 拒绝	

Non-HSK Vocabulary

50 而言	59 毕业生	68 科学技术
51 累计	60 发展中	69 艺术家
52 美好	61 月底	70 总部
53 收购	62 可持续发展	71 社会保险
54 葡萄酒	63 总量	72 大桥
55 走访	64 国家级	73 舞台
56 江阴	65 观看	74 中美
57 上海市	66 精品	
58 年内	67 基金会	

Lesson 36

Glossary

1 金 [jīn] surname Jin; surname Kim (Korean); Jurchen Jin dynasty (1115-1234) ◇ gold; chemical element Au; generic term for lustrous and ductile metals; money; golden; highly respected; one of the eight ancient musical instruments 八音 [bāyīn]

2 美 [měi] the Americas; abbr. for 美洲 [Měizhōu]; USA; abbr. for 美国 [Měiguó] ◇ beautiful; very satisfactory; good; to be pleased with oneself

3 奖 [jiǎng] prize; award; encouragement; CL: 个 [gè]

4 林 [lín] surname Lin ◇ woods; forest; CL: 片 [piàn]; circle(s) (i.e. specific group of people); a collection (of similar things)

5 批 [pī] to ascertain; to act on; to criticize; to pass on; classifier for batches, lots, military flights; tier (for the ranking of universities and colleges)

6 约 [yāo] to weigh in a balance or on a scale ◆ [yuē] to make an appointment; to invite; approximately; pact; treaty; to economize; to restrict; to reduce (a fraction); concise

7 购 [gòu] to buy; to purchase

8 评 [píng] to discuss; to comment; to criticize; to judge; to choose (by public appraisal)

9 言 [yán] words; speech; to say; to talk

10 丽 [lí] Korea ◆ [lì] beautiful

11 森 [sēn] forest

12 鹏 (*) [péng] Peng, large fabulous bird; roc

13 皮 [pí] surname Pi ◇ leather; skin; fur; pico- (one trillionth); CL: 张 [zhāng]

14 菲 (*) [fēi] abbr. for the Philippines 菲律宾 [Fēilǜbīn] ◇ luxuriant (plant growth); rich with fragrance; phenanthrene C14H10 ◆ [fěi] poor; humble; unworthy; radish (old)

15 剑 (*) [jiàn] double-edged sword; CL: 口 [kǒu], 把 [bǎ]; classifier for blows of a sword

16 燕 (*) [yān] Yan, a vassal state of Zhou in modern Hebei and Liaoning; north Hebei; the four Yan kingdoms of the Sixteen Kingdoms, namely: Former Yan 前燕 (337-370), Later Yan 后燕 (384-409), Southern Yan 南燕 (398-410), Northern Yan 北燕 (409-436); surname Yan ◆ [yàn] swallow (family Hirundinidae)

17 帅 (†) [shuài] handsome; graceful; smart; commander in chief

18 硬 (†) [yìng] hard; stiff; strong; firm; resolutely; doggedly; good (quality); able (person)

19 苦 (†) [kǔ] bitter; hardship; pain; to suffer; to bring suffering to; painstakingly

20 绝 [jué] to cut short; extinct; to disappear; to vanish; absolutely; by no means

21 断 [duàn] to break; to snap; to cut off; to give up or abstain from sth; to judge; (usu. used in the negative) absolutely, definitely, decidedly

22 累 [léi] surname Lei ◇ rope; to bind together; to twist around ◆ [lěi] to accumulate; to involve or implicate; continuous; repeated ◆ [lèi] tired; weary; to strain; to wear out; to work hard

23 判 [pàn] to judge; to sentence; to discriminate; to discern; obviously (different)

24 例 [lì] example; precedent; rule; case; instance

25 拒 [jù] to resist; to repel; to refuse

26 肤 [fū] skin

27 允 [yǔn] just; fair; to permit; to allow

28 出发 [chūfā] to start out; to set off

29 皮肤 [pífū] skin; CL: 层 [céng], 块 [kuài]

30 判断 [pànduàn] to decide; to determine; CL: 个 [gè]

Lesson 36

31 不管 [bùguǎn] no matter (what, how); regardless of; no matter

32 森林 [sēnlín] forest; CL: 片 [piàn]

33 不但 [bùdàn] not only (... but also...)

34 也许 [yěxǔ] perhaps; maybe

35 千万 [qiānwàn] ten million; countless; many; one must by all means

36 奖金 [jiǎngjīn] premium; award money; a bonus

37 语言 [yǔyán] language; CL: 门 [mén], 种 [zhǒng]

38 购物 [gòuwù] shopping

39 批评 [pīpíng] to criticize; criticism; CL: 个 [gè]

40 感动 [gǎndòng] to move (sb); to touch (sb emotionally); moving

41 允许 [yǔnxǔ] to permit; to allow

42 节约 [jiéyuē] to economize; to conserve (resources); economy; frugal

43 拒绝 [jùjué] to refuse; to decline; to reject

44 其次 [qícì] next; secondly

45 美丽 [měilì] beautiful

46 平时 [píngshí] ordinarily; in normal times; in peacetime

47 动作 [dòngzuò] movement; motion; action; CL: 个 [gè]

48 积累 [jīlěi] to accumulate; accumulation; cumulative; cumulatively

49 例如 [lìrú] for example; for instance; such as

50 而言 [éryán] with regard to (preceding phrase)

51 累计 [lěijì] to accumulate; cumulative

52 美好 [měihǎo] beautiful; fine

53 收购 [shōugòu] to purchase (from various places); to acquire (a company)

54 葡萄酒 [pútaojiǔ] (grape) wine

55 走访 [zǒufǎng] to visit; to travel to

56 江阴 [jiāngyīn] Jiangyin county level city in Wuxi 无锡 [Wúxī], Jiangsu

57 上海市 [shànghǎishì] Shanghai municipality in southeast China, abbr. 沪

58 年内 [niánnèi] during the current year

59 毕业生 [bìyèshēng] graduate

60 发展中 [fāzhǎnzhōng] developing; under development; in the pipeline

61 月底 [yuèdǐ] end of the month

62 可持续发展 [kěchíxùfāzhǎn] sustainable development

63 总量 [zǒngliàng] total; overall amount

64 国家级 [guójiājí] national level (e.g. nature reserve)

65 观看 [guānkàn] to watch; to view

66 精品 [jīngpǐn] quality goods; products

67 基金会 [jījīnhuì] foundation (institution supported by an endowment)

68 科学技术 [kēxuéjìshù] science and technology

69 艺术家 [yìshùjiā] artist; CL: 个 [gè], 位 [wèi], 名 [míng]

70 总部 [zǒngbù] general headquarters

71 社会保险 [shèhuìbǎoxiǎn] social security; abbr. to 社保

72 大桥 [dàqiáo] Da Qiao, one of the Two Qiaos, according to Romance of the Three Kingdoms 三国演义 [Sānguó Yǎnyì], the two great beauties of ancient China ◇ great bridge

73 舞台 [wǔtái] stage; arena; fig. in the limelight

74 中美 [zhōngměi] China–USA

Lesson 37

New Characters

1	2	3	4 *	5 *	6 *
则	警	整	袁	魏	尼

7 *	8 †	9 †	10	11 *	12 †
侯	厚	软	印	淮	梦

13 †	14 †	15 †	16	17	18
输	刀	酸	竟	象	弃

19	20	21	22	23
尤	察	忆	悉	否

Lesson 37

HSK Vocabulary

24	究竟	31	大约	38	周围
25	放弃	32	熟悉	39	爱情
26	否则	33	回忆	40	不得不
27	家具	34	空气	41	警察
28	尤其	35	信任	42	看法
29	合格	36	印象		
30	整理	37	气候		

Non-HSK Vocabulary

43	尤其是	52	快速发展	61	专用
44	民警	53	仅仅	62	现任
45	警方	54	下去	63	大多
46	整改	55	一代	64	夏季
47	通信	56	研究院	65	打开
48	之所以	57	排名	66	不了
49	全国人大	58	联网	67	检察
50	联合国	59	认证		
51	全民	60	上世纪		

Lesson 37

Glossary

1 则 [zé] conjunction used to express contrast with a previous sentence or clause; standard; norm; rule; to imitate; to follow; then; principle; classifier for written items (such as an official statement)

2 警 [jǐng] to alert; to warn; police

3 整 [zhěng] exactly; in good order; whole; complete; entire; in order; orderly; to repair; to mend; to renovate; to make sb suffer; to punish; to fix; to give sb a hard time

4 袁 (*) [yuán] surname Yuan ◇ long robe (old)

5 魏 (*) [wèi] surname Wei; name of vassal state of Zhou dynasty from 661 BC in Shanxi, one of the Seven Hero Warring States; Wei state, founded by Cao Cao 曹操, one of the Three Kingdoms from the fall of the Han; the Wei dynasty 221-265; Wei prefecture and Wei county at different historical periods ◇ tower over a palace gateway (old)

6 尼 (*) [ní] Buddhist nun; (often used in phonetic spellings)

7 侯 (*) [hóu] surname Hou ◇ marquis, second of the five orders of ancient Chinese nobility 五等爵位 [wǔděng juéwèi]; nobleman or high official

8 厚 (†) [hòu] thick; deep or profound; kind; generous; rich or strong in flavor; to favor; to stress

9 软 (†) [ruǎn] soft; flexible

10 印 [yìn] surname Yin; abbr. for 印度 [Yìndù] ◇ to print; to mark; to engrave; a seal; a print; a stamp; a mark; a trace; image

11 淮 (*) [huái] name of a river

12 梦 (†) [mèng] dream; CL: 场 [cháng], 个 [gè]

13 输 (†) [shū] to lose; to transport; to donate; to enter (a password)

14 刀 (†) [dāo] surname Dao ◇ knife; blade; single-edged sword; cutlass; CL: 把 [bǎ]; classifier for sets of one hundred sheets (of paper)

15 酸 (†) [suān] sour; sore; ache; acid

16 竟 [jìng] unexpectedly; actually; to go so far as to; indeed

17 象 [xiàng] elephant, CL: 只 [zhī]; shape; form; appearance; image under a mapping (math.); to imitate

18 弃 [qì] to abandon; to relinquish; to discard; to throw away

19 尤 [yóu] surname You ◇ outstanding; particularly, especially; a fault; to express discontentment against

20 察 [chá] to examine; to inquire; to observe; to inspect; to look into; obvious; clearly evident

21 忆 [yì] to recollect; to remember; memory

22 悉 [xī] in all cases; know

23 否 [fǒu] to negate; to deny; not ◆ [pǐ] clogged; evil

24 究竟 [jiūjìng] after all (when all is said and done); actually; outcome; result

25 放弃 [fàngqì] to renounce; to abandon; to give up

26 否则 [fǒuzé] if not; otherwise; else; or else

27 家具 [jiājù] furniture; CL: 件 [jiàn], 套 [tào]

28 尤其 [yóuqí] especially; particularly

29 合格 [hégé] qualified; meeting a standard; eligible (voter)

30 整理 [zhěnglǐ] to arrange; to tidy up; to sort out; to straighten out; to list systematically; to collate (data, files); to pack (luggage)

31 大约 [dàyuē] approximately; about

32 熟悉 [shúxī] to be familiar with; to know well

Lesson 37

33 回忆 [huíyì] to recall; recollection; CL: 个 [gè]

34 空气 [kōngqì] air; atmosphere

35 信任 [xìnrèn] to trust; to have confidence in

36 印象 [yìnxiàng] impression

37 气候 [qìhòu] climate; atmosphere; situation; CL: 种 [zhǒng]

38 周围 [zhōuwéi] surroundings; environment; to encompass

39 爱情 [àiqíng] romance; love (romantic); CL: 个 [gè]

40 不得不 [bùdébù] have no choice or option but to; cannot but; have to; can't help it; can't avoid

41 警察 [jǐngchá] police; policeman; policewoman; CL: 个 [gè]

42 看法 [kànfǎ] way of looking at a thing; view; opinion; CL: 个 [gè]

43 尤其是 [yóuqíshì] especially; most of all; above all; in particular

44 民警 [mínjǐng] civil police; PRC police; abbr. for 人民警察

45 警方 [jǐngfāng] police

46 整改 [zhěnggǎi] to reform; to rectify and improve

47 通信 [tōngxìn] to communicate

48 之所以 [zhīsuǒyǐ] the reason why

49 全国人大 [quánguóréndà] abbr. for National People's Congress (NPC)

50 联合国 [liánhéguó] United Nations

51 全民 [quánmín] entire population (of a country)

52 快速发展 [kuàisùfāzhǎn] rapid growth; rapid expansion

53 仅仅 [jǐnjǐn] barely; only; merely; only (this and nothing more)

54 下去 [xiàqu] to go down; to descend; to go on; to continue

55 一代 [yīdài] generation

56 研究院 [yánjiūyuàn] research institute; academy

57 排名 [páimíng] ranking; ordered list; to rank nth out of 100; to be placed; roll of honor

58 联网 [liánwǎng] network; cyber-

59 认证 [rènzhèng] to authenticate; to approve

60 上世纪 [shàngshìjì] last century

61 专用 [zhuānyòng] special; dedicated

62 现任 [xiànrèn] at the present; to hold an office; to occupy a post

63 大多 [dàduō] for the most part; many; most; the greater part; mostly

64 夏季 [xiàjì] summer

65 打开 [dǎkāi] to open; to show (a ticket); to turn on; to switch on

66 不了 [bùliǎo] unable to; without end

67 检察 [jiǎnchá] to inspect; check up (on)

Lesson 38

New Characters

1	2	3	4	5	6
将	案	景	松	贺	招

7 *	8 *	9 *	10 †	11	12 *
岭	穆	旭	挺	互	柳

13 *	14 †	15 †	16 †	17	18
俄	盐	抱	顿	肥	址

19	20	21	22	23
植	聘	仔	概	恐

Lesson 38

HSK Vocabulary

24	小说	31	本来	38	互相
25	植物	32	答案	39	竟然
26	地址	33	流行	40	长城
27	大概	34	将来	41	恐怕
28	轻松	35	风景	42	仔细
29	心情	36	祝贺	43	顾客
30	招聘	37	中文	44	减肥

Non-HSK Vocabulary

45	将会	54	意大利	63	电子商务
46	招商	55	大力发展	64	点评
47	报考	56	社保	65	国情
48	院校	57	周永康	66	减排
49	旅行社	58	小康社会	67	南海
50	地下	59	也就是	68	科技工作者
51	共同努力	60	海上	69	相当于
52	公交	61	江西		
53	招生	62	世博		

Lesson 38

Glossary

1 将 [jiāng] will; shall; to use; to take; to checkmate; just a short while ago ◆ [jiàng] general; commander-in-chief (military); king (chess piece); to command; to lead ◆ [qiāng] to desire; to invite; to request

2 案 [àn] (legal) case; incident; record; file; table

3 景 [jǐng] surname Jing ◇ bright; circumstance; scenery

4 松 [sōng] surname Song ◇ pine; CL: 棵 [kē] ◇ loose; to loosen; to relax

5 贺 [hè] surname He ◇ to congratulate

6 招 [zhāo] to recruit; to provoke; to beckon; to incur; to infect; contagious; a move (chess); a maneuver; device; trick; to confess

7 岭 (*) [lǐng] mountain range; mountain ridge

8 穆 (*) [mù] surname Mu ◇ solemn; reverent; calm; burial position in an ancestral tomb (old); old variant of 默

9 旭 (*) [xù] dawn; rising sun

10 挺 (†) [tǐng] to stick out; to (physically) straighten up; to endure or hold out; straight; stiff; outstanding; extraordinary; rather; quite; very; classifier for machine guns

11 互 [hù] mutual

12 柳 (*) [liǔ] surname Liu ◇ willow

13 俄 (*) [é] suddenly; very soon; Russian (Taiwan pr. [è])

14 盐 (†) [yán] salt; CL: 粒 [lì]

15 抱 (†) [bào] to hold; to carry (in one's arms); to hug or embrace; surround; cherish

16 顿 (†) [dùn] to stop; to pause; to arrange; to lay out; to kowtow; to stamp (one's foot); at once; classifier for meals, beatings, scoldings etc: time, bout, spell, meal

17 肥 [féi] fat; fertile; loose-fitting or large; to fertilize; to become rich by illegal means; fertilizer; manure

18 址 [zhǐ] location; site

19 植 [zhí] to plant

20 聘 [pìn] to engage (a teacher etc); to hire; to betroth; betrothal gift; to get married (of woman)

21 仔 [zǎi] variant of 崽 [zǎi] ◆ [zī] see 仔肩 [zījiān] ◆ [zǐ] meticulous; (of domestic animals or fowls) young

22 概 [gài] general; approximate

23 恐 [kǒng] afraid; frightened; to fear

24 小说 [xiǎoshuō] novel; fiction; CL: 本 [běn], 部 [bù]

25 植物 [zhíwù] botanical; plant; vegetation; CL: 种 [zhǒng]

26 地址 [dìzhǐ] address; CL: 个 [gè]

27 大概 [dàgài] roughly; probably; rough; approximate; about

28 轻松 [qīngsōng] gentle; relaxed

29 心情 [xīnqíng] mood; frame of mind; CL: 个 [gè]

30 招聘 [zhāopìn] recruitment; to invite applications for a job

31 本来 [běnlái] original; originally; at first; it goes without saying; of course

32 答案 [dá'àn] answer; solution; CL: 个 [gè]

33 流行 [liúxíng] to spread; to rage (of contagious disease); popular; fashionable; prevalent; (math.) manifold

34 将来 [jiānglái] in the future; future; the future; CL: 个 [gè]

35 风景 [fēngjǐng] scenery; landscape; CL: 个 [gè]

36 祝贺 [zhùhè] to congratulate; congratulations; CL: 个 [gè]

37 中文 [zhōngwén] Chinese; Chinese written language; Chinese writing

Lesson 38

38 互相 [hùxiāng] each other; mutually; mutual

39 竟然 [jìngrán] unexpectedly; to one's surprise; in spite of everything; in that crazy way; actually; to go as far as to

40 长城 [chángchéng] the Great Wall

41 恐怕 [kǒngpà] fear; to dread; I'm afraid that...; perhaps; maybe

42 仔细 [zǐxì] careful; attentive; cautious

43 顾客 [gùkè] client; customer; CL: 位 [wèi]

44 减肥 [jiǎnféi] to lose weight

45 将会 [jiānghuì] auxiliary verb introducing future action: may (be able to); will (cause); should (enable); going to

46 招商 [zhāoshāng] to seek investment or funding; investment promotion

47 报考 [bàokǎo] to enter oneself for an examination

48 院校 [yuànxiào] college; academy; educational institution

49 旅行社 [lǚxíngshè] travel agency

50 地下 [dìxià] underground; subterranean; covert

51 共同努力 [gòngtóngnǔlì] to work together; to collaborate

52 公交 [gōngjiāo] public transportation; mass transit

53 招生 [zhāoshēng] to enroll new students; recruitment

54 意大利 [yìdàlì] Italy; Italian

55 大力发展 [dàlìfāzhǎn] vigorous expansion; rapid development

56 社保 [shèbǎo] social insurance; abbr. for 社会保险

57 周永康 [zhōuyǒngkāng] Zhou Yongkang (1942-), PRC petroleum engineer and politician

58 小康社会 [xiǎokāngshèhuì] middle-class society

59 也就是 [yějiùshì] that is; i.e.

60 海上 [hǎishàng] maritime

61 江西 [jiāngxī] Jiangxi province (Kiangsi) in southeast China, abbr. 赣, capital Nanchang 南昌

62 世博 [shìbó] abbr. for 世界博览会 [Shìjiè Bólǎnhuì], World Expo

63 电子商务 [diànzǐshāngwù] e-commerce

64 点评 [diǎnpíng] to comment; a point by point commentary

65 国情 [guóqíng] current state of a country; national conditions; (US) State of the Union

66 减排 [jiǎnpái] to reduce emissions

67 南海 [nánhǎi] South China Sea

68 科技工作者 [kējìgōngzuòzhě] worker in science and technology

69 相当于 [xiāngdāngyú] equivalent to

Lesson 39

New Characters

1	2	3	4	5	6
区	处	像	既	温	味

7	8	9	10	11	12
缺	乘	故	怀	航	翻

13	14 *	15 *	16 *	17 *	18 *
失	玲	曰	琳	铝	鸿

19 †	20 †	21 †	22	23 †	24
赚	赢	页	密	俩	漫

25	26	27	28	29	30
暂	译	浪	败	激	疑

31	32
奋	估

Lesson 39

HSK Vocabulary

33	区别	40	温度	47	好处
34	翻译	41	合适	48	好像
35	留学	42	既然	49	兴奋
36	怀疑	43	航班	50	密码
37	乘坐	44	浪漫	51	故意
38	失败	45	暂时	52	味道
39	激动	46	估计	53	缺少

Non-HSK Vocabulary

54	书记处	63	情感	72	增速
55	质疑	64	以人为本	73	备受
56	航母	65	地板	74	学科
57	研究中心	66	拉开	75	内心
58	通行	67	计算机	76	负面
59	全方位	68	博客	77	山区
60	既有	69	中国科学院	78	那是
61	降雨	70	原因是		
62	既是	71	许可证		

Lesson 39

Glossary

1 区 [ōu] surname Ou ◆ [qū] area; region; district; small; distinguish; CL: 个 [gè]

2 处 [chǔ] to reside; to live; to dwell; to be in; to be situated at; to stay; to get along with; to be in a position of; to deal with; to discipline; to punish ◆ [chù] place; location; spot; point; office; department; bureau; respect; classifier for locations or items of damage: spot, point

3 像 [xiàng] to resemble; to be like; to look as if; such as; appearance; image; portrait

4 既 [jì] already; since; both... (and...)

5 温 [wēn] surname Wen ◇ warm; lukewarm; temperature; to warm up; mild; soft; tender; to review; to revise; epidemic

6 味 [wèi] taste; smell

7 缺 [quē] deficiency; lack; scarce; vacant post; to run short of

8 乘 [chéng] surname Cheng ◇ to ride; to mount; to make use of; to avail oneself of; to take advantage of; to multiply (mathematics); Buddhist sect or creed ◆ [shèng] four horse military chariot (archaic); four (archaic); generic term for history books

9 故 [gù] happening; instance; reason; cause; intentional; former; old; therefore; hence; (of people) to die, dead

10 怀 [huái] surname Huai ◇ bosom; heart; mind; to think of; to harbor in one's mind; to conceive (a child)

11 航 [háng] boat; ship; craft; to navigate; to sail; to fly

12 翻 [fān] to turn over; to flip over; to overturn; to rummage through; to translate; to decode; to double; to climb over or into; to cross

13 失 [shī] to lose; to miss; to fail

14 玲 (*) [líng] onomat. ting-a-ling (in compounds such as 玎玲 or 玲珑); tinkling of gem-pendants

15 曰 (*) [yuē] to speak; to say

16 琳 (*) [lín] gem

17 铝 (*) [lǚ] aluminum (chemistry)

18 鸿 (*) [hóng] eastern bean goose; great; large

19 赚 (†) [zhuàn] to earn; to make a profit ◆ [zuàn] to cheat; to swindle

20 赢 (†) [yíng] to beat; to win; to profit

21 页 (†) [yè] page; leaf

22 密 [mì] secret; confidential; close; thick; dense

23 俩 (†) [liǎ] two (colloquial equivalent of 两个); both; some

24 漫 [màn] free; unrestrained; to inundate

25 暂 [zàn] temporary; Taiwan pr. [zhàn]

26 译 [yì] to translate; to interpret

27 浪 [làng] wave; breaker; unrestrained; dissipated

28 败 [bài] be defeated; to defeat; loss

29 激 [jī] to arouse; to incite; to excite; to stimulate; sharp; fierce; violent

30 疑 [yí] to doubt; to misbelieve; to suspect

31 奋 [fèn] exert oneself

32 估 [gū] estimate ◆ [gù] old; second-hand (clothes)

33 区别 [qūbié] difference; to distinguish; to discriminate; to make a distinction; CL: 个 [gè]

34 翻译 [fānyì] to translate; to interpret; translator; interpreter; translation; interpretation; CL: 个 [gè], 位 [wèi], 名 [míng]

35 留学 [liúxué] to study abroad

36 怀疑 [huáiyí] to doubt; to suspect; doubt; suspicion; skeptical

37 乘坐 [chéngzuò] to ride (in a vehicle)

38 失败 [shībài] to be defeated; to lose; to fail (e.g. experiments); failure; defeat; CL: 次 [cì]

Lesson 39

39 激动 [jīdòng] to excite; to agitate; exciting

40 温度 [wēndù] temperature; CL: 个 [gè]

41 合适 [héshì] suitable; fitting; decent; to fit

42 既然 [jìrán] since; as; this being the case

43 航班 [hángbān] scheduled flight; flight number; plane; scheduled sailing; sailing number; passenger ship

44 浪漫 [làngmàn] romantic

45 暂时 [zànshí] temporary; provisional; for the time being

46 估计 [gūjì] to estimate; to reckon; CL: 个 [gè]

47 好处 [hǎochu] benefit; advantage; gain; profit; also pronounced [hǎo chù]; CL: 个 [gè]

48 好像 [hǎoxiàng] as if; to seem like

49 兴奋 [xīngfèn] excited; excitement

50 密码 [mìmǎ] code; secret code; password; pin number

51 故意 [gùyì] deliberately; on purpose

52 味道 [wèidao] flavor; smell; hint of

53 缺少 [quēshǎo] lack; shortage of; shortfall; to be short (of); to lack

54 书记处 [shūjichù] secretariat

55 质疑 [zhìyí] to call into question; to question (truth or validity)

56 航母 [hángmǔ] aircraft carrier; abbr. for 航空母舰

57 研究中心 [yánjiūzhōngxīn] research center

58 通行 [tōngxíng] to go through; a passage through; in general use; a pass or laissez-passer; a license (to a computer account)

59 全方位 [quánfāngwèi] all around; omni-directional; complete; holistic; comprehensive

60 既有 [jìyǒu] existing

61 降雨 [jiàngyǔ] precipitation; rainfall

62 既是 [jìshì] since, as; being the case that

63 情感 [qínggǎn] feeling; emotion; to move (emotionally)

64 以人为本 [yǐrénwéiběn] people-oriented

65 地板 [dìbǎn] floor

66 拉开 [lākāi] to pull open; to pull apart; to space out; to increase

67 计算机 [jìsuànjī] computer; calculator; CL: 台 [tái]

68 博客 [bókè] blog (loanword); weblog; blogger

69 中国科学院 [zhōngguókēxuéyuàn] Chinese Academy of Science

70 原因是 [yuányīnshì] the reason is ...

71 许可证 [xǔkězhèng] license; authorization; permit

72 增速 [zēngsù] to speed up; to accelerate; growth rate (economics)

73 备受 [bèishòu] to fully experience (good or bad)

74 学科 [xuékē] subject; branch of learning; course; academic discipline

75 内心 [nèixīn] heart; innermost being

76 负面 [fùmiàn] negative; the negative side

77 山区 [shānqū] mountain area; CL: 个 [gè]

78 那是 [nàshi] (coll.) of course; naturally; indeed

Lesson 40

New Characters

1	2	3	4	5 *	6 *
性	剧	导	辛	廖	肝

7 *	8 *	9 †	10 †	11 †	12 †
肾	沪	咸	呀	够	陪

13 †	14 †	15 *	16 †	17 †	18 †
弄	暗	郡	嘴	穷	脱

19 †	20 †	21	22	23	24
骗	尝	麻	烦	硕	歉

Lesson 40

HSK Vocabulary

25 性格	30 导游	35 难道
26 浪费	31 极其	36 麻烦
27 硕士	32 道歉	37 辛苦
28 相反	33 大夫	38 京剧
29 地球	34 加班	

Non-HSK Vocabulary

39 能够	48 收回	57 全球化
40 陪同	49 在职	58 深受
41 电视剧	50 长达	59 地处
42 科学研究	51 可持续	60 不利
43 再度	52 中国工程院	61 一句话
44 第二天	53 体内	62 分管
45 联通	54 合力	63 不合理
46 高科技	55 票价	
47 交给	56 天价	

Lesson 40

Glossary

1 性 [xìng] nature; character; property; quality; attribute; sexuality; sex; gender; suffix forming adjective from verb; suffix forming noun from adjective, corresponding to -ness or -ity; essence; CL: 个 [gè]

2 剧 [jù] drama; play; show; severe

3 导 [dǎo] to transmit; to lead; to guide; to conduct; to direct

4 辛 [xīn] (of taste) hot or pungent; hard; laborious; suffering; eighth of the ten heavenly stems 十天干; eighth in order; octa

5 廖 (*) [liào] surname Liao

6 肝 (*) [gān] liver; CL: 页 [yè], 个 [gè]

7 肾 (*) [shèn] kidney

8 沪 (*) [hù] short name for Shanghai

9 咸 (†) [xián] surname Xian ◇ all; everyone; each; widespread; harmonious ◇ salted; salty; stingy; miserly

10 呀 (†) [ya] (particle equivalent to 啊 after a vowel, expressing surprise or doubt)

11 够 (†) [gòu] to reach; to be enough

12 陪 (†) [péi] to accompany; to keep sb company; to assist; old variant of 赔 [péi]

13 弄 (†) [lòng] lane; alley ♦ [nòng] to do; to manage; to handle; to play with; to fool with; to mess with; to fix; to toy with

14 暗 (†) [àn] dark; gloomy; hidden; secret; muddled; obscure; in the dark ◇ to close (a door); to eclipse; muddled; stupid; ignorant

15 郡 (*) [jùn] canton; county; region

16 嘴 (†) [zuǐ] mouth; beak; spout (of teapot etc); CL: 张 [zhāng], 个 [gè]

17 穷 (†) [qióng] exhausted; poor

18 脱 (†) [tuō] to shed; to take off; to escape; to get away from

19 骗 (†) [piàn] to cheat; to swindle; to deceive; to fool; to hoodwink; to trick

20 尝 (†) [cháng] to taste; to try; already; ever; once ◇ to taste

21 麻 [má] surname Ma ◇ generic name for hemp, flax etc; hemp or flax fiber for textile materials; sesame; CL: 缕 [lǚ]; (of materials) rough or coarse; pocked; pitted; to have pins and needles or tingling; to feel numb

22 烦 [fán] to feel vexed; to bother; to trouble; superfluous and confusing; edgy

23 硕 [shuò] large; big

24 歉 [qiàn] to apologize; to regret; deficient

25 性格 [xìnggé] nature; disposition; temperament; character; CL: 个 [gè]

26 浪费 [làngfèi] to waste; to squander

27 硕士 [shuòshì] master's degree; learned person

28 相反 [xiāngfǎn] opposite; contrary

29 地球 [dìqiú] the Earth; planet; CL: 个 [gè]

30 导游 [dǎoyóu] tour guide; guidebook; to conduct a tour

31 极其 [jíqí] extremely

32 道歉 [dàoqiàn] to apologize

33 大夫 [dàifu] doctor; minister of state (in pre-Han states); CL: 个 [gè], 位 [wèi]

34 加班 [jiābān] to work overtime

35 难道 [nándào] don't tell me ...; could it be that...?

36 麻烦 [máfan] inconvenient; troublesome; annoying; to trouble or bother sb; to put sb to trouble

37 辛苦 [xīnkǔ] hard; exhausting; with much toil; thanks for your trouble

38 京剧 [jīngjù] Beijing opera; CL: 场 [chǎng], 出 [chū]

39 能够 [nénggòu] to be capable of; to be able to; can

40 陪同 [péitóng] to accompany

Lesson 40

41 电视剧 [diànshìjù] TV play; soap opera; CL: 部 [bù]

42 科学研究 [kēxuéyánjiū] scientific research

43 再度 [zàidù] once more; once again; one more time

44 第二天 [dì'èrtiān] next day; the morrow

45 联通 [liántōng] China United Telecommunications Corporation; abbr. to China Unicom or Unicom; abbr. of 中国联通 ◇ connection; link; to link together

46 高科技 [gāokējì] high tech; high technology

47 交给 [jiāogěi] to give; to deliver; to hand over

48 收回 [shōuhuí] to regain; to retake; to take back; to withdraw; to revoke

49 在职 [zàizhí] to be employed; to be in post; on-the-job

50 长达 [chángdá] to extend as long as; to lengthen out to

51 可持续 [kěchíxù] sustainable

52 中国工程院 [zhōngguógōngchéngyuàn] Chinese Academy of Engineering

53 体内 [tǐnèi] within the body; in vivo (vs in vitro); internal to

54 合力 [hélì] cooperate

55 票价 [piàojià] ticket price; fare; admission fee

56 天价 [tiānjià] extremely expensive; sky-high price

57 全球化 [quánqiúhuà] globalization

58 深受 [shēnshòu] to receive in no small measure

59 地处 [dìchǔ] to be located at; to be situated in

60 不利 [bùlì] unfavorable; disadvantageous; harmful; detrimental

61 一句话 [yījùhuà] in a word; in short

62 分管 [fēnguǎn] to be put in charge of; to be responsible for; branched passage

63 不合理 [bùhélǐ] unreasonable

Lesson 41

New Characters

1	2	3	4	5	6 *
列	傅	闹	聊	替	溢

7 †	8 *	9 *	10 †	11 †	12 *
寄	闫	缅	擦	撞	滇

13 *	14 †	15 †	16 †	17 †	18 †
鹿	丢	辣	汗	躺	棵

19	20	21	22
咱	骄	傲	惜

Lesson 41

HSK Vocabulary

23	差不多	29	排列	35	护士
24	到处	30	只好	36	有趣
25	聊天	31	可惜	37	咱们
26	代替	32	笔记本	38	师傅
27	热闹	33	洗衣机	39	优点
28	骄傲	34	正好		

Non-HSK Vocabulary

40	列入	49	赚钱	58	二手房
41	替代	50	风雨	59	不久前
42	好评	51	医改	60	小朋友
43	中等	52	有害	61	流失
44	故里	53	高温	62	拉萨
45	首发	54	切身	63	带给
46	科学院	55	效能	64	清洗
47	家族	56	修正		
48	出任	57	民办		

Lesson 41

Glossary

1 列 [liè] to arrange; to line up; row; file; series; column

2 傅 [fù] surname Fu ◇ tutor

3 闹 [nào] noisy; cacophonous; to make noise; to disturb; to vent (feelings); to fall ill; to have an attack (of sickness); to go in (for some activity); to joke

4 聊 [liáo] to chat; to depend upon (literary); temporarily; just; slightly

5 替 [tì] to substitute for; to take the place of; to replace; for; on behalf of; to stand in for

6 溢 (*) [yì] to overflow

7 寄 (†) [jì] to live (in a house); to lodge; to mail; to send; to entrust; to depend

8 闫 (*) [yán] variant of 阎; surname Yan

9 缅 (*) [miǎn] Myanmar (formerly Burma) (abbr. for 缅甸 [Miǎn diàn]) ◇ distant; remote; detailed

10 擦 (†) [cā] to wipe; to erase; rubbing (brush stroke in painting); to clean; to polish

11 撞 (†) [zhuàng] to hit; to strike; to meet by accident; to run into; to bump against; to bump into

12 滇 (*) [diān] abbr. for Yunnan province 云南 in southwest China

13 鹿 (*) [lù] deer

14 丢 (†) [diū] to lose; to put aside; to throw

15 辣 (†) [là] hot (spicy); pungent

16 汗 (†) [hàn] perspiration; sweat; CL: 滴 [dī], 头 [tóu], 身 [shēn]; to be speechless (out of helplessness, embarrassment etc) (Internet slang used as an interjection)

17 躺 (†) [tǎng] to recline; to lie down

18 棵 (†) [kē] classifier for trees, cabbages, plants etc

19 咱 [zán] I or me; we (including both the speaker and the person spoken to); [zá] [zǎ]

20 骄 [jiāo] proud; arrogant

21 傲 [ào] proud; arrogant; to despise; unyielding; to defy

22 惜 [xī] pity; regret; to rue; to begrudge; Taiwan pr. [xí]

23 差不多 [chàbuduō] almost; nearly; more or less; about the same; good enough; not bad

24 到处 [dàochù] everywhere

25 聊天 [liáotiān] to chat; to gossip

26 代替 [dàitì] instead; to replace; to substitute (X for Y, or a number in an algebraic expression)

27 热闹 [rènao] bustling with noise and excitement; lively

28 骄傲 [jiāo'ào] pride; arrogance; conceited; proud of sth

29 排列 [páiliè] array; arrangement; permutation (i.e. ordered choice of n elements out of m)

30 只好 [zhǐhǎo] without any better option; to have to; to be forced to

31 可惜 [kěxī] it is a pity; what a pity; unfortunately

32 笔记本 [bǐjìběn] notebook; CL: 本 [běn]

33 洗衣机 [xǐyījī] washer; washing machine; CL: 台 [tái]

34 正好 [zhènghǎo] just (in time); just right; just enough; to happen to; to chance to; by chance; it just so happens that

35 护士 [hùshi] nurse; CL: 个 [gè]

36 有趣 [yǒuqù] interesting; fascinating; amusing

37 咱们 [zánmen] we or us (including both the speaker and the person(s) spoken to); I or me; you; [zámen]

Lesson 41

38 师傅 [shīfu] master; qualified worker; respectful form of address for older men; CL: 个 [gè], 位 [wèi], 名 [míng]

39 优点 [yōudiǎn] merit; benefit; strong point; advantage; CL: 个 [gè]

40 列入 [lièrù] to include on a list

41 替代 [tìdài] to substitute for; to replace; to supersede

42 好评 [hǎopíng] favorable criticism; positive evaluation

43 中等 [zhōngděng] medium

44 故里 [gùlǐ] hometown; native place

45 首发 [shǒufā] first issue; first public showing

46 科学院 [kēxuéyuàn] academy of sciences; CL: 个 [gè]

47 家族 [jiāzú] household; clan

48 出任 [chūrèn] to take up a post; to start in a new job

49 赚钱 [zhuànqián] to earn money; money making

50 风雨 [fēngyǔ] wind and rain; the elements; trials and hardships

51 医改 [yīgǎi] reform of the medical system

52 有害 [yǒuhài] destructive; harmful; damaging

53 高温 [gāowēn] high temperature

54 切身 [qièshēn] direct; concerning oneself; personal

55 效能 [xiàonéng] efficacy; effectiveness

56 修正 [xiūzhèng] to revise; to amend

57 民办 [mínbàn] run by the local people; privately operated

58 二手房 [èrshǒufáng] second-hand house; house acquired indirectly through a middle-man

59 不久前 [bùjiǔqián] not long ago

60 小朋友 [xiǎopéngyǒu] children; CL: 个 [gè]

61 流失 [liúshī] drainage; to run off; to wash away

62 拉萨 [lāsà] Lhasa, capital city of Tibet autonomous region 西藏自治区

63 带给 [dàigěi] to carry to

64 清洗 [qīngxǐ] to wash; to clean; to purge

Lesson 42

New Characters

1	2	3	4	5	6
尔	勇	养	沙	签	耐

7 *	8	9 *	10 †	11 *	12 *
俞	厉	骏	剩	杭	玮

13 *	14	15 †	16 †	17	18
渝	握	抬	窄	默	偶

19	20	21	22	23	24
幽	肚	戚	燥	柿	愉

Lesson 42

HSK Vocabulary

25 随便	33 愉快	41 失望
26 入口	34 打印	42 西红柿
27 冷静	35 勇敢	43 沙发
28 握手	36 偶尔	44 肚子
29 签证	37 按时	45 干燥
30 幽默	38 养成	46 商量
31 亲戚	39 厉害	
32 耐心	40 样子	

Non-HSK Vocabulary

47 平米	56 性爱	65 护肤
48 干事	57 东南亚	66 外科
49 邮箱	58 限期	67 还说
50 一则	59 真情	68 死者
51 数百	60 首选	69 进修
52 性生活	61 语音	70 重温
53 细则	62 界定	71 流入
54 主要任务	63 高血压	
55 就是说	64 生命力	

Lesson 42

Glossary

1 尔 [ěr] thus; so; like that; you; thou

2 勇 [yǒng] brave

3 养 [yǎng] to raise (animals); to bring up (children); to keep (pets); to support; to give birth

4 沙 [shā] surname Sha ◇ granule; hoarse; raspy; sand; powder; CL: 粒 [lì]; abbr. for Tsar or Tsarist Russia

5 签 [qiān] sign one's name ◇ inscribed bamboo stick (used in divination, gambling, drawing lots etc); small wood sliver; a label; a tag

6 耐 [nài] capable of enduring; able to tolerate; patient; durable; hardy; resistant

7 俞 (*) [yú] surname Yu ◇ yes (used by Emperor or ruler); OK; to accede; to assent

8 厉 [lì] surname Li ◇ strict; severe

9 骏 (*) [jùn] spirited horse

10 剩 (†) [shèng] to remain; to be left; to have as remainder

11 杭 (*) [háng] surname Hang; Hangzhou

12 玮 (*) [wěi] (reddish jade); precious; rare

13 渝 (*) [yú] abbr. for Chongqing 重庆; old name of Jialing river 嘉陵江 in Sichuan

14 握 [wò] to hold; to grasp; to clench (one's fist); to master; classifier: a handful

15 抬 (†) [tái] to lift; to raise; (of two or more persons) to carry

16 窄 (†) [zhǎi] narrow; narrow-minded; badly off

17 默 [mò] silent; to write from memory

18 偶 [ǒu] accidental; image; pair; mate

19 幽 [yōu] remote; hidden away; secluded; serene; peaceful; to imprison; in superstition indicates the underworld; ancient district spanning Liaonang and Hebei provinces

20 肚 [dǔ] tripe ◆ [dù] belly

21 戚 [qī] surname Qi ◇ relative; grief (borrowed meaning from rarely used 慼); sorrow

22 燥 [zào] dry; parched; impatient

23 柿 [shì] persimmon

24 愉 [yú] pleased

25 随便 [suíbiàn] as one wishes; as one pleases; at random; negligent; casual; wanton

26 入口 [rùkǒu] entrance

27 冷静 [lěngjìng] calm; cool-headed

28 握手 [wòshǒu] to shake hands

29 签证 [qiānzhèng] visa; certificate; to certify; CL: 个 [gè]

30 幽默 [yōumò] (loanword) humor; humorous

31 亲戚 [qīnqi] a relative (i.e. family relation); CL: 门 [mén], 个 [gè], 位 [wèi]

32 耐心 [nàixīn] to be patient; patience

33 愉快 [yúkuài] cheerful; cheerily; delightful; pleasant; pleasantly; pleasing; happy; delighted

34 打印 [dǎyìn] to print; to seal; to stamp

35 勇敢 [yǒnggǎn] brave; courageous

36 偶尔 [ǒu'ěr] occasionally; once in a while; sometimes

37 按时 [ànshí] on time; before deadline; on schedule

38 养成 [yǎngchéng] to cultivate; to raise; to form (a habit); to acquire

39 厉害 [lìhai] difficult to deal with; difficult to endure; ferocious; radical; serious; terrible; violent; tremendous; awesome

40 样子 [yàngzi] manner; air; looks; aspect

41 失望 [shīwàng] disappointed; to lose hope; to despair

42 西红柿 [xīhóngshì] tomato; CL: 只 [zhī]

43 沙发 [shāfā] sofa; CL: 条 [tiáo], 张 [zhāng]

Lesson 42

44 肚子 [dùzi] belly; abdomen; stomach; CL: 个 [gè]

45 干燥 [gānzào] to dry (of weather, paint, cement etc); desiccation; dull; uninteresting; arid

46 商量 [shāngliang] to consult; to talk over; to discuss

47 平米 [píngmǐ] square meter; short for 平方米

48 干事 [gànshi] administrator; executive secretary

49 邮箱 [yóuxiāng] mailbox

50 一则 [yīzé] on the one hand

51 数百 [shùbǎi] several hundred

52 性生活 [xìngshēnghuó] sex life

53 细则 [xìzé] detailed rules and regulations; bylaws

54 主要任务 [zhǔyàorènwu] main task; principal duty

55 就是说 [jiùshìshuō] in other words; that is

56 性爱 [xìng'ài] sex; lovemaking

57 东南亚 [dōngnányà] Southeast Asia

58 限期 [xiànqī] to set a time limit; time limit; deadline

59 真情 [zhēnqíng] real situation; the truth

60 首选 [shǒuxuǎn] first choice; premium; to come first in the imperial examinations

61 语音 [yǔyīn] voice

62 界定 [jièdìng] definition; to delimit

63 高血压 [gāoxuèyā] high blood pressure; hypertension

64 生命力 [shēngmìnglì] vitality

65 护肤 [hùfū] skincare

66 外科 [wàikē] surgery; "external" medicine, i.e. surgical intervention, as opposed to 内科 [nèikē] "internal" treatment by administering drugs; surgical department

67 还说 [háishuō] to add (in speaking); to also say

68 死者 [sǐzhě] the dead; the deceased

69 进修 [jìnxiū] advanced studies; additional studies

70 重温 [chóngwēn] to learn sth over again; to review; to brush up

71 流入 [liúrù] to flow into; to drift into; influx; inflow

Lesson 43

New Characters

1	2	3	4	5	6
从	油	户	齐	传	虎

7	8	9	10	11 *	12
折	诚	窗	序	揽	泼

13 *	14 †	15 *	16 *	17 *	18 †
卿	扔	浆	熙	坠	敲

19	20	21	22	23
咳	钥	匙	嗽	恼

Lesson 43

HSK Vocabulary

24 加油站	32 缺点	40 从来
25 传真	33 打折	41 果然
26 起飞	34 大使馆	42 出差
27 活泼	35 顺序	43 老虎
28 性别	36 分之	44 窗户
29 整齐	37 钥匙	45 开玩笑
30 烦恼	38 网球	46 咳嗽
31 座位	39 诚实	

Non-HSK Vocabulary

47 传出	56 老龄化	65 整整
48 拉美	57 放宽	66 老龄
49 无不	58 性教育	67 出品
50 少量	59 总计	68 细心
51 具体情况	60 多久	69 研究报告
52 高尔夫	61 农作物	70 受害者
53 众人	62 估值	71 饮品
54 记住	63 引人注目	
55 合肥	64 案发	

Lesson 43

Glossary

1 从 [cōng] lax; yielding; unhurried ◆ [cóng] surname Cong ◇ from; via; passing through; through (a gap); past; ever (followed by negative, meaning never); (formerly pr. [zòng] and related to 纵) to follow; to comply with; to obey; to join; to engage in; adopting some mode of action or attitude; follower; retainer; accessory; accomplice; related by common paternal grandfather or earlier ancestor ◆ [zòng] second cousin

2 油 [yóu] oil; fat; grease; petroleum; to apply tung oil, paint or varnish; oily; greasy; glib; cunning

3 户 [hù] a household; door; family

4 齐 [qí] (name of states and dynasties at several different periods); surname Qi ◇ neat; even; level with; identical; simultaneous; all together; to even sth out

5 传 [chuán] to pass on; to spread; to transmit; to infect; to transfer; to circulate; to conduct (electricity) ◆ [zhuàn] biography; historical narrative; commentaries; relay station

6 虎 [hǔ] tiger; CL: 只 [zhī]

7 折 [shé] to break (e.g. stick or bone); a loss ◆ [zhē] to turn sth over; to turn upside-down; to tip sth out (of a container) ◆ [zhé] to break; to fracture; to snap; to suffer loss; to bend; to twist; to turn; to change direction; convinced; to convert into (currency); discount; rebate; tenth (in price); classifier for theatrical scenes; to fold; accounts book

8 诚 [chéng] honest; sincere; true

9 窗 [chuāng] shutter; window; CL: 扇 [shàn]

10 序 [xù] order; sequence; preface

11 揽 (*) [lǎn] to monopolize; to seize

12 泼 [pō] to splash; to spill; rough and coarse; brutish

13 卿 (*) [qīng] high ranking official (old); term of endearment between spouses (old); (from the Tang Dynasty onwards) term used by the emperor for his subjects (old); honorific (old)

14 扔 (†) [rēng] to throw; to throw away

15 浆 (*) [jiāng] broth; serum; to starch ◆ [jiàng] starch paste

16 熙 (*) [xī] prosperous; splendid

17 坠 (*) [zhuì] to fall; to drop; to weigh down

18 敲 (†) [qiāo] to hit; to strike; to tap; to rap; to knock; to rip sb off; to overcharge

19 咳 [hāi] sound of sighing ◆ [ké] cough

20 钥 [yuè] key; also pr. [yào]

21 匙 [chí] spoon

22 嗽 [sòu] cough

23 恼 [nǎo] to get angry

24 加油站 [jiāyóuzhàn] gas station

25 传真 [chuánzhēn] fax; facsimile

26 起飞 [qǐfēi] to take off (in an airplane)

27 活泼 [huópo] lively; vivacious; brisk; active

28 性别 [xìngbié] gender; sex; distinguishing between the sexes

29 整齐 [zhěngqí] orderly; neat; even; tidy

30 烦恼 [fánnǎo] to be worried; to be distressed; worries

31 座位 [zuòwèi] seat; CL: 个 [gè]

32 缺点 [quēdiǎn] weak point; fault; shortcoming; CL: 个 [gè]

33 打折 [dǎzhé] to give a discount

34 大使馆 [dàshǐguǎn] embassy; CL: 座 [zuò], 个 [gè]

35 顺序 [shùnxù] sequence; order

36 分之 [fēnzhī] (indicating a fraction)

37 钥匙 [yàoshi] key; CL: 把 [bǎ]

38 网球 [wǎngqiú] tennis; CL: 个 [gè]

Lesson 43

39 诚实 [chéngshí] honest; honesty; honorable; truthful

40 从来 [cónglái] always; at all times; never (if used in negative sentence)

41 果然 [guǒrán] really; sure enough; as expected; if indeed

42 出差 [chūchāi] to go on an official or business trip

43 老虎 [lǎohǔ] tiger; CL: 只 [zhī]

44 窗户 [chuānghu] window; CL: 个 [gè], 扇 [shàn]

45 开玩笑 [kāiwánxiào] to play a joke; to make fun of; to joke

46 咳嗽 [késou] to cough; CL: 阵 [zhèn]

47 传出 [chuánchū] to transmit outwards; to disseminate; efferent (nerve)

48 拉美 [lāměi] Latin America; abbr. for 拉丁美洲

49 无不 [wúbù] none lacking; none missing; everything is there; everyone without exception

50 少量 [shǎoliàng] a smidgen; a little bit; a few

51 具体情况 [jùtǐqíngkuàng] specific circumstances; actual situation

52 高尔夫 [gāo'ěrfū] golf

53 众人 [zhòngrén] everyone

54 记住 [jìzhu] to remember; to bear in mind; to learn by heart

55 合肥 [héféi] Hefei, capital of Anhui province 安徽省 in south central China

56 老龄化 [lǎolínghuà] ageing (population)

57 放宽 [fàngkuān] to relax restrictions

58 性教育 [xìngjiàoyù] sex education

59 总计 [zǒngjì] (grand) total

60 多久 [duōjiǔ] how long?

61 农作物 [nóngzuòwù] (farm) crops

62 估值 [gūzhí] valuation; estimation

63 引人注目 [yǐnrénzhùmù] to attract attention; eye-catching; conspicuous

64 案发 [ànfā] to investigate a crime on the spot; to occur (of a crime); to be discovered (of a crime)

65 整整 [zhěngzhěng] whole; full

66 老龄 [lǎolíng] old age; aging; aged; geriatric; the aged

67 出品 [chūpǐn] to produce an item; output; items that are produced

68 细心 [xìxīn] careful; attentive

69 研究报告 [yánjiūbàogào] research report

70 受害者 [shòuhàizhě] person who suffers damage, injury etc; a casualty; a victim; those injured and wounded

71 饮品 [yǐnpǐn] beverage

Lesson 44

New Characters

1	2	3	4	5	6
克	集	毛	堵	微	烟

7	8	9	10	11	12
扬	稍	抽	巧	羽	慕

13 *	14 *	15 *	16	17 *	18 †
涅	萃	靓	忽	甫	猜

19 *	20 †	21 †	22	23	24
昊	逛	懒	扮	巾	羡

25	26	27	28
乒	悔	怜	兵

Lesson 44

HSK Vocabulary

29	羽毛球	37	主意	45	打扮
30	稍微	38	乒乓球	46	做生意
31	忽然	39	表扬	47	得意
32	羡慕	40	抽烟	48	笑话
33	集合	41	后悔	49	堵车
34	对面	42	巧克力	50	毛巾
35	同情	43	日记		
36	可怜	44	受不了		

Non-HSK Vocabulary

51	吸烟	60	人流	69	使用者
52	先进集体	61	北美	70	绿茶
53	苦难	62	安全感	71	意味
54	后方	63	短暂	72	向阳
55	江阴市	64	有好处	73	西南部
56	申论	65	深感	74	急于
57	云集	66	角逐	75	无论如何
58	头奖	67	教导		
59	从来不	68	激光		

Lesson 44

Glossary

1 克 [kè] to be able to; to subdue; to restrain; to overcome; gram ◇ Ke (c. 2000 BC), seventh of the legendary Flame Emperors, 炎帝 [Yándì] descended from Shennong 神农 [Shénnóng] Farmer God ◇ to subdue; to overthrow

2 集 [jí] to gather; to collect; collected works; classifier for sections of a TV series etc: episode

3 毛 [máo] surname Mao ◇ hair; feather; down; wool; mildew; mold; coarse or semifinished; young; raw; careless; unthinking; nervous; scared; (of currency) to devalue or depreciate; classifier for Chinese fractional monetary unit (equal to one 角 [jiǎo], 1/10 yuán, or 10 fen 分 [fēn])

4 堵 [dǔ] to stop up; (to feel) stifled or suffocated; wall; classifier for walls

5 微 [wēi] surname Wei; ancient Chinese state near present day Chongqing; Taiwan pr. [wéi] ◇ tiny; miniature; profound; abtruse; to decline; one millionth part of; micro-; Taiwan pr. [wéi]

6 烟 [yān] cigarette or pipe tobacco; CL: 根 [gēn]; smoke; mist; vapour; CL: 缕 [lǚ]; tobacco plant; (of the eyes) to be irritated by smoke

7 扬 [yáng] to raise; to hoist; the action of tossing or winnowing; scattering (in the wind); to flutter; to propagate

8 稍 [shāo] somewhat; a little

9 抽 [chōu] to draw out; to pull out from in between; to remove part of the whole; (of certain plants) to sprout or bud; to whip or thrash

10 巧 [qiǎo] opportunely; coincidentally; as it happens; skillful; timely

11 羽 [yǔ] feather; 5th note in pentatonic scale

12 慕 [mù] admire

13 涅 (*) [niè] to blacken; abbr. for 涅槃 [nièpán]

14 萃 (*) [cuì] collect; collection; dense; grassy; thick; assemble; gather

15 靓 (*) [jìng] to make up (one's face); to dress; (of one's dress) beautiful ◆ [liàng] attractive; good-looking

16 忽 [hū] surname Hu ◇ to neglect; to overlook; to ignore; suddenly

17 甫 (*) [fǔ] (classical) barely just; just now

18 猜 (†) [cāi] to guess

19 昊 (*) [hào] surname Hao ◇ vast and limitless; the vast sky

20 逛 (†) [guàng] to stroll; to visit

21 懒 (†) [lǎn] lazy

22 扮 [bàn] to disguise oneself; to dress up; adorn

23 巾 [jīn] towel; general purpose cloth; women's headcovering (old); Kangxi radical 50

24 羡 [xiàn] to envy

25 乒 [pīng] onomat. ping; bing

26 悔 [huǐ] to regret

27 怜 [lián] to pity

28 乓 [pāng] onomat. bang

29 羽毛球 [yǔmáoqiú] shuttlecock; badminton; CL: 个 [gè]

30 稍微 [shāowēi] a little bit

31 忽然 [hūrán] suddenly; all of a sudden

32 羡慕 [xiànmù] to envy; to admire

33 集合 [jíhé] to gather; to assemble; set (mathematics)

34 对面 [duìmiàn] opposite

35 同情 [tóngqíng] compassion; relent; sympathize; sympathy

36 可怜 [kělián] pitiful; pathetic; to have pity on

37 主意 [zhǔyi] plan; idea; decision; CL: 个 [gè]

Lesson 44

38 乒乓球 [pīngpāngqiú] table tennis; ping-pong; ping pong; table tennis ball; CL: 个 [gè]

39 表扬 [biǎoyáng] to praise; to commend

40 抽烟 [chōuyān] to smoke (a cigarette, tobacco)

41 后悔 [hòuhuǐ] to regret; to repent

42 巧克力 [qiǎokèlì] chocolate (loanword); CL: 块 [kuài]

43 日记 [rìjì] diary; CL: 则 [zé], 本 [běn], 篇 [piān]

44 受不了 [shòubùliǎo] unbearable; unable to endure; can't stand

45 打扮 [dǎban] to decorate; to dress; to make up; to adorn; manner of dressing; style of dress

46 做生意 [zuòshēngyì] to do business

47 得意 [déyì] proud of oneself; pleased with oneself; complacent

48 笑话 [xiàohuà] joke; jest; CL: 个 [gè]; to laugh at; to mock

49 堵车 [dǔchē] traffic jam; choking

50 毛巾 [máojīn] towel; CL: 条 [tiáo]

51 吸烟 [xīyān] to smoke

52 先进集体 [xiānjìnjítǐ] collectives

53 苦难 [kǔnàn] suffering

54 后方 [hòufāng] the rear; far behind the front line

55 江阴市 [jiāngyīnshì] Jiangyin county level city in Wuxi 无锡 [Wúxī], Jiangsu

56 申论 [shēnlùn] to give a detailed exposition; to state in detail

57 云集 [yúnjí] to gather (in a crowd); to converge; to swarm

58 头奖 [tóujiǎng] first prize

59 从来不 [cóngláibù] never

60 人流 [rénliú] a stream of people; an abortion; abbr. of 人工流产手术

61 北美 [běiměi] North America

62 安全感 [ānquángǎn] sense of security

63 短暂 [duǎnzàn] of short duration; brief; momentary

64 有好处 [yǒuhǎochù] advantageous; a plus; good for; advisable; helpful

65 深感 [shēngǎn] feel deeply

66 角逐 [juézhú] to tussle; to contend; to contest

67 教导 [jiàodǎo] to instruct; to teach; guidance; teaching

68 激光 [jīguāng] laser

69 使用者 [shǐyòngzhě] user

70 绿茶 [lǜchá] green tea

71 意味 [yìwèi] meaning; implication; flavor; overtone

72 向阳 [xiàngyáng] Xiangyang district of Kiamusze or Jiamusi city 佳木斯 [Jiāmùsī], Heilongjiang; Xiangyang district of Hegang city 鹤岗 [Hègǎng], Heilongjiang ◊ facing the sun; exposed to the sun

73 西南部 [xīnánbù] southwest part

74 急于 [jíyú] anxious; impatient

75 无论如何 [wúlùnrúhé] anyhow; anyway; whatever

Lesson 45

New Characters

1	2	3	4	5	6
卡	叶	瓶	润	伤	散

7	8	9	10	11	12
湿	袋	误	掌	泪	塑

13	14	15 *	16 *	17 *	18 *
惊	拾	隋	焯	玫	渚

19 *	20
籽	谅

Lesson 45

HSK Vocabulary

21 散步	30 请假	39 表格
22 推迟	31 误会	40 流泪
23 镜子	32 难受	41 来得及
24 伤心	33 鼓掌	42 叶子
25 信用卡	34 准时	43 无聊
26 湿润	35 塑料袋	44 力气
27 收拾	36 来不及	45 原谅
28 约会	37 个子	
29 瓶子	38 吃惊	

Non-HSK Vocabulary

46 首页	55 举止	64 动情
47 有效性	56 破的	65 国际歌
48 受骗	57 激增	66 结业
49 利于	58 无处	67 雨量
50 马尔代夫	59 着实	68 百位
51 地标	60 门将	69 翻身
52 面料	61 中式	70 写成
53 伤员	62 果园	
54 肤色	63 百分之百	

Lesson 45

Glossary

1 卡 [kǎ] to stop; to block; card; CL: 张 [zhāng], 片 [piàn]; calorie ◆ [qiǎ] to block; to be stuck; to be wedged; customs station; a clip; a fastener; a checkpost; Taiwan pron. [kǎ]

2 叶 [xié] to be in harmony ◆ [yè] surname Ye ◇ leaf; page; lobe; (historical) period

3 瓶 [píng] bottle; vase; pitcher; CL: 个 [gè]; classifier for wine and liquids

4 润 [rùn] smooth; moist

5 伤 [shāng] to injure; injury; wound

6 散 [sǎn] leisurely; loosen; powdered medicine; to scatter; to come loose ◆ [sàn] to break up (of couples); to distribute; to let out; to fire or discharge (sb)

7 湿 [shī] moist; wet

8 袋 [dài] a pouch; bag; sack; pocket

9 误 [wù] mistake; error; to miss; to harm; to delay; to neglect; mistakenly

10 掌 [zhǎng] palm of the hand; sole of the foot; paw; horseshoe; to slap; to hold in one's hand; to wield

11 泪 [lèi] tears

12 塑 [sù] to model (a figure) in clay

13 惊 [jīng] to start; to be frightened; to be scared; alarm

14 拾 [shí] to pick up; to collate or arrange; ten (banker's anti-fraud numeral)

15 隋 (*) [suí] the Sui dynasty (581-617 AD); surname Sui

16 焯 (*) [chāo] to blanch (cooking); to scald

17 玫 (*) [méi] rose

18 渚 (*) [zhǔ] islet; bank

19 籽 (*) [zǐ] seeds

20 谅 [liàng] to forgive; to understand

21 散步 [sànbù] to take a walk; to go for a walk

22 推迟 [tuīchí] to postpone; to put off; to defer

23 镜子 [jìngzi] mirror; CL: 面 [miàn], 个 [gè]

24 伤心 [shāngxīn] to grieve; to be broken-hearted; to feel deeply hurt

25 信用卡 [xìnyòngkǎ] credit card

26 湿润 [shīrùn] moist

27 收拾 [shōushi] to put in order; to tidy up; to pack; to repair; to punish (colloquial); to manage

28 约会 [yuēhuì] appointment; engagement; date; CL: 次 [cì], 个 [gè]; to arrange to meet

29 瓶子 [píngzi] bottle; CL: 个 [gè]

30 请假 [qǐngjià] to request leave of absence

31 误会 [wùhuì] to misunderstand; to mistake; misunderstanding; CL: 个 [gè]

32 难受 [nánshòu] to feel unwell; to suffer pain; to be difficult to bear

33 鼓掌 [gǔzhǎng] to applaud; to clap

34 准时 [zhǔnshí] on time; punctual; on schedule

35 塑料袋 [sùliàodài] plastic bag

36 来不及 [láibují] there's not enough time (to do sth); it's too late (to do sth)

37 个子 [gèzi] height; stature; build; size

38 吃惊 [chījīng] to be startled; to be shocked; to be amazed

39 表格 [biǎogé] form; table; CL: 张 [zhāng], 份 [fèn]

40 流泪 [liúlèi] to shed tears

41 来得及 [láidejí] there's still time; able to do sth in time

42 叶子 [yèzi] foliage; leaf; CL: 片 [piàn]

43 无聊 [wúliáo] bored; boring; senseless

44 力气 [lìqi] strength; CL: 把 [bǎ]

45 原谅 [yuánliàng] to excuse; to forgive; to pardon

Lesson 45

46 首页 [shǒuyè] home page (of a website); title page; front page; first page; fig. beginning; cover letter

47 有效性 [yǒuxiàoxìng] validity

48 受骗 [shòupiàn] to be cheated; to be taken in; to be hoodwinked

49 利于 [lìyú] be beneficial; be good for

50 马尔代夫 [mǎ'ěrdàifū] the Maldives

51 地标 [dìbiāo] landmark

52 面料 [miànliào] material for making clothes; CL: 块 [kuài]

53 伤员 [shāngyuán] wounded person

54 肤色 [fūsè] skin color (race)

55 举止 [jǔzhǐ] bearing; manner; mien

56 破的 [pòdì] to hit the target; fig. to touch the main point in speaking

57 激增 [jīzēng] rapidly increasing

58 无处 [wúchù] nowhere

59 着实 [zhuóshí] truly; indeed; severely; harshly

60 门将 [ménjiàng] official gatekeeper; goalkeeper (soccer, hockey etc)

61 中式 [zhōngshì] Chinese style ◆ [zhòngshì] to pass an exam (or the imperial exam); to qualify

62 果园 [guǒyuán] orchard

63 百分之百 [bǎifēnzhībǎi] a hundred percent; out and out; absolutely

64 动情 [dòngqíng] to get excited; passionate; aroused to passion; to fall in love; on heat (of animals)

65 国际歌 [guójìgē] The Internationale

66 结业 [jiéyè] to finish school, esp. a short course; to complete a course

67 雨量 [yǔliàng] rainfall

68 百位 [bǎiwèi] the hundreds place (or column) in the decimal system

69 翻身 [fānshēn] to turn over; to free oneself; to emancipate oneself; to stand up

70 写成 [xiěchéng] to compile; to form through writing

Lesson 46

New Characters

1	2	3	4	5	6
垃	圾	售	货	桶	盒

7	8	9	10	11	12
暖	针	膏	貌	猴	饼

13	14 *	15 *	16 *	17 †	18 *
扰	倚	佰	痴	吵	泓

19 *	20	21	22 †	23	24
缨	厌	羞	笨	袜	饺

Lesson 46

HSK Vocabulary

25	牙膏	33	猴子	41	垃圾桶
26	饺子	34	讨厌	42	语法
27	理发	35	害羞	43	复印
28	流利	36	袜子	44	暖和
29	盒子	37	马虎	45	打针
30	礼貌	38	打扰	46	请客
31	顺便	39	抱歉	47	词典
32	饼干	40	售货员		

Non-HSK Vocabulary

48	供货商	57	首富	66	软件开发
49	背面	58	台中市	67	不快
50	海东	59	亲眼	68	子曰
51	重修	60	安全检查	69	台前
52	严查	61	亲生	70	西沙
53	冬瓜	62	附则	71	阅历
54	西周	63	眼皮	72	江汉
55	失利	64	美感		
56	吸入	65	绿叶		

Lesson 46

Glossary

1 垃 [lā] see 垃圾 [lājī]; Taiwan pr. [lè]

2 圾 [jī] see 垃圾 [lājī]; Taiwan pr. [sè]

3 售 [shòu] to sell; to make or carry out (a plan or intrigue etc)

4 货 [huò] goods; money; commodity; CL: 个 [gè]

5 桶 [tǒng] bucket; (trash) can; barrel (of oil etc); CL: 个 [gè], 只 [zhī]

6 盒 [hé] small box; case

7 暖 [nuǎn] warm; to heat; genial

8 针 [zhēn] injection; needle; pin; CL: 根 [gēn], 支 [zhī]

9 膏 [gāo] ointment; paste; CL: 帖 [tiě]

10 貌 [mào] appearance

11 猴 [hóu] monkey; CL: 只 [zhī]

12 饼 [bǐng] round flat cake; cookie; cake; pastry; CL: 张 [zhāng]

13 扰 [rǎo] to disturb

14 倚 (*) [yǐ] to lean on; to rely upon

15 佰 (*) [bǎi] hundred (banker's anti-fraud numeral)

16 痴 (*) [chī] imbecile; sentimental; stupid; foolish; silly

17 吵 (†) [chǎo] to quarrel; to make a noise; noisy; to disturb by making a noise

18 泓 (*) [hóng] clear; vast and deep; classifier for a body of clear water

19 缨 (*) [yīng] tassel; sth shaped like a tassel (e.g. a leaf etc); ribbon

20 厌 [yàn] to loathe

21 羞 [xiū] shy; ashamed; shame; bashful; variant of 馐 [xiū]; delicacies

22 笨 (†) [bèn] stupid; foolish; silly; slow-witted; clumsy

23 袜 [wà] socks; stockings

24 饺 [jiǎo] dumplings with meat filling

25 牙膏 [yágāo] toothpaste; CL: 管 [guǎn]

26 饺子 [jiǎozi] dumpling; pot-sticker; CL: 个 [gè], 只 [zhī]

27 理发 [lǐfà] a barber; hairdressing

28 流利 [liúlì] fluent

29 盒子 [hézi] case

30 礼貌 [lǐmào] courtesy; manners

31 顺便 [shùnbiàn] conveniently; in passing; without much extra effort

32 饼干 [bǐnggān] biscuit; cracker; cookie; CL: 片 [piàn], 块 [kuài]

33 猴子 [hóuzi] monkey; CL: 只 [zhī]

34 讨厌 [tǎoyàn] disgusting; troublesome; nuisance; nasty; to hate doing sth

35 害羞 [hàixiū] shy; embarrassed; bashful

36 袜子 [wàzi] socks; stockings; CL: 只 [zhī], 对 [duì], 双 [shuāng]

37 马虎 [mǎhu] careless; sloppy; negligent; skimpy

38 打扰 [dǎrǎo] to disturb; to bother; to trouble

39 抱歉 [bàoqiàn] to be sorry; to feel apologetic; sorry!

40 售货员 [shòuhuòyuán] salesperson; CL: 个 [gè]

41 垃圾桶 [lājītǒng] rubbish bin; Taiwan pr. [lè sè tǒng]

42 语法 [yǔfǎ] grammar

43 复印 [fùyìn] to photocopy; to duplicate a document

44 暖和 [nuǎnhuo] warm; nice and warm

45 打针 [dǎzhēn] to give or have an injection

46 请客 [qǐngkè] to give a dinner party; to entertain guests; to invite to dinner

47 词典 [cídiǎn] dictionary (of Chinese compound words); also written 辞典 [cídiǎn]; CL: 部 [bù], 本 [běn]

48 供货商 [gōnghuòshāng] supply of merchandise; a supplier

Lesson 46

49 背面 [bèimiàn] the back; the reverse side; the wrong side

50 海东 [hǎidōng] Haidong prefecture, Qinghai

51 重修 [chóngxiū] to reconstruct; to repair; to revamp

52 严查 [yánchá] to investigate strictly

53 冬瓜 [dōngguā] wax gourd (Cucurbitaceae, Benincasa hispida); white gourd; white hairy melon; Chinese squash

54 西周 [xīzhōu] Western Zhou (1027-771 BC)

55 失利 [shīlì] to lose; to suffer defeat

56 吸入 [xīrù] to breathe in; to suck in; to inhale

57 首富 [shǒufù] richest individual; top millionaire

58 台中市 [táizhōngshì] Taichung city in central Taiwan

59 亲眼 [qīnyǎn] with one's own eyes; personally

60 安全检查 [ānquánjiǎnchá] safety check; security inspection (at airports)

61 亲生 [qīnshēng] born to oneself (i.e. one's natural child); having born oneself (i.e. one's natural parent)

62 附则 [fùzé] supplementary provision; bylaw; additional article (law)

63 眼皮 [yǎnpí] eyelid

64 美感 [měigǎn] sense of beauty; aesthetic perception

65 绿叶 [lǜyè] green leaf

66 软件开发 [ruǎnjiànkāifā] software development

67 不快 [bùkuài] unhappy; in low spirits

68 子曰 [zǐyuē] Confucius says:

69 台前 [táiqián] Taiqian county in Puyang 濮阳 [Púyáng], Henan; front of the stage

70 西沙 [xīshā] see 西沙群岛 [Xīshā Qúndǎo]

71 阅历 [yuèlì] to experience; experience

72 江汉 [jiānghàn] Jianghan district of Wuhan city 武汉市 [Wǔhànshì], Hubei

Lesson 47

New Characters

1	2	3	4	5	6
钢	预	寒	凉	琴	填

7	8	9	10	11 *	12 *
弹	粗	孤	暑	藜	酵

13 *	14 *	15 *
棰	孪	铯

Lesson 47

HSK Vocabulary

16 孤单	19 寒假	22 预习
17 凉快	20 干杯	23 放暑假
18 填空	21 粗心	24 弹钢琴

Non-HSK Vocabulary

25 止咳	34 比划	43 参考资料
26 广安门	35 亮光	44 江油
27 及时性	36 断奶	45 高干
28 耳闻	37 正巧	46 变硬
29 了然	38 门禁	47 弄懂
30 次生	39 西北工业大学	48 划一
31 断送	40 败走	49 切切
32 名利双收	41 文身	
33 生啤酒	42 过客	

Lesson 47

Glossary

1 钢 [gāng] steel

2 预 [yù] to advance; in advance; beforehand; to prepare

3 寒 [hán] cold; poor; to tremble

4 凉 [liáng] the five Liang of the Sixteen Kingdoms, namely: Former Liang 前凉 (314-376), Later Liang 后凉 (386-403), Northern Liang 北凉 (398-439), Southern Liang 南凉 (397-414), Western Liang 西凉 (400-421) ◇ cool; cold

5 琴 [qín] guqin or zither, cf 古琴; musical instrument in general

6 填 [tián] to fill or stuff; (of a form etc) to fill in

7 弹 [dàn] crossball; bullet; shot; shell; ball ◆ [tán] to pluck (a string); to play (a string instrument); to spring or leap; to shoot (e.g. with a catapult); (of cotton) to fluff or tease; to flick; to flip; to accuse; to impeach; elastic (of materials)

8 粗 [cū] coarse; rough; thick (for cylindrical objects); unfinished; vulgar; rude; crude

9 孤 [gū] lone; lonely

10 暑 [shǔ] heat; hot weather; summer heat

11 藜 (*) [lí] name of weed plant (fat hen, goosefoot, pigweed etc); Chenopodium album

12 酵 (*) [jiào] yeast; leavening; fermentation; Taiwan pr. [xiào]

13 棰 (*) [chuí] to flog; whip

14 孪 (*) [luán] twins

15 铯 (*) [sè] cesium (chemistry)

16 孤单 [gūdān] lone; lonely; loneliness

17 凉快 [liángkuai] nice and cold; pleasantly cool

18 填空 [tiánkòng] to fill a job vacancy; to fill in a blank (e.g. on questionnaire or exam paper)

19 寒假 [hánjià] winter vacation

20 干杯 [gānbēi] to drink a toast; Cheers! (proposing a toast); Here's to you!; Bottoms up!; lit. dry cup

21 粗心 [cūxīn] careless; thoughtless

22 预习 [yùxí] to prepare a lesson

23 放暑假 [fàngshǔjià] have/spend the summer vacation

24 弹钢琴 [tángāngqín] play the piano

25 止咳 [zhǐké] to suppress coughing

26 广安门 [guǎng'ānmén] Guanganmen in Xuanwu 宣武区 district of southwest Beijing

27 及时性 [jíshíxìng] timeliness; promptness

28 耳闻 [ěrwén] to hear of; to hear about

29 了然 [liǎorán] to understand clearly; evident ◇ to understand clearly; evident

30 次生 [cìshēng] derivative; secondary; sub-

31 断送 [duànsòng] to forfeit (future profit, one's life etc); ruined

32 名利双收 [mínglìshuāngshōu] both fame and fortune (idiom); both virtue and reward

33 生啤酒 [shēngpíjiǔ] draft beer; unpasteurized beer

34 比划 [bǐhuà] to gesture; to use sign language; to gesticulate; to engage in body combat or martial art; to come to blows

35 亮光 [liàngguāng] light; beam of light; gleam of light; light reflected from an object

36 断奶 [duànnǎi] to wean

37 正巧 [zhèngqiǎo] just by chance; to happen to (just at the right time); opportune

38 门禁 [ménjìn] guarded entrance

39 西北工业大学 [xīběigōngyèdàxué] Northwestern Polytechnical University

40 败走 [bàizǒu] to run away (in defeat)

41 文身 [wénshēn] tattoo

Lesson 47

42 过客 [guòkè] passing traveler; transient guest; sojourner

43 参考资料 [cānkǎozīliào] reference material; bibliography

44 江油 [jiāngyóu] Jiangyou prefecture level city in Mianyang 绵阳 [Miányáng], north Sichuan

45 高干 [gāogàn] high cadre; top party member

46 变硬 [biànyìng] to stiffen

47 弄懂 [nòngdǒng] to make sense of; to grasp the meaning of; to figure out

48 划一 [huàyī] uniform; to standardize

49 切切 [qièqiè] urgently; eagerly; worried; (urge sb to) be sure to; it is absolutely essential to (follow the above instruction)

INDEX

This index includes every unique character appearing in all volumes of the *Eating the Dragon* series. Each character entry contains its Hanyu Pinyin pronunciation, and a list of lessons in which the character appears. Since this is a "global" index, numers may refer to lessons in another volume.

Index

呵 (†) ā 178
啊 (†) ā 18
阿 ā 22, 125, 137, 141, 184, 185, 186, 193
啊 (†) á 18
啊 (†) ǎ 18
啊 (†) à 18
啊 (†) a 18
哀 āi 165
哎 āi 197
唉 (†) āi 95
埃 (*) āi 79, 83
挨 (†) āi 169
挨 (†) ái 169
癌 ái 125, 163, 177, 178, 182
矮 (†) ǎi 23
蔼 ǎi 185, 195
唉 (†) ài 95
暧 ài 156
爱 (†) ài 3, 21, 22, 37, 42, 68, 72, 74, 86, 87, 89, 96, 97, 122, 135, 170, 171, 185, 190
碍 ài 91, 113, 136
艾 (*) ài 11
隘 ài 184
安 ān 22, 26, 30, 31, 35, 44, 46, 47, 63, 64, 75, 79, 81, 83, 88, 93, 94, 98, 105, 108, 110, 112, 113, 115, 116, 128, 140, 147, 148, 155, 168, 174, 182, 183, 185, 189, 198
庵 (*) ān 149
岸 (†) àn 76, 102, 196
按 àn 27, 42, 126, 137, 183
暗 (†) àn 40, 145, 150
案 àn 38, 43, 54, 102, 107, 109, 112, 123, 128, 132, 136, 144, 150, 152, 196
昂 áng 139
凹 āo 185
熬 (†) āo 142, 186, 195
敖 (*) áo 85

熬 (†) áo 142, 186, 195
傲 ào 41
奥 ào 165, 177, 192
岙 (*) ào 190
澳 (*) ào 74, 109, 115, 152
八 (†) bā 3, 6, 11, 137, 169
叭 bā 174
吧 (†) bā 9, 87
巴 bā 94, 95, 118, 125, 133, 144, 169, 170, 187, 194, 197
扒 (†) bā 165
疤 (†) bā 193
拔 bá 105, 116, 118, 175, 196
把 (†) bǎ 13, 60, 117, 141, 145, 160, 182, 190
伯 bà 190
坝 bà 198
把 (†) bà 13, 60, 117, 141, 145, 160, 182, 190
爸 bà 5, 181
罢 bà 153, 165
霸 bà 179
吧 (†) ba 9, 87
罢 ba 153, 165
掰 (†) bāi 185
白 (†) bái 9, 20, 21, 92, 94, 98, 115, 126, 175, 177, 180
伯 bǎi 190
佰 (*) bǎi 46
摆 (†) bǎi 64, 126, 183
柏 (*) bǎi 67, 70, 92
百 (†) bǎi 8, 20, 34, 42, 45, 58, 78, 86, 89, 94, 111, 119, 128, 138, 143, 148, 172, 176, 183, 195
拜 bài 98, 145, 165, 166, 168, 185, 194
败 bài 39, 47, 103, 115, 183
搬 (†) bān 20, 178
斑 bān 198

班 bān 11, 23, 34, 39, 40, 74, 91, 129, 154, 167
般 bān 16, 91, 146
颁 bān 119, 120
板 bǎn 24, 39, 64, 124, 126, 153, 182
版 bǎn 55, 65, 120, 138, 146, 170
钣 (*) bǎn 191
伴 bàn 70, 115, 120, 141, 161
办 bàn 16, 20, 23, 28, 41, 57, 67, 76, 104, 117, 118, 155
半 (†) bàn 18, 20, 21, 81, 83, 85, 93, 108, 125, 179, 197
扮 bàn 44, 115
拌 bàn 161
帮 bāng 9, 21
邦 (*) bāng 124
榜 bǎng 131, 136, 191
绑 bǎng 144, 148, 190
膀 bǎng 90
傍 bàng 84
棒 (†) bàng 78, 157, 194
磅 (†) bàng 170
膀 bàng 90
谤 bàng 156
剥 bāo 170
包 (†) bāo 17, 22, 26, 71, 87, 91, 107, 118, 128, 143, 151, 160, 167, 179, 191
炮 bāo 96
煲 (*) bāo 89
胞 bāo 122, 129, 173, 192
褒 (*) bāo 166
薄 (†) báo 68, 86, 122, 177
雹 báo 178
保 bǎo 27, 29, 31, 36, 38, 52, 63, 67, 68, 70, 72, 99, 100, 105, 109, 117, 122, 124, 131, 140, 142, 147,

163, 165, 167, 168, 180, 193
堡 bǎo 161, 167
宝 bǎo 66, 78, 83, 101, 169, 182
葆 (*) bǎo 80
饱 (†) bǎo 21, 158, 192
刨 (*) bào 175
报 bào 10, 18, 27, 34, 38, 43, 51, 62, 79, 84, 87, 88, 92, 97, 106, 107, 114, 116, 117, 124, 125, 133, 136, 139, 147, 155, 158, 160, 162, 174, 176, 187, 193, 195, 196
抱 (†) bào 38, 46, 85, 132, 180
暴 bào 126, 129, 140, 168
瀑 bào 144
爆 bào 114, 123, 128, 162, 183, 198
豹 (*) bào 94
鲍 (*) bào 78
卑 bēi 180, 181
悲 bēi 91, 165, 167, 171, 173, 177
杯 bēi 6, 47, 192
碑 bēi 139, 195
背 (†) bēi 19, 46, 58, 138, 173, 174
北 běi 2, 5, 6, 11, 16, 20, 44, 47, 64, 91, 112, 117, 136, 144, 147, 153, 159, 180, 191
倍 (†) bèi 56, 177
备 bèi 9, 23, 39, 54, 60, 95, 103, 110, 115, 118, 136, 152, 166, 172, 183, 186
惫 bèi 154
狈 bèi 190
背 (†) bèi 19, 46, 58, 138, 173, 174
被 (†) bèi 25, 93, 131, 175
贝 bèi 83, 163, 189

I–3

Index

辈 bèi 80, 163
奔 bēn 139, 151, 153, 167
本 (†) běn 2, 4, 6, 10, 12, 38, 39, 41, 49, 54, 68, 73, 74, 75, 82, 101, 104, 105, 107, 111, 113, 115, 120, 129, 132, 137, 140, 141, 142, 143, 150, 154, 158, 159, 162, 169, 174, 175, 178, 188
苯 (*) běn 80
奔 bèn 139, 151, 153, 167
笨 (†) bèn 46, 196
崩 bēng 159
甭 (†) béng 190
蹦 (†) bèng 172
迸 bèng 176
逼 bī 170, 198
鼻 bí 22, 193
彼 bǐ 73, 167
比 (†) bǐ 7, 15, 16, 47, 52, 56, 57, 71, 72, 86, 110, 137, 151, 154, 171, 181, 195
笔 bǐ 24, 41, 159, 162, 186, 189
鄙 bǐ 180
壁 bì 94, 98, 189, 194
币 bì 32, 94, 113
庇 bì 191
弊 bì 147, 164, 179, 188
弼 (*) bì 160
必 bì 15, 23, 62, 63, 72, 79, 80, 86, 88, 93, 138, 145, 152, 179
比 (†) bì 7, 15, 16, 47, 52, 56, 57, 71, 72, 86, 110, 137, 151, 154, 171, 181, 195
毕 bì 31, 36, 69, 130
璧 (*) bì 96
痹 bì 173
碧 bì 192
秘 bì 68, 72, 73, 106, 118, 165

臂 (†) bì 143
蔽 bì 142
辟 bì 119
避 bì 60, 85, 88, 129, 153, 196
闭 bì 73, 84, 127, 136, 153, 176
陛 (*) bì 194
编 biān 62, 76, 79, 93, 130, 143, 160, 173, 198
边 biān 11, 12, 19, 105, 109, 112, 133, 140, 145, 149, 183
鞭 biān 96, 175
匾 (*) biǎn 181
扁 (†) biǎn 147, 148
贬 biǎn 185, 193
便 biàn 11, 18, 42, 46, 111, 121, 130, 133, 198
变 biàn 16, 30, 47, 53, 109, 121, 128, 137, 144, 145, 146, 169, 175, 182, 193
辨 biàn 172, 173
辩 biàn 88, 146, 161, 164, 181
辫 biàn 189
遍 biàn 32, 139
边 bian 11, 12, 19, 105, 109, 112, 133, 140, 145, 149, 183
标 biāo 26, 45, 50, 58, 85, 88, 97, 102, 113, 120, 142, 150, 152, 158, 169, 188, 196
飙 biāo 148
表 biǎo 11, 13, 18, 26, 32, 44, 45, 54, 55, 63, 65, 72, 82, 98, 105, 127, 130, 147, 171, 174, 190
憋 (†) biē 160
鳖 (*) biē 185
别 (†) bié 10, 14, 39, 43, 52, 67, 74, 82, 107, 116, 124, 136, 154, 165, 187, 194

别 (†) biè 10, 14, 39, 43, 52, 67, 74, 82, 107, 116, 124, 136, 154, 165, 187, 194
宾 bīn 20, 61, 167
彬 (*) bīn 6
斌 (*) bīn 19
滨 bīn 140, 151
濒 bīn 168
兵 bīng 82, 105, 106, 171, 188
冰 bīng 20, 98, 159, 166, 178
屏 bīng 147, 155
丙 (†) bǐng 85
屏 bǐng 147, 155
炳 (*) bǐng 77
饼 bǐng 46
并 bìng 32, 107, 112, 121, 141, 145, 150, 171
病 bìng 12, 20, 24, 79, 82, 86, 88, 92, 104, 114, 126, 148, 150, 160, 161, 173, 179, 182, 196
剥 bō 170
拨 bō 129, 182, 196
播 bō 35, 52, 88, 92, 114, 117, 165, 174
波 bō 151, 160, 171, 188, 195
玻 bō 71
伯 bó 190
勃 bó 161, 162, 173, 175
博 bó 34, 35, 38, 39, 51, 60, 116, 146, 154, 174
搏 bó 126, 173, 174
柏 (*) bó 67, 70, 92
泊 bó 136, 182
渤 (*) bó 186
脖 bó 90
膊 bó 93
舶 bó 130
薄 (†) bó 68, 86, 122, 177
铂 (*) bó 174
驳 bó 168

簸 bǒ 174
柏 (*) bò 67, 70, 92
簸 bò 174
薄 (†) bò 68, 86, 122, 177
卜 (*) bo 156
哺 bū 162
卜 (*) bǔ 156
哺 bǔ 162
捕 bǔ 125, 155, 178
补 bǔ 64, 65, 75, 83, 92, 103, 107, 127, 137, 165, 170, 182
不 (†) bù 1, 3, 4, 5, 6, 8, 10, 12, 17, 19, 21, 22, 27, 28, 32, 36, 37, 40, 41, 43, 44, 45, 46, 48, 57, 62, 63, 68, 70, 71, 72, 79, 81, 83, 85, 86, 87, 89, 91, 92, 93, 94, 95, 96, 97, 98, 112, 113, 117, 120, 121, 124, 125, 126, 127, 128, 131, 132, 134, 135, 138, 139, 144, 147, 148, 156, 157, 158, 159, 161, 162, 164, 168, 170, 171, 175, 176, 177, 178, 179, 181, 182, 183, 185, 186, 187, 188, 189, 190, 191, 192, 193, 194, 195
哺 bù 162
埠 (*) bù 164
布 bù 53, 57, 69, 70, 73, 100, 107, 120, 130, 139, 144, 173, 196
怖 bù 85
步 bù 12, 14, 20, 22, 45, 56, 57, 70, 73, 79, 97, 105, 109, 119, 147, 156, 176, 177
簿 (*) bù 170, 171
部 bù 29, 31, 32, 33, 35, 36, 44, 48, 49, 62, 66, 67, 71, 82,

I-4

Index

83, 84, 89, 102, 107, 109, 112, 116, 122, 123, 125, 140, 142, 178, 188, 190
擦 (†) cā 41, 140, 183
猜 (†) cāi 44, 128
才 (†) cái 14, 16, 20, 51, 152, 164
材 cái 30, 69, 76, 89, 113, 132
裁 cái 65, 126, 138, 140, 164, 184, 196
财 cái 62, 80, 98, 99, 108, 110, 115, 170, 177, 182, 197
彩 cǎi 34, 90, 92, 95, 102, 111, 147, 149, 173
睬 cǎi 194
踩 (†) cǎi 83
采 cǎi 53, 54, 104, 127, 131, 137, 144, 190, 196
菜 (†) cài 4, 23, 61, 187, 196
蔡 (*) cài 35, 79
採 cài 53, 54, 104, 127, 131, 137, 144, 190, 196
参 cān 14, 33, 47, 50, 65, 83, 84, 115, 127, 163
餐 cān 70, 84, 110, 132, 149
惭 cán 96
残 cán 82, 135, 148, 168, 175
蚕 (*) cán 161, 170
惨 cǎn 177
灿 càn 133
仓 cāng 132, 187
沧 cāng 192
舱 (†) cāng 151
苍 cāng 177
藏 cáng 98, 101, 106, 138, 154, 168, 184
操 cāo 90, 94, 103, 152, 182, 195
嘈 cáo 185
曹 (*) cáo 5

槽 (*) cáo 89
草 (†) cǎo 19, 72, 95, 107, 130, 132, 134, 182, 193
操 cào 90, 94, 103, 152, 182, 195
侧 cè 139
册 cè 63, 150
厕 cè 83
测 cè 94, 103, 108, 111, 115, 128, 137, 153, 159, 177
策 cè 48, 88, 97, 102, 111, 114, 131, 132, 153, 175
岑 (*) cén 163
层 (†) céng 18, 28, 65, 106, 108, 132, 144, 176, 180
曾 céng 57, 91
蹭 (*) cèng 187
叉 chā 98, 135
差 (†) chā 18, 41, 43, 74, 107, 116, 137, 166, 171, 187, 191, 195
插 (†) chā 78, 94
锸 (*) chā 198
叉 chá 98, 135
察 chá 37, 66, 101, 107, 112, 124, 156, 180, 193, 195
查 chá 15, 23, 24, 27, 46, 64, 78, 85, 90, 107, 132, 141, 151, 154, 165
茬 (*) chá 170
茶 (†) chá 5, 44, 187
叉 chǎ 98, 135
刹 chà 155, 184
岔 (†) chà 176
差 (†) chà 18, 41, 43, 74, 107, 116, 137, 166, 171, 187, 191, 195
诧 chà 185
差 (†) chāi 18, 41, 43, 74, 107, 116, 137, 166, 171, 187, 191, 195

拆 (†) chāi 74
钗 (*) chāi 164
柴 chái 96, 129
掺 (*) chān 152, 188
搀 (†) chān 195
单 chán 17, 19, 23, 47, 48, 74, 75, 77, 82, 86, 89, 91, 119, 166, 168, 185, 186, 189, 195
崭 chán 125
禅 (*) chán 149
缠 chán 185
馋 (†) chán 192
产 chǎn 48, 52, 57, 58, 62, 69, 74, 77, 83, 84, 86, 91, 94, 99, 100, 102, 107, 108, 109, 113, 116, 119, 124, 125, 128, 135, 138, 139, 146, 150, 157, 158, 161, 164, 165, 177, 185
阐 chǎn 127
颤 chàn 184
昌 chāng 192
猖 chāng 191
偿 cháng 66, 107, 134, 144, 178
场 cháng 9, 25, 61, 77, 78, 80, 89, 90, 95, 99, 108, 114, 117, 119, 121, 122, 126, 127, 129, 131, 134, 140, 141, 151, 152, 166, 168, 192, 193, 197
尝 (†) cháng 40, 113, 134
常 cháng 8, 17, 32, 64, 67, 68, 78, 81, 85, 94, 101, 104, 113, 115, 117, 131, 145, 164, 168, 177, 180, 190, 192
肠 (*) cháng 73, 132, 158, 189
裳 cháng 184
长 (†) cháng 8, 9, 10, 11, 19, 20, 23, 26,

32, 34, 35, 38, 40, 59, 65, 68, 70, 72, 73, 76, 78, 81, 86, 91, 92, 101, 104, 106, 107, 109, 113, 118, 120, 125, 132, 136, 137, 138, 142, 143, 146, 147, 152, 154, 157, 163, 170, 172, 174, 188, 189, 194, 196
厂 chǎng 65, 84, 87, 156, 181, 192
场 chǎng 9, 25, 61, 77, 78, 80, 89, 90, 95, 99, 108, 114, 117, 119, 121, 122, 126, 127, 129, 131, 134, 140, 141, 151, 152, 166, 168, 192, 193, 197
敞 chǎng 149, 152
倡 chàng 76, 113, 144
唱 chàng 12, 21, 129, 140
畅 chàng 122, 143, 145, 169, 182
抄 (†) chāo 85, 139
焯 (*) chāo 45
超 chāo 18, 23, 27, 93, 115, 118, 152, 159, 193
钞 chāo 166
嘲 cháo 188
朝 (†) cháo 65, 73, 83, 95, 113, 119, 146, 173, 192, 198
潮 cháo 119, 121, 127, 169
吵 (†) chǎo 46, 92
炒 (†) chǎo 71, 73, 174
车 chē 6, 10, 11, 12, 16, 18, 21, 44, 62, 78, 80, 89, 92, 93, 94, 125, 127, 129, 130, 133, 141, 155, 156, 160, 165, 167, 183, 187, 191, 192, 195, 197, 198
尺 chě 97, 156

I-5

Index

扯 chě 168
彻 chè 64, 101
撤 chè 124, 176
澈 chè 155
辙 chè 197
沉 chén 86, 143, 154, 164, 171, 176, 177, 187
琛 (*) chēn 171
尘 chén 89, 97, 186
忱 (*) chén 168
晨 chén 117, 143, 147
沈 (*) chén 5, 68, 141
沉 chén 86, 143, 154, 164, 171, 176, 177, 187
臣 chén 155
辰 chén 150
陈 chén 128, 148, 149, 152, 158
称 (†) chèn 49, 63, 70, 82, 88, 89, 108, 111, 133, 134, 157, 179, 187, 196
衬 chèn 23
趁 (†) chèn 81
撑 chēng 105
称 (†) chēng 49, 63, 70, 82, 88, 89, 108, 111, 133, 134, 157, 179, 187, 196
乘 chéng 39, 169, 176, 198
呈 chéng 104
城 chéng 13, 19, 21, 23, 38, 64, 74, 97, 102, 103, 115, 116, 123, 146, 161, 165, 168, 169, 180, 181, 187, 189, 193, 197
惩 chéng 148, 151
成 chéng 14, 16, 25, 28, 32, 33, 34, 35, 42, 45, 49, 50, 52, 56, 59, 63, 70, 73, 75, 81, 87, 93, 96, 101, 103, 105, 108, 109, 116, 120, 133, 140, 148, 166, 168, 179, 187, 195, 198

承 chéng 57, 65, 74, 105, 113, 117, 118, 165, 179
晟 (*) chéng 183
橙 (†) chéng 175, 183
澄 chéng 134
盛 (†) chéng 107, 145, 149, 165, 169, 178, 180, 185, 192
程 chéng 26, 40, 55, 56, 61, 62, 70, 71, 78, 81, 131, 132, 139, 142, 165, 175, 198
诚 chéng 43, 90, 110, 118, 139, 142
秤 (†) chèng 192
称 (†) chèng 49, 63, 70, 82, 88, 89, 108, 111, 133, 134, 157, 179, 187, 196
吃 (†) chī 3, 12, 45, 71, 79, 90, 158, 176
痴 (*) chī 46, 93
匙 chí 43
持 chí 26, 31, 36, 40, 52, 54, 56, 67, 90, 109, 128, 193
池 chí 78, 97, 179
迟 chí 23, 45, 145, 167, 180, 189
驰 chí 139, 186
侈 chǐ 143
尺 chǐ 97, 156
耻 chǐ 189, 193
齿 chǐ 198
斥 chì 149
炽 (*) chì 190
翅 chì 90
赤 chì 154, 190, 194, 197
充 chōng 50, 59, 64, 88, 95, 97, 122, 132, 134, 150, 160, 161, 163
冲 (†) chōng 65, 96, 110, 114, 141, 163, 188
崇 chóng 116, 145, 166, 194

虫 chóng 184, 185
重 chóng 13, 15, 24, 26, 28, 29, 32, 33, 42, 46, 60, 68, 73, 80, 81, 82, 90, 104, 107, 109, 110, 114, 133, 136, 138, 141, 143, 144, 155, 159, 161, 162, 165, 173, 180, 182, 184, 193
宠 chǒng 89
冲 (†) chòng 65, 96, 110, 114, 141, 163, 188
抽 chōu 44, 78, 85, 94, 145, 183
仇 chóu 196
愁 chóu 93
畴 chóu 136
稠 chóu 196
筹 chóu 118, 134, 139, 153, 155
绸 chóu 70, 145
踌 chóu 194
酬 chóu 139, 154, 166
丑 (†) chǒu 91, 185
臭 (†) chòu 83, 168, 171
出 chū 6, 9, 11, 14, 18, 20, 21, 30, 31, 32, 33, 35, 36, 41, 43, 51, 54, 55, 58, 63, 65, 67, 69, 71, 83, 84, 91, 93, 96, 102, 113, 114, 118, 123, 124, 132, 137, 139, 144, 145, 147, 150, 156, 160, 163, 167, 175, 181, 182, 183, 188, 191, 195, 197, 198
初 chū 71, 74, 81, 88, 105, 122, 138, 150
厨 chú 21
滁 (*) chú 198
蹰 chú 194
除 chú 16, 81, 82, 84, 93, 111, 118, 127, 141, 145, 157

储 chǔ 115, 135, 140, 155, 166, 168
处 chǔ 39, 40, 41, 44, 45, 51, 58, 64, 69, 73, 76, 79, 81, 87, 90, 114, 118, 126, 130, 151, 156, 170, 177, 178, 183, 190
楚 chǔ 19
础 chǔ 26, 58, 187
处 chù 39, 40, 41, 44, 45, 51, 58, 64, 69, 73, 76, 79, 81, 87, 90, 114, 118, 126, 130, 151, 156, 170, 177, 178, 183, 190
畜 chù 149, 157
触 chù 63, 97, 166
揣 (*) chuāi 171
揣 (*) chuǎi 171
川 chuān 194
穿 (†) chuān 10, 75, 86, 123, 126, 147, 176
传 chuán 43, 49, 50, 52, 63, 65, 67, 75, 76, 78, 90, 91, 93, 95, 96, 107, 120, 124, 133, 137, 148, 153, 156, 158, 183, 184, 186, 192
船 (†) chuán 10, 97, 130, 141, 180
喘 chuǎn 198
串 (†) chuàn 134, 166, 169, 184
创 chuāng 53, 56, 60, 67, 73, 75, 92, 99, 102, 118, 133, 135, 139, 142, 155, 167
疮 (*) chuāng 168
窗 chuāng 43, 69, 89, 189
幢 (†) chuáng 142
床 chuáng 12, 108, 160, 189
闯 (†) chuǎng 79
创 chuàng 53, 56, 60, 67, 73, 75, 92, 99, 102, 118, 133, 135, 139, 142, 155, 167

I-6

Index

吹 (†) chuī 71, 189, 191
垂 chuí 148
棰 (*) chuí 47
椎 chuí 183
锤 (†) chuí 142
春 (†) chūn 16, 23, 65, 66, 67, 180, 196
椿 (*) chūn 179
唇 chún 172
椿 (*) chún 179
淳 (*) chún 177
纯 chún 74, 135, 159, 162
醇 (*) chún 148, 150
蠢 chǔn 191
缀 chuò 158
刺 cī 65, 90
差 (†) cī 18, 41, 43, 74, 107, 116, 137, 166, 171, 187, 191, 195
慈 cí 184, 187, 195
瓷 cí 103
磁 cí 97, 155
祠 (*) cí 134
茨 (*) cí 134, 138
词 cí 23, 46, 144, 152, 157
辞 cí 78, 97, 121, 186, 198
雌 cí 193
此 cǐ 27, 29, 31, 54, 60, 63, 64, 69, 71, 73, 74, 80, 81, 111, 115, 134, 147, 157, 198
伺 cì 183
刺 cì 65, 90
次 (†) cì 7, 9, 10, 11, 21, 22, 29, 31, 33, 36, 47, 62, 67, 73, 80, 88, 92, 106, 110, 123, 132, 143; 160, 169, 184, 188, 197
赐 (*) cì 158
从 cōng 43, 44, 57, 58, 71, 73, 75, 76, 83, 88, 120, 138, 151, 195
匆 cōng 94
聪 cōng 21, 183
葱 (*) cōng 23, 86

丛 (†) cóng 154
从 cóng 43, 44, 57, 58, 71, 73, 75, 76, 83, 88, 120, 138, 151, 195
凑 còu 187
粗 cū 47, 168, 194
促 cù 49, 66, 74, 118, 187, 196
卒 (*) cù 92
醋 (†) cù 83
蹿 (*) cuān 163
攒 (†) cuán 153
窜 (†) cuàn 170
催 (†) cuī 80
崔 (*) cuī 70
摧 cuī 175
衰 cuī 137, 157, 170
粹 cuì 135, 187
翠 (*) cuì 133
脆 cuì 84, 141
萃 (*) cuì 44
村 cūn 26, 31, 85, 111
存 cún 50, 72, 81, 109, 129, 140, 150, 196, 197
寸 cùn 194
搓 (†) cuō 171
磋 cuō 122
厝 (*) cuò 182
挫 cuò 157
措 cuò 51, 64, 186
错 (†) cuò 11, 19, 23, 67, 165, 171, 182
搭 (†) dā 118, 119, 127, 150
答 dā 10, 38, 80, 117, 161, 187
打 dá 5, 12, 20, 23, 32, 37, 42, 43, 44, 46, 73, 86, 91, 92, 96, 98, 105, 114, 129, 147, 156, 159, 160, 163, 168, 173, 179, 186, 187, 189, 194, 196
瘩 dá 186
答 dá 10, 38, 80, 117, 161, 187

达 dá 32, 40, 49, 64, 68, 71, 82, 86, 98, 109, 118, 124, 135, 140, 158, 169, 184
打 dǎ 5, 12, 20, 23, 32, 37, 42, 43, 44, 46, 73, 86, 91, 92, 96, 98, 105, 114, 129, 147, 156, 159, 160, 163, 168, 173, 179, 186, 187, 189, 194, 196
大 (†) dà 1, 4, 5, 6, 8, 11, 15, 16, 17, 21, 22, 24, 28, 29, 35, 36, 37, 38, 40, 43, 47, 50, 54, 55, 60, 62, 64, 65, 69, 71, 72, 74, 75, 76, 77, 81, 82, 83, 86, 87, 90, 92, 93, 95, 97, 104, 105, 111, 112, 113, 115, 116, 121, 122, 125, 127, 129, 130, 132, 136, 137, 138, 140, 142, 143, 146, 147, 149, 152, 154, 155, 156, 158, 159, 162, 164, 165, 169, 170, 174, 177, 180, 182, 184, 185, 188, 189, 190, 192, 193, 194, 195, 196, 197
呆 (†) dāi 81, 191
待 dāi 62, 63, 70, 88, 119, 156, 177, 194, 197
傣 (*) dǎi 93
歹 dǎi 156
代 dài 26, 28, 32, 37, 41, 45, 52, 57, 62, 65, 71, 79, 95, 113, 125, 132, 134, 135, 136, 139, 141, 142, 149, 157, 187, 189, 190
埭 (*) dài 96
大 (†) dài 1, 4, 5, 6, 8, 11, 15, 16, 17, 21, 22, 24, 28, 29, 35,

36, 37, 38, 40, 43, 47, 50, 54, 55, 60, 62, 64, 65, 69, 71, 72, 74, 75, 76, 77, 81, 82, 83, 86, 87, 90, 92, 93, 95, 97, 104, 105, 111, 112, 113, 115, 116, 121, 122, 125, 127, 129, 130, 132, 136, 137, 138, 140, 142, 143, 146, 147, 149, 152, 154, 155, 156, 158, 159, 162, 164, 165, 169, 170, 174, 177, 180, 182, 184, 185, 188, 189, 190, 192, 193, 194, 195, 196, 197
岱 (*) dài 137
带 (†) dài 15, 16, 23, 33, 41, 74, 94, 97, 98, 104, 127, 165, 171, 174, 185
待 dài 62, 63, 70, 88, 119, 156, 177, 194, 197
怠 dài 195
戴 (†) dài 35, 170
袋 dài 45, 89, 179
贷 dài 58, 123, 156, 179, 196
逮 dài 125
丹 (*) dān 65, 195
单 dān 17, 19, 23, 47, 48, 74, 75, 77, 82, 86, 89, 91, 119, 166, 168, 185, 186, 189, 195
担 dān 19, 57, 80, 109, 117
耽 dān 86
胆 dǎn 98, 121, 150, 189, 196
但 dàn 8, 36
弹 dàn 47, 124, 144, 156
惮 dàn 178
担 dàn 19, 57, 80, 109, 117

I-7

Index

旦 dàn 62, 82, 85, 182
氮 (*) dàn 167
淡 (†) dàn 72, 92, 145, 160, 176, 181, 186, 189
石 dàn 80, 85, 92, 104, 122, 141, 154, 158, 166, 169, 174, 175, 186, 188
蛋 dàn 11, 22, 91, 115, 177
诞 dàn 112, 150
当 dāng 16, 18, 21, 22, 28, 29, 38, 59, 61, 62, 88, 96, 101, 108, 112, 113, 122, 125, 127, 131, 133, 144, 150, 151, 159, 162, 164, 171, 187, 193, 195
党 (†) dǎng 99, 100, 102, 103, 106, 107, 108, 109, 110, 114, 119, 122, 123, 124, 130, 134, 145, 158, 192
挡 (†) dǎng 78, 165, 194
当 dàng 16, 18, 21, 22, 28, 29, 38, 59, 61, 62, 88, 96, 101, 108, 112, 113, 122, 125, 127, 131, 133, 144, 150, 151, 159, 162, 164, 171, 187, 193, 195
挡 (†) dàng 78, 165, 194
档 dàng 68, 109, 132, 150
荡 dàng 151, 185, 189
刀 (†) dāo 37, 92, 154, 193, 195
叨 dāo 182
倒 (†) dǎo 62, 93, 98, 143, 153, 173, 181, 187, 196
导 dǎo 40, 44, 48, 52, 53, 58, 63, 73, 79, 101, 111, 113, 124, 143, 146, 153, 159, 167, 173, 174
岛 (†) dǎo 57, 62, 77, 83, 85, 147, 151, 169, 188
捣 dǎo 186
蹈 dǎo 117
倒 (†) dào 62, 93, 98, 143, 153, 173, 181, 187, 196
到 (†) dào 7, 9, 10, 11, 17, 18, 23, 32, 33, 35, 41, 49, 54, 65, 66, 68, 79, 82, 86, 87, 114, 116, 121, 131, 148, 158, 162, 169, 177
悼 dào 190
盗 dào 138
稻 dào 174
道 dào 18, 24, 27, 30, 39, 40, 51, 58, 59, 63, 65, 70, 73, 79, 86, 87, 88, 94, 101, 121, 122, 125, 132, 141, 142, 154, 157, 158, 162, 165, 166, 179, 181, 186, 189, 190
得 (†) dé 7, 9, 11, 12, 18, 20, 28, 34, 37, 44, 45, 57, 65, 66, 70, 81, 91, 92, 93, 98, 128, 131, 140, 145, 149, 152, 162, 167, 171, 176, 177, 178, 181, 183, 185, 187, 190, 192, 194
德 dé 58, 60, 68, 84, 95, 140, 154, 159, 165, 176, 184, 188, 194
地 (†) de 13, 14, 20, 21, 22, 23, 29, 31, 38, 39, 40, 45, 49, 51, 57, 65, 70, 82, 85, 86, 88, 94, 96, 97, 100, 109, 111, 113, 116, 117, 119, 122, 123, 124, 125, 127, 131, 136, 142, 143, 145, 147, 149, 153, 154, 155, 159, 162, 165, 167, 171, 176, 179, 183, 184, 195, 198
底 de 33, 36, 63, 64, 83, 169
得 (†) de 7, 9, 11, 12, 18, 20, 28, 34, 37, 44, 45, 57, 65, 66, 70, 81, 91, 92, 93, 98, 128, 131, 140, 145, 149, 152, 162, 167, 171, 176, 177, 178, 181, 183, 185, 187, 190, 192, 194
的 (†) de 1, 3, 4, 6, 31, 45, 68, 69, 87, 114, 145, 172, 189
得 (†) děi 7, 9, 11, 12, 18, 20, 28, 34, 37, 44, 45, 57, 65, 66, 70, 81, 91, 92, 93, 98, 128, 131, 140, 145, 149, 152, 162, 167, 171, 176, 177, 178, 181, 183, 185, 187, 190, 192, 194
灯 (†) dēng 17, 183, 184, 191
登 dēng 59, 79, 80, 95, 124, 125, 132, 169
蹬 (†) dēng 193
等 (†) děng 7, 10, 22, 41, 65, 70, 77, 85, 86, 88, 93, 120, 121, 126, 127, 163, 176, 180, 186, 195
凳 (*) dèng 182
澄 dèng 134
瞪 (†) dèng 185
邓 (*) dèng 17, 127, 152
低 (†) dī 14, 22, 30, 62, 72, 119, 140, 149, 185
堤 dī 198
滴 (†) dī 80, 91
敌 dí 72, 191
狄 (*) dí 12
的 (†) dí 1, 3, 4, 6, 31, 45, 68, 69, 87, 114, 145, 172, 189
笛 (*) dí 155
荻 (*) dí 181
迪 (*) dí 68, 86, 92, 172
底 dǐ 33, 36, 63, 64, 83, 169
抵 dǐ 118, 135, 141, 157, 174, 187
地 (†) dì 13, 14, 20, 21, 22, 23, 29, 31, 38, 39, 40, 45, 49, 51, 57, 65, 70, 82, 85, 86, 88, 94, 96, 97, 100, 109, 111, 113, 116, 117, 119, 122, 123, 124, 125, 127, 131, 136, 142, 143, 145, 147, 149, 153, 154, 155, 159, 162, 165, 167, 171, 176, 179, 183, 184, 195, 198
帝 dì 75, 87, 191
弟 dì 11, 69, 86, 146, 166
的 (†) dì 1, 3, 4, 6, 31, 45, 68, 69, 87, 114, 145, 172, 189
第 dì 7, 9, 10, 11, 19, 33, 40, 64, 71, 88, 114, 186, 198
缔 dì 148, 175
蒂 dì 183
递 dì 63, 152
滇 (*) diān 41
颠 diān 174, 181
典 diǎn 24, 46, 58, 80, 106, 127
点 (†) diǎn 2, 4, 5, 11, 12, 20, 22, 26, 30, 38, 41, 43, 57, 78, 91, 92, 93, 97, 112, 119, 123, 129, 132, 141, 148, 149, 153, 158, 164, 179, 191
碘 (*) diǎn 84
佃 (*) diàn 190

I-8

Index

垫 (†) diàn 147
奠 diàn 113
店 diàn 6, 19, 21, 86, 135, 137
惦 diàn 179
殿 diàn 164, 189
淀 diàn 154
电 diàn 3, 5, 6, 12, 18, 20, 23, 34, 38, 40, 65, 70, 73, 75, 77, 78, 83, 84, 85, 92, 97, 130, 134, 137, 146, 147, 148, 155, 160, 174, 181
甸 (*) diàn 148
钿 (*) diàn 189
叼 (†) diāo 193
雕 diāo 121, 148
吊 (†) diào 144
掉 (†) diào 35
调 diào 19, 21, 24, 27, 35, 50, 52, 53, 76, 90, 91, 96, 98, 108, 110, 116, 118, 139, 141, 156, 158, 159, 161, 168
钓 (†) diào 90, 147
爹 (*) diē 133
跌 (†) diē 123, 153
叠 dié 173
碟 (*) dié 91, 98, 197
蝶 dié 90
谍 dié 167
丁 (†) dīng 63, 180
叮 dīng 149
盯 (†) dīng 138
钉 dīng 188, 194
顶 (†) dǐng 64, 75, 158
鼎 (*) dǐng 121
定 dìng 15, 18, 20, 22, 24, 26, 30, 42, 51, 52, 54, 62, 67, 69, 71, 73, 83, 84, 94, 105, 108, 110, 113, 115, 120, 121, 124, 125, 129, 139, 141, 147, 148, 152, 154, 157, 161, 167, 175, 179, 193, 198

订 dìng 81, 107, 128, 167
丢 (†) diū 41, 181, 193, 198
东 dōng 4, 5, 19, 24, 32, 35, 42, 46, 58, 79, 85, 88, 90, 108, 118, 121, 128, 145, 146, 165, 178, 197, 198
冬 (†) dōng 19, 46, 130
懂 (†) dǒng 11, 47, 176
董 dǒng 104, 123, 169, 192
冻 (†) dòng 75, 166
动 dòng 9, 12, 18, 21, 25, 31, 33, 34, 36, 39, 45, 54, 58, 61, 66, 67, 68, 69, 77, 79, 89, 93, 94, 101, 102, 110, 112, 113, 114, 116, 121, 122, 129, 131, 136, 139, 141, 146, 147, 148, 151, 164, 170, 176, 178, 183, 186, 187, 188, 191, 192
栋 (†) dòng 112
洞 (†) dòng 61, 77, 155, 173, 176, 180, 188
兜 (†) dōu 156, 174
都 (†) dōu 1, 32, 34, 116, 133, 180, 196
抖 dǒu 97, 184
斗 dǒu 57, 79, 107, 108, 174, 181, 190
陡 dǒu 178
斗 dòu 57, 79, 107, 108, 174, 181, 190
痘 (*) dòu 146
窦 (*) dòu 146
读 (†) dòu 4, 5, 19, 25, 70, 130, 178, 195
豆 dòu 80, 95, 139
逗 (†) dòu 94
督 dū 99, 118, 198
都 (†) dū 1, 32, 34, 116, 133, 180, 196

毒 dú 79, 83, 96, 104, 106, 130, 152, 169, 196
牍 (*) dú 191
独 dú 59, 60, 75, 86, 87, 89, 93, 123, 142, 152, 157, 172, 184
读 (†) dú 4, 5, 19, 25, 70, 130, 178, 195
堵 dǔ 44, 160
睹 dǔ 161
笃 (*) dǔ 165, 166
笃 (*) dǔ 161
肚 dǔ 42
赌 dǔ 154
妒 dù 179
度 dù 31, 33, 39, 40, 49, 55, 58, 69, 70, 74, 76, 80, 82, 103, 111, 112, 117, 119, 121, 126, 128, 139, 145, 149, 155, 156, 174, 184
杜 dù 126, 167, 182
渡 dù 126
肚 dù 42
端 (†) duān 112, 128, 147, 149, 152, 158, 165, 166, 172, 195
短 (†) duǎn 17, 44, 66, 77, 116, 184, 196
断 duàn 36, 47, 48, 73, 117, 138, 150, 174, 175, 184, 193, 196
段 (†) duàn 15, 17, 54, 80, 84, 136, 162, 188
锻 duàn 19
堆 (†) duī 78, 96, 154, 165
追 duī 59, 111, 144, 178, 190
兑 duì 137, 165
对 duì 6, 17, 35, 44, 49, 54, 55, 58, 60, 62, 63, 66, 70, 72, 94, 112, 129, 131, 132, 135, 137, 141, 144, 153, 162, 165, 179, 188, 195, 196

队 duì 75, 77, 83, 102, 103, 106, 112, 130, 150
吨 (†) dūn 53
墩 (*) dūn 80
敦 dūn 137
蹲 (†) dūn 84
囤 dùn 153
盾 dùn 56
钝 (*) dùn 184
顿 (†) dùn 38, 124, 151, 180
哆 duō 194
多 (†) duō 1, 4, 5, 10, 21, 28, 33, 35, 37, 41, 43, 50, 58, 71, 76, 82, 88, 96, 98, 112, 116, 122, 125, 128, 135, 169, 180, 181, 194
夺 duó 123, 133, 183
度 duó 31, 33, 39, 40, 49, 55, 58, 69, 70, 74, 76, 80, 82, 103, 111, 112, 117, 119, 121, 126, 128, 139, 145, 149, 155, 156, 174, 184
铎 (*) duó 166
垛 (*) duǒ 24
朵 duǒ 23
躲 duǒ 98
垛 (*) duò 24
堕 duò 170
惰 duò 189
驮 (*) duò 182
阿 ē 22, 125, 137, 141, 184, 185, 186, 193
俄 (*) é 38, 125
哦 (†) é 133
峨 (*) é 174, 176
蚵 (*) é 195
额 é 131, 133, 141, 146, 157, 160, 178
鹅 (*) é 160
恶 ě 78, 141, 146, 171, 182, 185, 187, 190, 198

I-9

Index

恶 è 78, 141, 146, 171, 182, 185, 187, 190, 198
遏 è 117
鄂 (*) è 142, 180, 181
饿 (†) è 23, 159
嗯 (†) ēn 183
恩 ēn 179, 189
嗯 (†) èn 183
嗯 (†) en 183
儿 ér 5, 6, 22, 31, 66, 98, 126, 141, 146, 151, 190, 192, 194, 197, 198
而 ér 15, 17, 31, 36, 58, 69, 72, 90, 121, 127, 149, 162, 164, 167, 175, 180, 182, 183, 197
尔 ěr 42, 43, 45, 82, 119, 134, 151, 163, 172, 179, 180, 181, 185, 188
耳 ěr 23, 47, 180, 188
饵 (*) ěr 196
二 (†) èr 2, 4, 9, 11, 19, 21, 40, 41, 88, 91, 118, 121, 122, 148, 163, 185
发 fā 14, 18, 20, 21, 23, 24, 25, 26, 29, 33, 36, 37, 38, 41, 42, 43, 46, 50, 52, 55, 57, 60, 63, 64, 67, 70, 71, 73, 78, 82, 83, 86, 93, 97, 100, 103, 109, 113, 114, 115, 116, 117, 119, 121, 125, 132, 134, 138, 139, 140, 154, 160, 172, 173, 175, 176, 180, 181, 182, 183, 188, 190, 191
乏 fá 61, 128, 185
伐 fá 109
罚 fá 69, 148, 195
阀 (*) fá 169
法 fǎ 16, 18, 20, 23, 27, 29, 30, 33, 35, 37, 46, 53, 57, 58, 62, 63, 64, 65, 66, 67, 88, 95, 104, 106, 116, 121, 122, 128, 131, 140, 155, 156, 160, 161, 172, 185, 189, 196
发 fà 14, 18, 20, 21, 23, 24, 25, 26, 29, 33, 36, 37, 38, 41, 42, 43, 46, 50, 52, 55, 57, 60, 63, 64, 67, 70, 71, 73, 78, 82, 83, 86, 93, 97, 100, 103, 109, 113, 114, 115, 116, 117, 119, 121, 125, 132, 134, 138, 139, 140, 154, 160, 172, 173, 175, 176, 180, 181, 182, 183, 188, 190, 191
帆 fān 178
番 (†) fān 111
翻 fān 39, 45, 145, 149, 153, 186, 196, 198
凡 fán 77, 137, 171
樊 (*) fán 138
烦 fán 40, 43, 96
繁 fán 60, 82, 94, 115, 139, 142, 155, 186, 191
反 fǎn 29, 35, 40, 64, 65, 68, 69, 75, 89, 108, 115, 123, 132, 134, 158, 161, 168, 170, 171, 173, 177, 182, 189, 190
返 fǎn 82, 124
泛 fàn 54, 145
犯 fàn 92, 102, 120, 166, 171
范 fàn 28, 101, 103, 120, 124, 136, 140, 151, 176
贩 fàn 152
饭 fàn 6, 71, 98
坊 (*) fāng 74
方 fāng 14, 17, 18, 19, 20, 21, 22, 25, 29, 30, 35, 37, 39, 44, 48, 51, 54, 62, 71, 76, 83, 87, 91, 105, 107, 108, 110, 113, 116, 130, 137, 138, 142, 155, 160, 162, 172, 173, 174, 181
芳 (*) fāng 19, 172
坊 (*) fáng 74
妨 fáng 91, 120
房 fáng 11, 17, 19, 21, 41, 57, 90, 91, 95, 119, 156, 171, 182
肪 fáng 119
防 fáng 60, 78, 89, 100, 106, 107, 111, 112, 132, 148, 151, 160
仿 fǎng 75, 83, 155
纺 fǎng 129
舫 (*) fǎng 174
访 fǎng 32, 34, 36, 53, 119, 136, 146, 154, 165
放 (†) fàng 15, 20, 24, 37, 43, 47, 54, 57, 58, 63, 71, 72, 81, 110, 116, 117, 136, 140, 142, 145, 168, 171, 191
啡 fēi 11
菲 (*) fēi 36, 87
霏 (*) fēi 183
非 fēi 8, 11, 76, 84, 106, 107, 115, 146, 155, 177
飞 fēi 5, 43, 85, 88, 157, 163, 178, 182, 186, 188, 197
肥 féi 38, 43, 94, 156, 179
匪 fěi 195
菲 (*) fěi 36, 87
诽 fěi 156
废 fèi 97, 134, 157, 162, 164, 165, 193, 197
沸 fèi 166, 184
肺 (†) fèi 76
费 fèi 31, 40, 52, 56, 80, 87, 103, 125, 135, 157
分 fēn 4, 29, 35, 40, 43, 45, 49, 50, 52, 53, 60, 62, 66, 69, 70, 81, 82, 84, 88, 90, 97, 110, 116, 118, 119, 120, 124, 129, 130, 133, 134, 135, 138, 145, 147, 148, 149, 157, 158, 163, 165, 172, 180, 194
吩 fēn 187
氛 fēn 70, 108
纷 fēn 59, 94, 108
芬 (*) fēn 78, 98, 172
酚 (*) fēn 157
坟 fén 184
汾 (*) fén 173, 180
焚 (*) fén 173
粉 fěn 160, 167, 169, 175
份 (†) fèn 29, 31, 61, 114, 115, 120, 131, 137, 152, 183
分 fèn 4, 29, 35, 40, 43, 45, 49, 50, 52, 53, 60, 62, 66, 69, 70, 81, 82, 84, 88, 90, 97, 110, 116, 118, 119, 120, 124, 129, 130, 133, 134, 135, 138, 145, 147, 148, 149, 157, 158, 163, 165, 172, 180, 194
奋 fèn 39, 57, 82, 131, 136, 138
愤 fèn 79
粪 (*) fèn 6
丰 fēng 29, 128, 142, 148, 158, 178
封 fēng 96, 127, 135, 152, 161
峰 fēng 111, 124, 152
枫 (*) fēng 130
疯 fēng 74
蜂 fēng 96, 192
锋 fēng 194
风 fēng 24, 38, 41, 57, 61, 74, 82, 89, 96, 98, 105, 125, 127, 128, 131, 136, 138,

I-10

Index

140, 156, 158, 164, 168, 173, 176, 178, 182, 183, 184, 186
冯 (*) féng 18
缝 féng 196
逢 (†) féng 127, 198
讽 fěng 90
凤 (*) fèng 5
奉 fèng 107, 190, 196
缝 fèng 196
佛 fó 75, 87, 97, 98, 108
否 fǒu 37, 52, 67, 73, 84, 155, 173, 188, 191
夫 fū 10, 40, 43, 45, 65, 112, 116, 119, 122, 168, 185, 196
敷 fū 184, 197
肤 fū 36, 42, 45
伏 fú 146, 185, 186
佛 fú 75, 87, 97, 98, 108
俘 fú 188
夫 fú 10, 40, 43, 45, 65, 112, 116, 119, 122, 168, 185, 196
孚 (*) fú 153
幅 (†) fú 63, 64, 71, 74, 88, 119, 124, 150, 153, 172, 179
弗 (*) fú 129, 188
扶 (†) fú 67, 112
服 fú 5, 11, 13, 20, 22, 23, 66, 69, 78, 80, 83, 84, 87, 91, 143, 145, 151, 155, 157, 190, 192, 193, 195
浮 fú 172, 195
福 fú 31, 74, 94, 97, 98, 108, 188, 193
符 fú 30, 70, 87, 133
芙 (*) fú 160
袱 fú 167
辐 fú 112
俯 fǔ 197
府 fǔ 48, 57, 60, 76, 143, 165, 183, 190
抚 fǔ 162, 171, 198
斧 (*) fǔ 176

甫 (*) fǔ 44, 167
腐 fǔ 80, 95, 103, 108, 115, 139, 154, 171, 173
辅 fǔ 79, 97, 127, 166
付 fù 84, 87, 103, 135, 162, 186
傅 fù 41
副 (†) fù 99, 101, 102, 107, 109, 113, 118, 120, 126, 139, 146, 157, 169, 194, 196
附 fù 89, 187
复 fù 23, 33, 46, 58, 68, 73, 77, 82, 111, 117, 119, 151, 158, 160, 173, 182
妇 fù 57, 74, 116, 134, 157, 164, 166
富 fù 29, 46, 71, 93, 110, 116, 119, 131, 133, 137
服 fù 5, 11, 13, 20, 22, 23, 66, 69, 78, 80, 83, 84, 87, 91, 143, 145, 151, 155, 157, 190, 192, 193, 195
父 fù 32, 33, 151, 159, 171, 194
缚 fù 154
腹 fù 146
覆 fù 104, 129, 145, 174
负 fù 28, 39, 80, 109, 152, 162, 163, 169, 173, 180, 186, 196
赋 fù 114
赴 fù 143, 153, 174
附 fù 18, 46, 121, 133, 151, 166, 192
嘎 (*) gá 146
尬 gà 125
该 gāi 14, 81, 197
改 gǎi 30, 32, 37, 41, 48, 53, 57, 62, 76, 79, 109, 130, 157
丐 gài 188
概 gài 38, 61, 75, 179
溉 gài 132

盖 (†) gài 67, 104, 129, 138, 154, 162, 163, 186
钙 (*) gài 133
尴 gān 125
干 gān 21, 29, 42, 46, 47, 84, 93, 98, 114, 115, 121, 126, 133, 139, 156, 161, 164, 175, 183, 187
杆 gān 158
甘 gān 193, 195, 196
肝 (*) gān 40, 87, 163
苷 (*) gān 188
酐 (*) gān 193
感 gǎn 21, 31, 33, 35, 36, 39, 44, 46, 60, 72, 85, 95, 113, 118, 124, 136, 140, 161, 177, 198
敢 (†) gǎn 19, 42, 112, 195
杆 gǎn 158
赶 gǎn 79, 90, 121, 150
干 gàn 21, 29, 42, 46, 47, 84, 93, 98, 114, 115, 121, 126, 133, 139, 156, 161, 164, 175, 183, 187
赣 (*) gàn 91, 179
刚 gāng 20, 106, 137
扛 (†) gāng 141
杠 gāng 158
纲 gāng 96, 107, 152
缸 (*) gāng 154
钢 gāng 47, 72, 89, 94, 149, 193
岗 gǎng 102, 132
港 gǎng 115, 152, 162, 167
杠 gàng 158
糕 gāo 22, 89
膏 gāo 46
高 gāo 5, 6, 13, 22, 23, 31, 33, 34, 40, 41, 42, 43, 47, 58, 59, 64, 68, 78, 80, 85, 92, 94, 106, 108, 109, 110, 111, 112, 116, 119, 120, 121,

126, 130, 131, 132, 137, 140, 144, 152, 157, 159, 165, 168, 175, 176, 180, 182, 190, 192, 195
搞 (†) gǎo 57, 73
稿 gǎo 138, 183, 187
告 gào 9, 30, 43, 51, 82, 97, 108, 114, 130, 131, 133, 136, 138, 150, 168, 174, 184, 186, 196, 198
郜 (*) gào 166
割 (†) gē 148, 172
哥 gē 12, 189, 192
圪 (*) gē 170
戈 (*) gē 139, 181
搁 (†) gē 174
歌 gē 12, 45, 90, 98, 129, 130, 145
疙 gē 186
胳 gē 93
鸽 gē 95
搁 (†) gé 174
格 gé 26, 30, 37, 40, 45, 61, 77, 96, 104, 123, 134, 135, 137, 141
葛 (*) gé 132, 179
阁 (*) gé 76
隔 gé 94, 137, 166, 171
革 gé 48, 52, 57, 121, 163, 164, 188
合 gě 30, 34, 37, 39, 40, 43, 44, 48, 50, 53, 56, 58, 60, 62, 68, 70, 77, 78, 89, 96, 102, 115, 120, 121, 123, 127, 129, 134, 141, 142, 154, 169, 171, 172, 173, 174, 176, 183, 187, 192, 194, 196
盖 (†) gě 67, 104, 129, 138, 154, 162, 163, 186
葛 (*) gě 132, 179
个 (†) gè 1, 2, 5, 10, 21, 22, 33, 45, 49, 53,

I-11

Index

60, 63, 67, 92, 121, 125, 144, 176
各 (†) gè 25, 28, 29, 31, 33, 34, 35, 57, 108, 113, 116, 143, 168, 170, 188
给 (†) gěi 7, 40, 41, 82, 101, 125, 140, 197
根 gēn 14, 54, 132, 138, 141, 150, 169, 183
跟 (†) gēn 16, 75, 115, 136, 165, 171, 188
庚 (*) gēng 145
更 (†) gēng 48, 50, 55, 63, 74, 109, 115, 167, 170
耕 gēng 119, 196
耿 (*) gěng 133
更 (†) gèng 48, 50, 55, 63, 74, 109, 115, 167, 170
供 gōng 26, 34, 46, 70, 120, 125, 151, 162, 166
公 gōng 7, 9, 10, 11, 12, 16, 17, 23, 28, 30, 31, 34, 35, 38, 50, 53, 59, 61, 67, 68, 76, 84, 85, 88, 92, 96, 105, 106, 107, 108, 112, 115, 117, 126, 130, 134, 136, 137, 148, 158, 161, 163, 165, 167, 172, 173, 176, 178, 184, 186, 191
功 gōng 28, 50, 65, 88, 94, 120, 161, 164, 170, 172, 175, 181, 184, 189, 192
宫 gōng 164, 165, 193
工 gōng 1, 10, 11, 12, 19, 20, 22, 26, 30, 31, 34, 35, 38, 40, 47, 51, 59, 61, 62, 65, 70, 73, 79, 81, 84, 87, 89, 96, 101, 108, 109, 114, 120, 130, 151, 153, 155,

158, 161, 166, 168, 178, 179, 180, 181, 198
弓 (*) gōng 162
恭 gōng 188
攻 gōng 121, 132, 147
躬 gōng 166
龚 (*) gōng 139
巩 gǒng 107
汞 (*) gǒng 162
供 gòng 26, 34, 46, 70, 120, 125, 151, 162, 166
共 gòng 12, 16, 17, 19, 22, 27, 34, 38, 65, 72, 83, 100, 101, 104, 107, 109, 115, 123, 133, 148, 158, 161
贡 gòng 53, 90
勾 gōu 170
句 gōu 24, 40, 119
沟 gōu 57
钩 gōu 194
狗 (†) gǒu 5
苟 gǒu 175
勾 gòu 170
够 (†) gòu 40, 62
构 gòu 51, 60, 63, 76, 77, 91, 92, 99, 142, 144, 157
购 gòu 36, 54, 92, 104, 111, 152
估 gū 39, 43, 105, 198
姑 gū 81, 95, 194
孤 gū 47, 142, 146, 174
辜 gū 162
古 gǔ 71, 74, 80, 83, 89, 91, 93, 110, 122, 131, 133, 164, 169, 186
滑 gǔ 89, 98
股 gǔ 72, 114, 115, 121, 137, 146, 163, 174
谷 gǔ 140, 158, 174, 195
贾 (*) gǔ 20, 64
骨 gǔ 90, 114
鼓 gǔ 30, 45, 76, 176

估 gù 39, 43, 105, 198
固 gù 67, 85, 107, 123, 124, 135, 142, 150, 157, 175, 178, 181, 183
故 gù 39, 41, 55, 93, 102, 124, 134, 185, 193
雇 gù 91, 148, 192
顾 gù 20, 38, 106, 113, 134, 139, 154, 155, 156, 186, 191
刮 guā 24
瓜 guā 11, 46, 80
剐 (*) guǎ 193
寡 (*) guǎ 165, 166
挂 (†) guà 34, 76, 78, 127, 140
乖 (*) guāi 89
拐 guǎi 97, 187
怪 guài 22, 89, 98, 181, 186
关 guān 6, 8, 13, 15, 17, 29, 35, 48, 67, 70, 71, 73, 74, 79, 86, 91, 100, 111, 129, 130, 141, 144, 150, 159, 163, 171, 196
冠 guān 65
官 (†) guān 55, 56, 83, 98, 105, 122, 124, 137, 140, 151, 157, 173, 196
棺 (*) guān 169
观 guān 30, 33, 36, 57, 62, 64, 66, 71, 79, 91, 115, 119, 120, 125, 142, 144, 146, 151, 153, 157, 158
管 guǎn 25, 31, 36, 40, 76, 88, 93, 94, 101, 103, 116, 123, 125, 129, 134, 147, 148, 163, 170, 185, 190, 193
馆 guǎn 6, 20, 22, 43, 60, 76, 80, 91, 119, 186
冠 guàn 65

惯 guàn 18, 146
灌 guàn 132, 181
罐 guàn 94
观 guàn 30, 33, 36, 57, 62, 64, 66, 71, 79, 91, 115, 119, 120, 125, 142, 144, 146, 151, 153, 157, 158
贯 guàn 101, 123, 125, 170
光 (†) guāng 29, 35, 44, 47, 67, 77, 86, 89, 93, 95, 109, 111, 115, 119, 123, 125, 139, 146, 149, 152, 171, 183, 198
广 guǎng 30, 32, 35, 47, 50, 54, 56, 61, 64, 92, 105, 114, 137, 189, 194
逛 (†) guàng 44
归 guī 150, 154, 156, 166, 169, 170, 172, 179
硅 (*) guī 157
规 guī 26, 35, 51, 63, 64, 87, 99, 101, 120, 121, 123, 157, 168, 176
轨 guǐ 122, 149, 167
鬼 guǐ 98, 167
柜 guì 86
桂 (*) guì 71, 194
贵 (†) guì 10, 66, 95, 106, 113, 115, 117, 131, 139, 153, 181
跪 (†) guì 159, 196
滚 (†) gǔn 82, 89, 152, 173
棍 gùn 194
郭 (*) guō 4
锅 (†) guō 73, 197
国 guó 1, 3, 4, 5, 9, 13, 18, 19, 21, 23, 24, 25, 26, 27, 32, 35, 36, 37, 38, 39, 40, 45, 49, 59, 60, 63, 64, 68, 70, 72, 75, 76, 77, 81, 87, 88, 89, 90, 91, 94, 98,

I-12

Index

99, 100, 104, 106, 108, 110, 111, 113, 114, 116, 123, 125, 128, 131, 132, 134, 137, 141, 142, 148, 149, 153, 155, 158, 159, 168, 169, 180, 187, 188, 195, 198
虢 (*) guó 164
果 guǒ 4, 11, 13, 22, 29, 43, 45, 52, 76, 82, 87, 100, 150, 159
裹 guǒ 87
过 (†) guò 7, 15, 16, 23, 24, 25, 26, 27, 28, 47, 71, 72, 80, 82, 85, 86, 88, 95, 115, 117, 119, 126, 130, 136, 138, 147, 153, 164, 168, 182, 183, 197, 198
哈 (†) hā 61, 151
哈 (†) hǎ 61, 151
咳 hāi 43, 47
嗨 (†) hāi 193
孩 hái 8, 69, 112
还 (†) hái 7, 9, 14, 42, 137, 144, 166, 182
海 hǎi 33, 36, 38, 46, 68, 71, 83, 87, 91, 96, 98, 113, 116, 127, 133, 137, 140, 142, 145, 153, 154, 163, 165, 167, 194, 196
害 hài 22, 41, 42, 43, 46, 65, 66, 84, 109, 116, 130, 131, 161, 175, 178, 182, 191
酣 (*) hān 24
函 (*) hán 79
含 hán 71, 139, 177
寒 hán 47, 159, 190
涵 hán 108
韩 (*) hán 17, 19, 165
厂 hǎn 65, 84, 87, 156, 181, 192
喊 (†) hǎn 74, 181
罕 hǎn 123

憾 hàn 72
捍 hàn 149
旱 hàn 121
汉 hàn 6, 12, 46, 68, 76, 114
汗 (†) hàn 41, 137
瀚 (*) hàn 165
翰 hàn 88
杭 (*) háng 42, 108
航 háng 39, 87, 109, 126, 128, 143, 163, 182, 188
行 háng 10, 15, 16, 21, 24, 25, 38, 39, 49, 50, 51, 53, 54, 65, 67, 69, 75, 76, 84, 85, 88, 100, 101, 103, 104, 116, 118, 121, 123, 124, 127, 131, 134, 136, 139, 143, 144, 149, 157, 158, 163, 164, 168, 173, 183, 186
蒿 (*) hāo 156
号 (†) háo 8, 12, 22, 34, 69, 78, 108, 125, 126, 129, 133, 143, 160, 176, 186
壕 (*) háo 163
毫 háo 84, 119, 128
豪 háo 71, 76, 157, 195
好 (†) hǎo 2, 5, 12, 22, 24, 31, 32, 36, 39, 41, 44, 52, 55, 73, 82, 91, 119, 122, 144, 147, 151, 163, 164, 171, 174, 177, 190
郝 (*) hǎo 130
号 (†) hào 8, 12, 22, 34, 69, 78, 108, 125, 126, 129, 133, 143, 160, 176, 186
好 (†) hào 2, 5, 12, 22, 24, 31, 32, 36, 39, 41, 44, 52, 55, 73, 82, 91, 119, 122, 144, 147, 151, 163, 164, 171, 174, 177, 190

昊 (*) hào 44
浩 (*) hào 73, 91, 180, 185
皓 (*) hào 153
耗 hào 123, 157
呵 (†) hē 178
喝 (†) hē 4
何 hé 29, 44, 50, 83, 93, 110, 181
合 hé 30, 34, 37, 39, 40, 43, 44, 48, 50, 53, 56, 58, 60, 62, 68, 70, 77, 78, 89, 96, 102, 115, 120, 121, 123, 127, 129, 134, 141, 142, 154, 169, 171, 172, 173, 174, 176, 183, 187, 192, 194, 196
和 (†) hé 1, 12, 46, 56, 91, 96, 100, 104, 123, 145, 148, 149, 156, 158, 163, 167, 171, 181, 185, 192, 195, 196
核 hé 52, 75, 96, 103, 113, 122, 173, 181, 182
河 (†) hé 16, 18, 64, 66, 75, 81, 94, 98, 112, 114, 121, 158, 182, 192, 193
盒 hé 46, 158
禾 (*) hé 87
荷 (†) hé 131, 177
阂 hé 171
吓 (†) hè 80, 165
和 (†) hè 1, 12, 46, 56, 91, 96, 100, 104, 123, 145, 148, 149, 156, 158, 163, 167, 171, 181, 185, 192, 195, 196
喝 (†) hè 4
荷 (†) hè 131, 177
褐 (*) hè 180
贺 hè 38, 92
赫 (*) hè 136, 154
鹤 (*) hè 134
嘿 (†) hēi 181

黑 (†) hēi 9, 24, 71, 76, 82, 145, 173, 186, 187, 191
痕 hén 135
很 (†) hěn 1, 11
狠 hěn 187
恨 (†) hèn 83, 190
亨 (*) hēng 169
哼 (†) hēng 162
恒 héng 138
横 (†) héng 72, 98, 149, 157
珩 (*) héng 188
衡 héng 65, 94, 134, 173
横 (†) hèng 72, 98, 149, 157
哄 (†) hōng 163, 195
烘 (†) hōng 190
轰 hōng 148
宏 hóng 125, 127
弘 (*) hóng 133, 135
泓 (*) hóng 46
洪 hóng 123, 143, 154, 156, 166, 188
红 (†) hóng 8, 10, 17, 24, 42, 132, 143, 151, 157, 169
虹 hóng 92
鸿 (*) hóng 39, 173, 189
哄 (†) hǒng 163, 195
哄 (†) hòng 163, 195
侯 (*) hóu 37
喉 hóu 180, 186
猴 hóu 46
吼 (†) hǒu 167
候 hòu 3, 19, 37, 72, 83, 85, 88, 128, 136, 148, 162, 183
厚 (†) hòu 37, 122, 141, 152, 173, 187
后 hòu 16, 17, 19, 28, 29, 31, 33, 44, 65, 76, 92, 115, 116, 127, 129, 133, 138, 139, 142, 149, 151, 156, 159, 174, 178, 187, 191, 196, 197
乎 hū 17, 62, 93, 172

I-13

Index

呼 hū 74, 81, 88, 91, 94, 111, 181, 187
忽 hū 44, 73, 134, 172
和 (†) hú 1, 12, 46, 56, 91, 96, 100, 104, 123, 145, 148, 149, 156, 158, 163, 167, 171, 181, 185, 192, 195, 196
壶 (†) hú 81
湖 hú 136, 169, 177, 181, 183, 186
狐 (*) hú 187
糊 hú 82, 93, 177
胡 hú 84, 95, 98, 154, 188
葫 hú 197
蝴 hú 90
虎 hǔ 43, 46, 180
互 hù 38, 56, 58, 66, 75, 101, 114, 136, 155
户 hù 43, 70, 72, 79, 100, 103, 153
护 hù 21, 27, 41, 42, 53, 68, 78, 87, 93, 133, 142, 146, 155, 160, 165
沪 (*) hù 40, 58, 68, 139
糊 hù 82, 93, 177
化 huā 13, 16, 18, 19, 20, 31, 32, 40, 43, 58, 65, 69, 70, 77, 79, 84, 87, 88, 90, 92, 95, 108, 111, 113, 115, 116, 120, 121, 128, 129, 137, 141, 144, 148, 149, 156, 158, 160, 165, 166, 189, 190
花 (†) huā 16, 21, 23, 79, 81, 86, 95, 128, 135, 143, 182, 198
划 huá 27, 47, 90, 97, 99, 111, 135, 153, 157, 168
华 huá 71, 79, 82, 84, 87, 95, 103, 104, 106, 115, 117, 124, 128, 134, 139, 141, 142, 143, 149, 159, 182, 195
滑 huá 89, 98
猾 huá 96
骅 (*) huá 173
划 huà 27, 47, 90, 97, 99, 111, 135, 153, 157, 168
化 huà 13, 16, 18, 19, 20, 31, 32, 40, 43, 58, 65, 69, 70, 77, 79, 84, 87, 88, 90, 92, 95, 108, 111, 113, 115, 116, 120, 121, 128, 129, 137, 141, 144, 148, 149, 156, 158, 160, 165, 166, 189, 190
华 huà 71, 79, 82, 84, 87, 95, 103, 104, 106, 115, 117, 124, 128, 134, 139, 141, 142, 143, 149, 159, 182, 195
画 (†) huà 17, 20, 74, 76, 77, 112, 118, 130, 131, 151, 170, 197
话 huà 5, 17, 23, 31, 35, 40, 44, 68, 83, 86, 97, 126, 146, 160, 163, 187, 190, 193, 196
徊 huái 155
怀 huái 39, 70, 82, 85, 127, 133, 139, 146
淮 (*) huái 37, 91, 112, 147
坏 (†) huài 20, 66, 147, 183
欢 huān 4, 9, 123, 170, 171
桓 (*) huán 91
环 huán 14, 23, 31, 68, 92, 102, 112, 135, 158, 188
还 (†) huán 7, 9, 14, 42, 137, 144, 166, 182

缓 huǎn 64, 142, 156, 176, 180, 190
唤 (*) huàn 166
幻 huàn 86
患 huàn 102, 109, 156, 197
换 (†) huàn 16, 71, 74, 76, 90, 165, 170
焕 (*) huàn 143, 162
痪 huàn 156
慌 huāng 97, 143, 196
荒 huāng 175, 186, 187
煌 huáng 108
皇 huáng 75, 92, 150
磺 (*) huáng 195
黄 (†) huáng 15, 64, 80, 95, 114, 151, 167, 177, 179, 181, 189, 192
恍 huǎng 193
晃 huǎng 183, 189
谎 huǎng 187
晃 huàng 183, 189
徽 (*) huī 22, 64, 115
恢 huī 58
挥 huī 52, 58, 179
晖 (*) huī 22
灰 (†) huī 80, 89, 98
辉 huī 108, 111
回 (†) huí 4, 10, 23, 34, 37, 40, 65, 66, 84, 106, 114, 116, 122, 124, 129, 133, 146, 148, 150, 157, 166, 189
悔 huǐ 44, 190
毁 huǐ 143, 166, 190
会 (†) huì 1, 4, 10, 14, 17, 19, 22, 25, 32, 35, 36, 38, 45, 55, 59, 61, 67, 70, 71, 73, 74, 75, 78, 82, 84, 87, 91, 98, 100, 104, 105, 109, 113, 116, 117, 123, 124, 129, 130, 131, 133, 134, 136, 140, 141, 143, 144, 147, 149, 159, 166, 168, 169, 171, 172, 173, 181, 196
卉 (*) huì 155
惠 huì 59, 76, 79, 118, 155, 188, 192
慧 huì 64
汇 huì 82, 107, 157, 162, 166, 191, 193
绘 huì 130
蕙 (*) huì 187
讳 huì 186
贿 huì 134
婚 hūn 19, 66, 70, 73, 76, 173
昏 hūn 163, 181
浑 hún 166
混 hún 127, 129, 150, 176, 183, 191
魂 hún 130
混 hùn 127, 129, 150, 176, 183, 191
和 (†) huó 1, 12, 46, 56, 91, 96, 100, 104, 123, 145, 148, 149, 156, 158, 163, 167, 171, 181, 185, 192, 195, 196
活 huó 25, 26, 42, 43, 69, 75, 83, 98, 105, 182, 187, 190, 197
伙 huǒ 70, 86, 115, 120, 161, 174, 194
火 huǒ 6, 78, 96, 125, 128, 133, 143, 151, 167, 171, 176, 180, 184, 188, 190, 195, 197
和 (†) huò 1, 12, 46, 56, 91, 96, 100, 104, 123, 145, 148, 149, 156, 158, 163, 167, 171, 181, 185, 192, 195, 196
惑 huò 130, 151, 181
或 huò 15, 72, 110
祸 huò 195
获 huò 28, 63, 71, 73, 118, 120, 132, 142

I-14

Index

货 huò 46, 91, 113, 133, 135, 143, 145, 161, 170
霍 huò 179, 180
几 (†) jī 15, 17, 22, 60, 73, 78, 85, 93, 119, 126, 128, 138, 141, 155, 177
击 jī 87, 90, 105, 110, 121, 123, 139, 150, 175, 178, 183
叽 (*) jī 187
圾 jī 46, 63, 83, 96
基 jī 26, 28, 36, 49, 58, 67, 100, 102, 111, 133, 140, 141, 143, 169, 187, 189
奇 jī 22, 72, 82, 114, 120, 128, 162, 167, 183
姬 (*) jī 154
居 jī 22, 29, 66, 74, 81, 109, 148, 159, 198
机 jī 5, 6, 8, 9, 17, 19, 21, 24, 32, 35, 39, 41, 76, 80, 83, 89, 91, 92, 95, 99, 100, 101, 105, 108, 111, 113, 126, 128, 130, 131, 136, 142, 143, 144, 146, 151, 158, 167, 168, 176, 180, 182, 187, 188, 191, 194, 197
激 jī 39, 44, 45, 65, 67, 85, 110, 111, 114, 191, 198
矶 (*) jī 177
积 jī 26, 36, 53, 85, 90, 154, 155, 158, 179
肌 jī 77
讥 jī 197
饥 jī 159
鸡 jī 11, 190, 192
亟 (*) jí 164
即 jí 33, 59, 104, 111, 121, 122
及 jí 29, 45, 47, 48, 59, 83, 96, 97, 101, 110, 157, 161, 177, 185

吃 (†) jí 3, 12, 45, 71, 79, 90, 158, 176
吉 jí 152, 158, 194, 196, 197
嫉 jí 179
急 jí 23, 35, 44, 67, 82, 85, 91, 92, 135, 145, 159, 164, 168, 170, 179, 182, 191, 195
极 (†) jí 17, 26, 40, 94, 96, 121, 128, 133, 144, 151
疾 jí 82, 104
籍 jí 88, 130, 164, 170
级 jí 21, 29, 34, 36, 60, 62, 66, 74, 75, 81, 115, 117, 118, 120, 124, 144, 148, 150, 155, 164, 195
辑 jí 62, 77, 149
集 jí 44, 53, 58, 73, 79, 96, 99, 109, 112, 114, 120, 131, 134, 136, 161, 182
几 (†) jǐ 15, 17, 22, 60, 73, 78, 85, 93, 119, 126, 128, 138, 141, 155, 177
己 jǐ 13, 98, 188
挤 jǐ 88, 93
给 (†) jǐ 7, 40, 41, 82, 101, 125, 140, 197
冀 (*) jì 125, 198
剂 jì 141, 173, 185
季 jì 21, 37, 70, 111, 145, 166, 183
寂 jì 86, 177
寄 (†) jì 41, 153, 173, 180
忌 jì 178, 186
技 jì 25, 26, 35, 36, 38, 40, 83, 108, 126, 132, 160, 163, 174, 175, 176
既 jì 39, 143
暨 (*) jì 5
济 jì 25, 29, 93, 119, 126, 143, 149, 166, 169
祭 (*) jì 150

系 jì 6, 13, 29, 49, 58, 91, 97, 98, 99, 101, 111, 137, 144, 159, 162, 171, 196
纪 jì 32, 37, 59, 65, 67, 72, 79, 95, 119, 123, 129, 150, 164, 185
继 jì 27, 68, 113, 162, 174
绩 jì 16, 65, 67, 161
计 jì 27, 36, 39, 43, 49, 57, 61, 71, 75, 82, 94, 103, 107, 111, 115, 121, 126, 138, 162, 185
记 jì 20, 25, 33, 39, 41, 43, 44, 59, 70, 99, 101, 118, 129, 158, 166, 169, 171, 179, 184, 196
迹 jì 72, 78, 93, 119, 135, 139, 146, 149, 180, 190
际 jì 25, 28, 33, 45, 65, 89, 90, 91, 94, 141, 153
骑 (†) jì 20
骥 (*) jì 179
佳 jiā 160, 180, 185
加 jiā 14, 15, 16, 18, 27, 32, 40, 43, 50, 52, 80, 87, 101, 111, 117, 124, 125, 126, 133, 135, 167, 184, 185, 192, 193
嘉 jiā 61, 92
夹 jiā 97, 176
家 (†) jiā 2, 4, 8, 11, 13, 19, 23, 24, 36, 37, 41, 49, 53, 66, 69, 72, 77, 81, 88, 89, 90, 94, 96, 101, 106, 109, 110, 111, 113, 114, 116, 117, 121, 123, 126, 128, 136, 143, 153, 154, 161, 164, 172, 181, 184, 187
茄 (*) jiā 158
夹 jiá 97, 176

假 (†) jiǎ 35, 45, 47, 70, 79, 82, 89, 96, 126, 127, 135, 160, 188, 193, 195
甲 (†) jiǎ 69, 173, 174, 180
贾 (*) jiǎ 20, 64
钾 (*) jiǎ 147
价 jià 26, 40, 53, 55, 66, 67, 69, 74, 77, 109, 115, 119, 120, 125, 131, 139, 140, 149, 156, 180, 182, 195
假 (†) jià 35, 45, 47, 70, 79, 82, 89, 96, 126, 127, 135, 160, 188, 193, 195
嫁 (†) jià 80
架 jià 92, 95, 112, 142, 148, 156, 194, 198
稼 (*) jià 166
驾 jià 68, 98, 133
兼 jiān 134, 139, 155
坚 jiān 26, 62, 68, 71, 105, 116, 149, 157, 169, 176
尖 jiān 88, 165, 189
浅 (†) jiān 74
渐 jiān 33, 82, 163
煎 (†) jiān 87
监 jiān 99, 101, 107, 108, 118, 134, 155, 170, 177
肩 jiān 90
艰 jiān 65, 79, 118, 174
间 jiān 7, 11, 19, 24, 28, 51, 54, 80, 98, 105, 118, 119, 125, 129, 131, 144, 166, 167
鹣 (*) jiān 198
俭 jiǎn 181
减 jiǎn 30, 38, 118, 138, 161, 163
剪 jiǎn 92, 173, 195
拣 (†) jiǎn 176
捡 (†) jiǎn 82
柬 jiǎn 196

I-15

Index

检 jiǎn 15, 24, 37, 46, 84, 90, 103, 105, 112, 115, 124, 145, 158, 177
简 jiǎn 17, 72, 82, 83, 86, 95, 111, 144, 152, 164, 175, 195
茧 (*) jiǎn 92, 170
锏 (*) jiǎn 95
件 (†) jiàn 8, 23, 27, 46, 59, 61, 73, 75, 92, 96, 97, 100, 102, 138, 151, 162, 177, 179
健 jiàn 14, 21, 84, 95, 98, 103, 109, 192
剑 (*) jiàn 36
建 jiàn 48, 49, 51, 53, 56, 60, 64, 66, 68, 74, 83, 84, 89, 98, 102, 107, 118, 120, 122, 135, 139, 141, 146, 156, 176, 191
渐 jiàn 33, 82, 163
溅 (†) jiàn 185
监 jiàn 99, 101, 107, 108, 118, 134, 155, 170, 177
箭 jiàn 143
舰 jiàn 156
荐 jiàn 48
见 jiàn 6, 10, 11, 12, 20, 27, 68, 92, 97, 117, 121, 123, 148, 153, 163, 164, 165, 170, 185, 188, 194
谏 (*) jiàn 164
贱 (*) jiàn 165
践 jiàn 52, 180
鉴 jiàn 112, 115, 130, 154
键 jiàn 29, 84
间 jiàn 7, 11, 19, 24, 28, 51, 54, 80, 98, 105, 118, 119, 125, 129, 131, 144, 166, 167
僵 jiāng 188
姜 (*) jiāng 10

将 jiāng 38, 45, 72, 104, 116, 129, 144, 168
江 jiāng 35, 36, 38, 44, 46, 47, 74, 76, 93, 97, 153, 158, 161, 167, 168, 169, 179, 186, 188, 191, 193
浆 (*) jiāng 43, 139, 191
疆 jiāng 145
奖 jiǎng 36, 44, 92, 106, 111, 119, 120, 125, 161, 163, 193, 197
桨 (†) jiǎng 184
蒋 (*) jiǎng 10, 80
讲 (†) jiǎng 16, 17, 22, 75, 77, 92, 113, 114, 115, 148, 171
将 jiàng 38, 45, 72, 104, 116, 129, 144, 168
强 jiàng 52, 53, 58, 60, 61, 64, 66, 68, 79, 80, 86, 89, 91, 108, 126, 130, 131, 143, 164, 195
浆 (*) jiàng 43, 139, 191
酱 jiàng 91
降 jiàng 30, 32, 39, 74, 90, 150, 166, 171, 172
交 jiāo 27, 28, 38, 40, 68, 69, 71, 84, 86, 88, 93, 94, 96, 102, 107, 108, 112, 117, 126, 135, 145, 151, 154, 161, 168, 192
姣 (*) jiāo 159
娇 jiāo 195
教 jiāo 12, 18, 25, 30, 43, 44, 63, 69, 75, 88, 127, 139, 148, 153, 155, 163, 165, 178, 181, 183, 190
椒 jiāo 84
浇 (†) jiāo 85
焦 jiāo 112, 168

胶 jiāo 96, 141
蕉 jiāo 23
郊 jiāo 85
骄 jiāo 41
鹪 (*) jiāo 98
嚼 jiáo 175
矫 (*) jiáo 185
搅 jiǎo 161
狡 jiǎo 96
皎 (*) jiǎo 180
矫 (*) jiǎo 185
绞 (*) jiǎo 184
缴 jiǎo 113
脚 (†) jiǎo 19, 22, 176, 189, 190
角 (†) jiǎo 19, 20, 44, 58, 64, 94, 126, 129, 146, 164, 180, 185, 188, 191
饺 jiǎo 46
叫 (†) jiào 4, 6
教 jiào 12, 18, 25, 30, 43, 44, 63, 69, 75, 88, 127, 139, 148, 153, 155, 163, 165, 178, 181, 183, 190
校 jiào 3, 19, 38, 59, 90, 96, 109, 117, 153
窖 (*) jiào 137
觉 jiào 6, 9, 31, 63, 159, 171, 172, 181, 187, 190
较 jiào 15, 20, 23, 62, 119, 136, 155, 185
酵 (*) jiào 47, 78
接 (†) jiē 17, 27, 28, 63, 65, 66, 70, 72, 75, 118, 124, 131, 142, 161, 164
揭 jiē 144, 180
皆 (†) jiē 114
结 jiē 16, 19, 32, 45, 50, 51, 73, 91, 95, 96, 100, 103, 124, 125, 147, 159, 166, 170, 175, 182, 187, 197
街 jiē 18, 134, 145, 177, 188

阶 jiē 54, 73, 80, 84, 132, 150, 155
劫 jié 157
截 jié 102, 188
捷 jié 175
杰 jié 118, 196
桔 jié 98
洁 jié 110, 113, 162, 170
碣 (*) jié 190, 195
竭 jié 177, 179
结 jié 16, 19, 32, 45, 50, 51, 73, 91, 95, 96, 100, 103, 124, 125, 147, 159, 166, 170, 175, 182, 187, 197
节 jié 18, 19, 21, 36, 64, 66, 78, 93, 94, 96, 102, 110, 121, 133, 152, 166, 177, 186, 193
姐 jiě 5, 11, 143, 193
解 jiě 14, 22, 33, 58, 64, 70, 71, 81, 97, 111, 116, 127, 134, 141, 148, 157, 165, 167, 174, 180, 181, 184, 192
介 jiè 8, 68, 70, 72, 80, 95, 106
借 (†) jiè 18, 84, 112, 115, 153, 156, 192
届 (†) jiè 49, 111, 116, 117
戒 jiè 86, 89, 186
界 jiè 13, 34, 42, 114, 119, 122, 143, 145, 150, 151, 186, 192
解 jiè 14, 22, 33, 58, 64, 70, 71, 81, 97, 111, 116, 127, 134, 141, 148, 157, 165, 167, 174, 180, 181, 184, 192
诫 jiè 150
价 jiè 26, 40, 53, 55, 66, 67, 69, 74, 77, 109, 115, 119, 120, 125, 131, 139, 140,

I-16

Index

149, 156, 180, 182, 195
今 jīn 3, 17, 57, 59, 64, 142, 146
巾 jīn 44, 94, 96, 185, 194
斤 jīn 10
津 jīn 191
禁 jīn 35, 47, 82, 104, 129, 135
筋 jīn 197
襟 (*) jīn 175, 176
金 jīn 36, 49, 64, 67, 73, 85, 92, 95, 98, 101, 102, 108, 137, 149, 150, 157, 164, 172, 173, 179, 180, 182, 186, 189
仅 jǐn 27, 37, 147
尽 jǐn 31, 67, 87, 97, 105, 127, 179, 190, 196
槿 (*) jǐn 161
瑾 (*) jǐn 12
紧 jǐn 34, 67, 74, 79, 97, 109, 124, 171, 191
谨 jǐn 75, 80
锦 jǐn 198
劲 jìn 98, 161, 183, 187
尽 jìn 31, 67, 87, 97, 105, 127, 179, 190, 196
晋 jìn 134, 148, 181
浸 jìn 140, 164
禁 jìn 35, 47, 82, 104, 129, 135
近 (†) jìn 14, 17, 18, 66, 79, 83, 129, 134, 138, 153, 154, 164, 166, 170
进 (†) jìn 8, 12, 14, 25, 27, 31, 32, 34, 42, 44, 49, 56, 57, 61, 62, 66, 73, 74, 86, 100, 104, 121, 123, 131, 132, 134, 135, 149, 163, 172, 187, 197

京 jīng 2, 6, 11, 12, 16, 18, 40, 58, 68, 147, 153, 180
兢 jīng 169
惊 jīng 45, 96, 132, 142, 143, 162, 186
晶 jīng 159
睛 jīng 11
精 jīng 26, 34, 36, 71, 88, 109, 125, 128, 130, 132, 140, 142, 152, 157, 160, 161, 168, 174, 176, 180, 189, 196
经 jīng 7, 15, 17, 19, 25, 28, 29, 31, 33, 50, 57, 58, 60, 67, 71, 77, 85, 90, 98, 103, 115, 124, 126, 143, 151, 166, 180, 188, 192
茎 (†) jīng 173
荆 (†) jīng 145
井 (†) jǐng 114, 149, 175
景 jǐng 38, 57, 58, 76, 85, 87, 109, 121
警 jǐng 37, 83, 117, 130, 140, 160, 174, 185
颈 jǐng 183
净 jìng 21, 83, 159
劲 jìng 98, 161, 183, 187
境 jìng 14, 23, 67, 68, 122, 133, 145, 156, 169, 185, 195
婧 (*) jìng 23
径 jìng 108, 149, 181
敬 jìng 79, 89, 92, 96, 138, 166, 173, 174, 183, 188, 189
竞 jìng 30, 63, 77, 83, 120, 137, 154
竟 jìng 37, 38, 69
镜 jìng 22, 45, 119
靓 (*) jìng 44
靖 (*) jìng 135, 179, 183

静 jìng 22, 42, 83, 169, 170, 177
揪 (*) jiū 96
究 jiū 35, 37, 39, 40, 43, 62, 77, 111, 144, 162, 166
纠 jiū 108, 118
久 (†) jiǔ 18, 41, 43, 80, 128, 134, 142, 146, 165
九 (†) jiǔ 4, 21, 71, 163, 170
酒 jiǔ 19, 20, 36, 47, 83, 87, 115, 130, 186
就 (†) jiù 7, 8, 22, 23, 38, 42, 56, 64, 77, 93, 101, 117, 127, 128, 130, 149, 153, 160, 181
救 (†) jiù 66, 82, 91, 93, 110, 116, 144, 149, 150, 159, 169, 170
旧 (†) jiù 18, 121, 151, 158
臼 (*) jiù 96
舅 jiù 94
居 jū 22, 29, 66, 74, 81, 109, 148, 159, 198
拘 jū 137, 183
据 jū 14, 54, 67, 75, 79, 91, 103, 104, 114, 121, 134
车 jū 6, 10, 11, 12, 16, 18, 21, 44, 62, 78, 80, 89, 92, 93, 94, 125, 127, 129, 130, 133, 141, 155, 156, 160, 165, 167, 183, 187, 191, 192, 195, 197, 198
鞠 jū 166
局 jú 95, 96, 101, 103, 104, 105, 107, 109, 116, 120, 121, 122, 124, 137, 147, 157, 159, 165, 183
桔 jú 98
菊 (*) jú 129, 143

举 jǔ 15, 18, 28, 45, 61, 64, 97, 139, 144, 147, 154, 165, 180, 187, 188
咀 jǔ 175
柜 jǔ 86
沮 jǔ 177
矩 jǔ 87, 162
莒 (*) jǔ 93
俱 jù 66, 74, 156, 178, 184, 185
具 jù 35, 37, 43, 52, 60, 77, 84, 95, 149, 170
剧 jù 40, 76, 93, 126, 130, 132, 145, 146, 177
句 jù 24, 40, 119
巨 jù 54, 72, 79, 92, 155, 163, 172
惧 jù 145, 188
拒 jù 36, 192
据 jù 14, 54, 67, 75, 79, 91, 103, 104, 114, 121, 134
渠 jù 101, 187
瞿 (*) jù 24
聚 jù 82, 109, 112, 116, 127, 168, 170, 176
足 jù 12, 56, 57, 78, 80, 92, 113, 115, 122, 130, 131, 165, 181, 192, 197
距 jù 35, 107, 142, 157
钜 (*) jù 189
圈 (†) juān 59, 85, 195
娟 (*) juān 74
捐 (†) juān 78, 131, 147, 158
卷 (†) juǎn 64, 86, 151
倦 juàn 182, 183
卷 (†) juàn 64, 86, 151
圈 (†) juàn 59, 85, 195
决 jué 14, 15, 21, 62, 67, 69, 102, 122, 130, 154, 155, 191, 197
掘 jué 113
爵 (*) jué 92
绝 jué 36, 63, 98, 117, 125, 126, 158, 162,

I-17

Index

178, 182, 184, 187, 196
脚 (†) jué 19, 22, 176, 189, 190
蕨 (*) jué 196
觉 jué 6, 9, 31, 63, 159, 171, 172, 181, 187, 190
角 (†) jué 19, 20, 44, 58, 64, 94, 126, 129, 146, 164, 180, 185, 188, 191
军 jūn 58, 65, 71, 74, 81, 94, 103, 113, 116, 117, 124, 133, 137, 159, 177, 183, 188
君 (*) jūn 5
均 jūn 56, 78, 86, 88, 108, 160
菌 jūn 120, 134, 158
钧 (*) jūn 79
俊 jùn 93
峻 jùn 120
菌 jùn 120, 134, 158
郡 (*) jùn 40
骏 (*) jùn 42
咖 kā 11
喀 (*) kā 150, 171
卡 kǎ 45, 92, 153, 179, 192
开 (†) kāi 2, 7, 12, 18, 24, 34, 37, 39, 43, 46, 50, 51, 54, 57, 60, 61, 62, 67, 76, 83, 93, 99, 109, 119, 121, 124, 126, 129, 137, 141, 143, 152, 154, 156, 162, 164, 165, 166, 167, 169, 171, 173, 182
凯 (*) kǎi 10, 94
岂 kǎi 198
恺 (*) kǎi 93
慨 kǎi 124, 155
刊 kān 132, 135, 145
勘 kān 153, 156
堪 kān 135, 190
看 kān 6, 12, 17, 36, 37, 79, 86, 92, 95, 106, 113, 114, 119, 120, 124, 130, 152, 171, 176, 190
坎 (*) kǎn 147, 181
嵌 kǎn 150
砍 (†) kǎn 83
看 kàn 6, 12, 17, 36, 37, 79, 86, 92, 95, 106, 113, 114, 119, 120, 124, 130, 152, 171, 176, 190
康 kāng 14, 38, 133, 139, 192
慷 kāng 155
扛 (†) káng 141
抗 kàng 84, 121, 129, 157, 158
炕 (*) kàng 89
拷 (*) kǎo 128
烤 kǎo 85, 180
考 kǎo 9, 23, 30, 38, 47, 59, 63, 65, 77, 88, 101, 103, 106, 111, 122, 141, 145, 153, 181
犒 (*) kào 192
靠 kào 74, 83, 107, 172
柯 (*) kē 77, 184
棵 (†) kē 41
珂 (*) kē 90
磕 (†) kē 178
科 kē 26, 35, 36, 38, 39, 40, 41, 42, 61, 69, 74, 85, 94, 96, 128, 132, 134, 136, 147, 155, 156, 159, 180, 189
颗 (†) kē 67, 150
咳 ké 43, 47
可 kě 7, 8, 21, 35, 36, 39, 40, 41, 44, 62, 63, 68, 74, 78, 85, 86, 87, 92, 93, 94, 97, 109, 111, 116, 121, 127, 143, 146, 158, 162, 168, 172, 181, 190, 193, 195, 196
渴 (†) kě 22, 131
克 kè 44, 66, 69, 79, 87, 96, 108, 147, 155, 166, 174, 188, 193, 196, 197
刻 (†) kè 20, 58, 68, 76, 90, 148, 171, 176
嗑 (*) kè 97
客 kè 6, 9, 10, 20, 38, 39, 46, 47, 64, 76, 103, 108, 130, 143, 152, 174, 184
恪 (*) kè 158
课 (†) kè 10, 70, 86, 97, 110, 147, 164, 187, 197
啃 (†) kěn 154
垦 (*) kěn 86
恳 kěn 90, 193, 196
肯 kěn 30, 172, 196
坑 (†) kēng 129
空 kōng 19, 37, 47, 54, 84, 95, 109, 126, 133, 137, 150, 176, 178, 180, 183, 194, 196
孔 (†) kǒng 113, 189
恐 kǒng 38, 85, 96, 134, 143, 145, 165, 178
控 kòng 53, 72, 108, 130, 177
空 kòng 19, 37, 47, 54, 84, 95, 109, 126, 133, 137, 150, 176, 178, 180, 183, 194, 196
口 (†) kǒu 15, 21, 23, 42, 55, 56, 58, 69, 72, 79, 84, 85, 95, 112, 115, 123, 125, 126, 129, 137, 138, 154, 159, 160, 162, 165, 170, 172, 180, 181, 190, 191
扣 kòu 198
哭 (†) kū 21, 184
枯 kū 166, 177
苦 (†) kǔ 36, 40, 44, 65, 76, 90, 98, 158, 175, 195, 196
库 kù 94, 129, 132, 148, 174
裤 kù 23, 92
酷 kù 148, 185
夸 (†) kuā 89
挎 (†) kuà 191
跨 (†) kuà 107, 110, 113, 137, 157, 182
会 (†) kuài 1, 4, 10, 14, 17, 19, 22, 25, 32, 35, 36, 38, 45, 55, 59, 61, 67, 70, 71, 73, 74, 75, 78, 82, 84, 87, 91, 98, 100, 104, 105, 109, 113, 116, 117, 123, 124, 129, 130, 131, 133, 134, 136, 140, 141, 143, 144, 147, 149, 159, 166, 168, 169, 171, 172, 173, 181, 196
块 (†) kuài 4, 109, 123, 124, 175
快 (†) kuài 8, 10, 15, 32, 37, 42, 46, 47, 90, 92, 105, 171, 172, 176, 187, 190
筷 kuài 23
宽 (†) kuān 34, 43, 149
款 kuǎn 58, 69, 81, 87, 127, 134, 153, 161, 162, 179, 186, 194
匡 (*) kuāng 90
筐 (†) kuāng 179
狂 kuáng 74, 191
况 kuàng 25, 32, 43, 58, 83, 166
旷 kuàng 197
框 kuàng 112
眶 kuàng 184
矿 kuàng 87, 89, 122, 138, 153, 176, 192, 198
亏 kuī 90, 96, 119, 197
奎 (*) kuí 78
魁 (*) kuí 77
愧 kuì 96, 148
溃 kuì 159
馈 kuì 123, 148

I-18

Index

坤 (*) kūn 11
昆 kūn 184
琨 (*) kūn 91
锟 (*) kūn 76
捆 kǔn 144
困 kùn 29, 77, 109, 185
廓 kuò 166
扩 kuò 28, 119, 122, 127, 135, 163
括 kuò 26, 75
阔 kuò 114, 143, 159
啦 (†) lā 131
喇 lā 174
垃 lā 46, 63, 83, 96
拉 (†) lā 28, 39, 41, 43, 87, 131, 156, 174, 185, 191, 193
喇 lǎ 174
腊 (*) là 155
落 là 65, 72, 89, 90, 97, 99, 134, 146, 148, 164, 170, 191, 198
蜡 là 96
辣 (†) là 41, 84
啦 (†) la 131
徕 (*) lái 194
来 (†) lái 2, 4, 5, 9, 11, 12, 16, 17, 31, 33, 38, 43, 44, 45, 50, 51, 52, 70, 71, 85, 86, 100, 106, 114, 115, 118, 124, 135, 138, 140, 142, 146, 150, 155, 162, 164, 175, 179, 183, 184, 187, 194, 196, 198
莱 (*) lái 73, 166, 192
赖 lài 120, 148, 177, 194
兰 (*) lán 18, 145, 151, 196
婪 lán 175
岚 lán 132
拦 (†) lán 87, 185
栏 lán 112
澜 (*) lán 76
篮 lán 12
蓝 (†) lán 19, 22, 78, 139, 175
懒 (†) lǎn 44, 189

揽 (*) lǎn 43
览 lǎn 60, 74, 81, 116, 146, 166
滥 làn 145, 156
烂 (†) làn 81, 133, 173
廊 láng 136
狼 (†) láng 80, 190
郎 láng 158
朗 lǎng 166, 192, 195
浪 làng 39, 40, 88, 150, 171
捞 (†) lāo 138, 168
劳 láo 58, 66, 68, 75, 89, 98, 151, 175, 182, 192, 195, 197
唠 láo 182
牢 láo 123, 124, 129, 190
姥 lǎo 97
老 lǎo 4, 12, 31, 43, 58, 64, 67, 69, 74, 89, 92, 93, 97, 117, 129, 137, 143, 164, 173, 181, 186, 187, 188
劳 lào 58, 66, 68, 75, 89, 98, 151, 175, 182, 192, 195, 197
唠 lào 182
涝 (*) lào 140, 143
络 lào 99, 122, 162, 188, 197
落 lào 65, 72, 89, 90, 97, 99, 134, 146, 148, 164, 170, 191, 198
乐 lè 10, 17, 24, 57, 66, 71, 85, 87, 123, 133, 148, 165, 166, 192, 195, 197
勒 (*) lè 74
了 (†) le 1, 4, 9, 14, 16, 33, 37, 44, 47, 81, 89, 93, 94, 152, 161, 195
勒 (*) lēi 74
嫘 (*) léi 98
累 léi 36
雷 (†) léi 59, 89, 158, 188
磊 (*) lěi 74

累 lěi 36
蕾 (*) lěi 131
泪 lèi 45, 184
类 (†) lèi 53, 57, 59, 66, 74, 75, 79, 91, 110, 118, 129, 137, 155
累 lèi 36
冷 (†) lěng 5, 42, 162, 185, 186
愣 (†) lèng 178
丽 lí 36, 143, 144, 151, 180
厘 lí 71
梨 (†) lí 81
犁 (*) lí 180
璃 lí 71
离 (†) lí 10, 12, 18, 35, 70, 98, 131, 137, 157, 172, 187
藜 (*) lí 47
黎 lí 144
李 lǐ 24, 65, 66, 93, 166, 184, 189
理 lǐ 19, 20, 25, 33, 34, 37, 40, 46, 51, 54, 55, 56, 57, 59, 60, 65, 70, 73, 74, 76, 78, 80, 85, 88, 90, 102, 106, 113, 114, 116, 120, 126, 127, 129, 130, 132, 136, 144, 148, 157, 159, 160, 162, 168, 169, 172, 176, 178, 179, 189, 192, 193, 194, 198
礼 lǐ 21, 46, 73, 98, 127, 145, 147, 183, 186
里 (†) lǐ 2, 4, 6, 10, 22, 28, 41, 66, 68, 94, 95, 107, 125, 139, 161, 184, 188
锂 (*) lǐ 178
鲤 (*) lǐ 179
丽 lì 36, 143, 144, 151, 180
例 lì 36, 56, 60, 77, 112, 116, 146, 147, 175, 191

俐 lì 194
利 lì 32, 38, 40, 45, 46, 47, 50, 60, 62, 63, 66, 69, 71, 83, 103, 108, 111, 115, 117, 123, 129, 133, 156, 157, 165, 170, 179, 185, 190, 191, 194, 196
力 lì 14, 17, 18, 23, 26, 30, 31, 32, 34, 35, 38, 40, 42, 44, 45, 53, 58, 63, 65, 66, 68, 71, 79, 80, 81, 82, 87, 95, 102, 104, 105, 110, 111, 124, 125, 126, 127, 131, 132, 135, 139, 141, 143, 150, 157, 158, 163, 165, 166, 167, 170, 171, 176, 178, 179, 183, 184, 185, 194, 198
励 lì 30, 106, 110, 138
历 lì 13, 31, 46, 62, 73, 83, 97, 110, 124, 135, 139, 140, 146, 179
厉 lì 42, 128, 164
吏 (*) lì 162
痢 (*) lì 189
砺 (*) lì 168
立 lì 49, 50, 59, 65, 71, 76, 89, 91, 97, 102, 105, 113, 117, 123, 124, 126, 133, 144, 151, 160, 167, 174, 188
粒 (†) lì 79, 150
莉 (*) lì 121
郦 (*) lì 97
隶 lì 177
俩 (†) liǎ 39, 193
帘 lián 89, 188
廉 lián 110, 138, 180
怜 lián 44
联 lián 29, 37, 40, 53, 74, 101, 109, 122, 123, 129, 132, 137, 140, 165, 169, 171,

I-19

Index

176, 178, 181, 182, 188, 191
莲 (*) lián 72, 186
连 (†) lián 29, 57, 72, 79, 87, 92, 93, 94, 118, 129, 142, 166, 170, 171, 173, 177, 185
敛 (*) liǎn 176, 177
脸 (†) liǎn 19, 175
恋 liàn 86, 182
敛 (*) liàn 176, 177
炼 liàn 19, 91, 138, 180, 193
练 liàn 22, 61, 75, 83, 128, 169, 193, 195
链 liàn 93, 108, 118
凉 liáng 47, 98, 184, 186
梁 liáng 118, 169, 194, 198
粮 liáng 64, 98
良 liáng 52, 66, 68, 86, 157, 159, 170, 173
量 liáng 28, 29, 31, 36, 42, 43, 45, 53, 67, 78, 81, 88, 112, 116, 128, 132, 135, 137, 140, 146, 149, 155, 186
两 (†) liǎng 7, 9, 24, 102, 110, 111, 149, 187, 196
亮 liàng 5, 11, 22, 23, 47, 155, 156, 162
晾 (†) liàng 174
谅 liàng 45, 157, 180
辆 (†) liàng 17, 18
量 liàng 28, 29, 31, 36, 42, 43, 45, 53, 67, 78, 81, 88, 112, 116, 128, 132, 135, 137, 140, 146, 149, 155, 186
靓 (*) liàng 44
疗 liáo 56, 70, 77, 80, 88, 90
聊 liáo 41, 45
辽 liáo 159, 182

了 (†) liǎo 1, 4, 9, 14, 16, 33, 37, 44, 47, 81, 89, 93, 94, 152, 161, 195
廖 (*) liào 40
料 liào 30, 35, 45, 47, 55, 63, 149, 155, 164, 167, 168, 170
列 liè 41, 58, 62, 84, 91, 101, 127, 128, 139, 151, 154, 171
劣 liè 78, 88, 150, 156, 184
烈 liè 61, 63, 67, 77, 145, 163, 164, 167, 184, 190
猎 liè 187
裂 liè 129, 175
临 lín 56, 67, 79, 95, 108, 168, 172, 180
林 lín 36, 64, 74, 89, 121, 125, 158, 160, 166, 180
淋 (†) lín 162, 187
琳 (*) lín 39
磷 (*) lín 12
邻 lín 22, 154, 168
霖 (*) lín 145
麟 (*) lín 83
吝 lìn 195
淋 (†) lìn 162, 187
赁 lìn 116
令 líng 76, 82, 121, 149, 170, 172, 175, 184
伶 líng 194
凌 líng 117
灵 líng 75, 122, 130, 140, 173, 176, 179, 194
玲 (*) líng 39
翎 (*) líng 184
菱 líng 136
铃 (†) líng 90, 197
陵 líng 156, 184, 189
零 (†) líng 5, 69, 91, 92, 97, 157, 174, 198
龄 líng 34, 43

令 lǐng 76, 82, 121, 149, 170, 172, 175, 184
岭 (*) lǐng 38, 169, 182
领 lǐng 48, 49, 58, 64, 75, 82, 98, 104, 111, 119, 127, 133, 141, 145, 146, 152, 162, 163, 165, 167, 186
令 lìng 76, 82, 121, 149, 170, 172, 175, 184
另 lìng 30, 34, 35, 155
溜 (†) liū 178, 194
刘 (*) liú 3, 87, 114, 159
流 liú 27, 33, 38, 41, 42, 44, 45, 46, 69, 70, 73, 76, 80, 88, 89, 108, 110, 112, 119, 129, 144, 146, 150, 159, 173, 181, 194
浏 liú 81, 166
留 (†) liú 33, 34, 39, 62, 67, 80, 135, 137, 140, 146, 149, 151, 182, 186
瘤 liú 113
硫 (*) liú 154
柳 (*) liǔ 38, 193
六 (†) liù 3, 10, 148
陆 liù 66, 88, 105, 124
隆 lōng 109, 155, 170
咙 lóng 180
笼 lóng 169, 184, 197
聋 lóng 194
隆 lóng 109, 155, 170
龙 (†) lóng 54, 76, 92, 122, 147, 159, 173, 177, 184, 193
垄 lǒng 117
拢 lǒng 172
笼 lǒng 169, 184, 197
弄 (†) lòng 40, 47, 89, 191
搂 (†) lōu 172
楼 (†) lóu 16, 23, 77, 120, 148, 158, 172
搂 (†) lǒu 172

漏 (†) lòu 75, 77, 151, 173, 197
陋 lòu 164, 179
露 (†) lòu 70, 83, 87, 92, 118, 129, 140, 144, 181
撸 (*) lū 193
卢 (*) lú 67
炉 lú 191
芦 lú 197
虏 lǔ 188
鲁 lǔ 194
录 lù 59, 72, 74, 78, 81, 89, 125, 152, 162
潞 (*) lù 95
璐 (*) lù 149
碌 lù 134
禄 (*) lù 22
赂 lù 134
路 (†) lù 8, 9, 12, 20, 30, 59, 60, 97, 98, 112, 118, 125, 137, 139, 145, 156, 169, 175, 186, 188, 190, 198
陆 lù 66, 88, 105, 124
露 (†) lù 70, 83, 87, 92, 118, 129, 140, 144, 181
鹿 (*) lù 41, 178, 185
驴 (*) lǘ 86
侣 lǚ 161
吕 (*) lǚ 19, 173
屡 lǚ 169
履 lǚ 104
旅 lǚ 7, 10, 20, 21, 38, 88, 139, 146
铝 (*) lǚ 39, 173
律 lǜ 27, 34, 63, 65, 123, 124, 142
氯 (*) lǜ 169
滤 lǜ 153
率 lǜ 62, 63, 81, 82, 86, 88, 90, 93, 94, 123, 127, 129, 135, 138, 168, 182
绿 (†) lǜ 18, 19, 32, 44, 46, 175
虑 lǜ 30, 88, 154, 193
掠 lüè 183

I-20

Index

略 lüè 86, 94, 96, 97, 99, 113, 114, 120, 134, 146, 176, 178
挛 (*) luán 47
栾 (*) luán 12
乱 (†) luàn 34, 95, 129, 150, 186, 188
伦 lún 197
沦 (*) lún 151
纶 (*) lún 178
论 lún 31, 44, 55, 65, 72, 73, 77, 80, 88, 100, 103, 106, 122, 126, 127, 141, 169, 188
轮 lún 88, 110, 127, 166, 180
论 lùn 31, 44, 55, 65, 72, 73, 77, 80, 88, 100, 103, 106, 122, 126, 127, 141, 169, 188
啰 luō 198
箩 (*) luó 198
罗 (*) luó 9, 97, 131, 183, 190, 194, 196
螺 luó 194
逻 luó 77, 130
裸 (*) luǒ 75, 76
洛 (*) luò 69, 148, 180
络 luò 99, 122, 162, 188, 197
落 luò 65, 72, 89, 90, 97, 99, 134, 146, 148, 164, 170, 191, 198
雒 (*) luò 193
骆 (*) luò 6
啰 luo 198
妈 mā 5
抹 mā 165, 189
么 má 2, 4, 5, 6, 9, 21, 67, 76, 136, 141, 162
麻 má 40, 155, 169, 173, 176, 189, 194
吗 (†) mǎ 4
玛 (*) mǎ 124
码 mǎ 34, 39, 84, 124, 141, 160

马 mǎ 10, 23, 45, 46, 79, 108, 124, 143, 150, 156, 173, 191, 196
骂 (†) mà 77, 96, 179
么 ma 2, 4, 5, 6, 9, 21, 67, 76, 136, 141, 162
吗 (†) ma 4
嘛 (†) ma 134
埋 mái 175, 179, 185, 195
买 (†) mǎi 3, 24, 54, 77, 82
卖 (†) mài 9, 65, 77, 135, 143, 152, 153, 175
脉 mài 164, 166, 173, 182, 198
迈 (†) mài 106, 157
麦 mài 75, 96
埋 mán 175, 179, 185, 195
瞒 mán 151, 160
蔓 mán 131
蛮 mán 172
馒 mán 84
满 mǎn 18, 21, 56, 59, 82, 117, 158, 177, 190
慢 (†) màn 11, 135, 161, 190, 195
曼 (*) màn 20, 194
漫 màn 39, 61, 118, 136, 153
蔓 màn 131
忙 (†) máng 11, 21, 92, 94, 134, 142, 196
氓 máng 181
盲 máng 128, 191, 198
芒 máng 152
茫 máng 177, 178
猫 (†) māo 5, 21
毛 máo 44, 67, 88, 95, 183
矛 máo 56
茅 (*) máo 83, 106, 115
髦 máo 92
卯 (*) mǎo 162
峁 (*) mǎo 190

冒 mào 21, 86, 127, 161
帽 mào 22
茂 mào 180, 186
貌 mào 46, 120, 188
贸 mào 59, 60, 69, 90, 96, 153, 157, 167
么 me 2, 4, 5, 6, 9, 21, 67, 76, 136, 141, 162
媒 méi 99, 106, 107, 122, 124
枚 (†) méi 117, 187
梅 (*) méi 18
楣 (*) méi 98
没 (†) méi 3, 6, 12, 94, 152, 155, 165, 195, 197
煤 méi 64, 122, 157
玫 (*) méi 45
眉 méi 95, 176
糜 (*) méi 188
酶 (*) méi 88
霉 méi 93
每 (†) měi 8, 9, 33, 67, 120, 144, 169
美 měi 36, 43, 44, 46, 49, 52, 68, 69, 76, 79, 81, 84, 92, 95, 124, 125, 132, 137, 153, 161, 167, 169, 174, 177, 178, 180
镁 (*) měi 168
妹 mèi 11, 193
昧 mèi 156, 183
谜 mèi 98, 191
魅 mèi 66
闷 mēn 187, 198
门 (†) mén 9, 21, 31, 45, 47, 48, 77, 109, 120, 121, 123, 126, 140, 150, 155, 166, 176, 192, 193, 197
闷 mèn 187, 198
们 men 1, 2, 4, 5, 41, 74, 88, 107, 112, 192
蒙 (†) mēng 109, 110, 131
氓 méng 181

盟 méng 109, 111, 118, 125
萌 méng 163
蒙 (†) méng 109, 110, 131
猛 měng 167, 178
蒙 (†) měng 109, 110, 131
孟 (*) mèng 10, 189, 193
梦 (†) mèng 37, 86, 111, 168
眯 (†) mī 182
弥 mí 127, 153
眯 (*) mí 182
谜 mí 98, 191
迷 mí 77, 93, 97, 140, 153, 160, 162, 163, 181, 184
糜 (*) mí 178
弭 (*) mǐ 186
米 mǐ 6, 17, 42, 71, 78, 119, 154, 188
靡 (*) mǐ 178
密 mì 39, 61, 68, 73, 109, 131, 142, 145, 149, 151, 161, 171, 176, 196
泌 mì 138
秘 mì 68, 72, 73, 106, 118, 165
蜜 mì 96
觅 mì 178
棉 mián 86, 98, 175
眠 mián 88
绵 (*) mián 150
免 miǎn 31, 60, 85, 91, 126, 137, 139, 180, 192
勉 miǎn 138, 164
缅 (*) miǎn 41, 139
面 miàn 6, 10, 19, 20, 22, 23, 25, 35, 39, 44, 45, 46, 49, 53, 55, 56, 62, 65, 72, 76, 89, 92, 104, 113, 114, 116, 119, 120, 121, 124, 126, 127, 132, 139, 141, 142, 146, 158, 168, 171,

I-21

Index

172, 175, 183, 185, 193, 194
描 miáo 84, 130
苗 miáo 96, 153, 160, 196
渺 miáo 192
秒 (†) miǎo 68, 153
妙 miào 83, 167, 175
庙 miào 82, 84
灭 miè 82, 133, 166, 167, 183, 186
蔑 miè 189, 191
民 mín 29, 30, 31, 32, 34, 35, 37, 41, 52, 55, 57, 59, 67, 68, 71, 72, 76, 81, 82, 90, 98, 104, 105, 106, 108, 110, 119, 122, 125, 127, 137, 140, 143, 147, 159, 184, 187, 188, 189, 192
敏 mǐn 86, 118, 155, 175, 179
闵 (*) mǐn 142
闽 (*) mǐn 23
名 míng 5, 11, 19, 22, 23, 30, 34, 37, 47, 70, 74, 81, 82, 88, 93, 116, 120, 121, 132, 141, 149, 155, 157, 158, 165, 168, 173, 175, 184, 188, 190, 194
明 míng 5, 11, 21, 32, 33, 51, 52, 55, 61, 63, 70, 73, 75, 77, 82, 95, 97, 106, 114, 136, 144, 152, 158, 159, 179, 182, 193
铭 míng 181
鸣 míng 148, 198
命 mìng 32, 42, 52, 68, 76, 80, 107, 117, 132, 157, 162, 163, 164, 175, 178, 184, 188
谬 miù 187
摸 (†) mō 70, 149, 198

摩 mó 78, 126, 131, 140
摸 (†) mó 70, 149, 198
模 mó 51, 64, 79, 82, 83, 100, 103, 128, 151, 155
磨 mó 157, 158, 169, 179
膜 (†) mó 126, 192
谟 (*) mó 171
魔 mó 167, 172, 179
抹 mǒ 165, 189
万 (†) mò 13, 20, 22, 36, 58, 85, 89, 93, 163, 185, 189
墨 mò 198
寞 mò 86
抹 mò 165, 189
末 mò 21, 167, 192
没 (†) mò 3, 6, 12, 94, 152, 155, 165, 195, 197
沫 mò 129, 195
漠 mò 75
磨 mò 157, 158, 169, 179
秣 (*) mò 97
脉 mò 164, 166, 173, 182, 198
莫 mò 175, 180
陌 mò 78
默 mò 42, 86, 139, 166
谋 móu 141, 144, 163, 168, 177
某 (†) mǒu 49
模 mú 51, 64, 79, 82, 83, 100, 103, 128, 151, 155
亩 (*) mǔ 4
姆 mǔ 142
姥 mǔ 97
母 mǔ 33, 39, 176, 187, 190, 191
募 (*) mù 159
墓 mù 184
幕 mù 62, 84, 90, 96, 136, 139, 161
慕 mù 44
木 mù 95, 160, 169, 180, 196

沐 mù 157
牧 mù 149, 150
目 mù 18, 31, 43, 48, 50, 76, 78, 90, 93, 112, 119, 128, 132, 147, 148, 161, 165, 168, 185
睦 mù 167
穆 (*) mù 38
拿 (†) ná 16, 20, 147, 181, 197
哪 (†) nǎ 5, 6, 10, 21, 66, 78, 92
那 (†) nǎ 3, 4, 6, 10, 17, 39, 72, 122, 184
娜 (*) nà 72
纳 nà 113, 116, 120, 141, 144, 150, 154, 196, 198
那 (†) nà 3, 4, 6, 10, 17, 39, 72, 122, 184
钠 (*) nà 141
哪 (†) na 5, 6, 10, 21, 66, 78, 92
乃 (*) nǎi 72, 110
奶 nǎi 10, 22, 47, 140
奈 nài 73, 181
耐 nài 42, 96, 180, 182
南 (†) nán 15, 18, 20, 23, 38, 42, 44, 64, 66, 68, 74, 76, 84, 93, 98, 110, 118, 119, 120, 133, 135, 142, 145, 156, 167, 168, 169, 170, 185, 191, 193
楠 (*) nán 11
男 nán 10, 62, 67, 126, 142
难 (†) nán 15, 20, 23, 29, 33, 40, 44, 45, 69, 89, 92, 118, 128, 129, 135, 137, 172, 181, 186, 190
难 (†) nàn 15, 20, 23, 29, 33, 40, 44, 45, 69, 89, 92, 118, 128, 129, 135, 137, 172, 181, 186, 190
囊 (*) náng 152

挠 náo 170, 183
恼 nǎo 43, 190
脑 nǎo 5, 81, 89, 98, 197
闹 nào 41, 192
讷 (*) nè 187
呢 (†) ne 3
哪 (†) něi 5, 6, 10, 21, 66, 78, 92
内 (†) nèi 25, 27, 33, 35, 36, 39, 40, 68, 85, 108, 110, 111, 123, 131, 134, 156, 161, 190
嫩 (†) nèn 79
能 (†) néng 2, 3, 8, 12, 16, 18, 21, 26, 32, 40, 41, 50, 53, 63, 67, 71, 81, 93, 105, 106, 108, 112, 121, 127, 128, 135, 150, 157, 158, 161, 167, 181, 185
呢 (†) nī 3
妮 (*) nī 81
倪 (*) ní 144
呢 (†) ní 3
尼 (*) ní 37, 92, 125, 158, 172, 192
泥 ní 120, 170
你 (†) nǐ 2, 5, 147
拟 nǐ 147
泥 nì 120, 170
腻 nì 179
逆 (*) nì 22
年 (†) nián 1, 3, 4, 5, 8, 9, 10, 11, 17, 19, 21, 33, 34, 36, 55, 57, 59, 63, 69, 70, 73, 77, 79, 80, 82, 85, 87, 93, 100, 103, 108, 111, 117, 118, 119, 124, 128, 129, 131, 134, 141, 147, 152, 162, 167, 168, 171, 174, 181, 187, 188
粘 nián 93
碾 (*) niǎn 167

I-22

Index

念 niàn 59, 61, 62, 85, 95, 110, 119, 149, 150, 169, 170
娘 niáng 81, 148
酿 niàng 134, 146
鸟 (†) niǎo 21
尿 (*) niào 151
捏 (†) niē 154
涅 (*) niè 44
聂 (†) niè 82, 90
您 (†) nín 8
凝 níng 116, 127, 150, 178, 183
宁 níng 93, 123, 135, 139, 155, 157, 159, 165, 196
拧 (†) níng 172
拧 (†) nǐng 172
宁 nìng 93, 123, 135, 139, 155, 157, 159, 165, 196
拧 (†) nìng 172
牛 niú 10, 12, 92, 140, 153, 161, 191
扭 niǔ 145, 162, 187
纽 niǔ 198
农 nóng 26, 34, 43, 51, 52, 87, 121, 126, 146, 163, 177, 178
浓 (†) nóng 73, 122, 184
弄 (†) nòng 40, 47, 89, 191
奴 nú 177, 198
努 nǔ 14, 38
怒 nù 79
女 nǚ 5, 6, 10, 57, 60, 69, 87, 88, 110, 126
虐 nüè 156
暖 nuǎn 46, 71, 166
娜 (*) nuó 72
挪 (†) nuó 160
糯 (*) nuò 188
诺 nuò 105, 111, 163
哦 (†) ó 133
哦 (†) ò 133
区 ōu 39, 49, 56, 57, 59, 60, 61, 64, 79, 82, 85, 89, 90, 99, 100, 110, 113, 122, 124, 125, 131, 142, 145, 147, 148, 150, 153, 157, 161, 171, 183, 184, 188, 191, 193, 194, 198
欧 ōu 102, 111, 125, 151, 162, 178
殴 ōu 163
偶 ǒu 42, 82, 147
呕 ǒu 156
趴 (†) pā 153
扒 (†) pá 165
爬 pá 24
帕 (*) pà 68
怕 pà 22, 38, 78, 85
拍 (†) pāi 57, 65, 105, 130, 143, 152
徘 pái 155
排 pái 30, 37, 38, 41, 75, 85, 95, 110, 118, 130, 136, 147, 149, 155, 188
牌 pái 74, 76, 81, 83, 95, 100, 154, 196
派 (†) pài 56, 63, 93, 135, 145, 173, 194
攀 pān 169
潘 (*) pān 11
番 (†) pān 111
盘 pán 23, 84, 86, 97, 147, 171, 189
般 pán 16, 91, 146
判 pàn 36, 66, 122, 123, 138, 139, 147, 184
叛 pàn 173
板 pàn 24, 39, 64, 124, 126, 153, 182
畔 (†) pàn 148
盼 pàn 91, 133
乓 pāng 44
膀 pāng 90
庞 páng 122
旁 páng 11, 149, 188, 198
膀 páng 90
胖 (†) pàng 22
抛 pāo 153, 192, 197
泡 pāo 129, 140
刨 (*) páo 175
炮 páo 96
袍 páo 172
跑 pǎo 12, 24, 157, 162
泡 pào 129, 140
炮 pào 96
疱 (*) pào 195
培 péi 55, 74, 100, 104, 153, 198
裴 (*) péi 87
赔 péi 66, 144
陪 (†) péi 40
佩 pèi 91, 92, 161
沛 pèi 160
配 pèi 60, 63, 75, 93, 102, 110, 119, 133, 134, 147, 160, 173, 180
霈 (*) pèi 191
喷 pēn 98, 183
盆 (†) pén 81, 176, 192
喷 pèn 98, 183
烹 pēng 138
彭 (*) péng 19
朋 péng 4, 41, 164
棚 (*) péng 11, 79
硼 (*) péng 173, 174
篷 péng 150
膨 péng 133
蓬 péng 173
鹏 (*) péng 36
捧 (†) pěng 140, 189
碰 pèng 97
丕 (*) pī 186
劈 (†) pī 176
匹 (†) pī 86
坯 (*) pī 176
批 pī 36, 57, 65, 107, 119, 140, 147
披 (†) pī 81, 118
啤 pí 19, 47, 83
疲 pí 75, 154, 182
皮 pí 36, 46, 91, 92, 94, 96, 163
脾 pí 160
蜱 (*) pí 139
铍 (*) pí 188
劈 (†) pǐ 176
匹 (†) pǐ 86
否 pǐ 37, 52, 67, 73, 84, 155, 173, 188, 191
僻 pì 167
屁 pì 163
譬 pì 151
辟 pì 119
偏 piān 163, 166, 167, 173
扁 (†) piān 147, 148
片 piān 17, 19, 34, 76, 77, 81, 86, 89, 97, 110, 128, 140, 162, 168, 171, 173, 175
篇 (†) piān 32, 88
便 pián 11, 18, 42, 46, 111, 121, 130, 133, 198
匾 (*) pián 181
片 piàn 17, 19, 34, 76, 77, 81, 86, 89, 97, 110, 128, 140, 162, 168, 171, 173, 175
骗 (†) piàn 40, 45, 127, 146
漂 piāo 5, 172
飘 (†) piāo 79, 146, 176
朴 piáo 85, 142
漂 piǎo 5, 172
漂 piào 5, 172
票 (†) piào 9, 40, 72, 73, 77, 89, 98, 102, 112, 131, 166, 167, 177, 193
撇 (*) piē 186
撇 (*) piě 186
拼 pīn 126, 157
苹 pín 4
贫 pín 109, 112, 185
频 pín 59, 115, 135, 144, 147
品 pǐn 27, 30, 36, 43, 48, 51, 54, 61, 62, 65, 72, 73, 91, 94, 100, 105, 106, 119, 125, 128, 134, 137, 138, 140, 143, 144, 146, 149, 151, 161, 162, 164, 192, 197
榀 (*) pǐn 195
聘 pìn 38, 90
乒 pīng 44
冯 (*) píng 18

I-23

Index

凭 (†) píng 69, 152
坪 (*) píng 135
屏 píng 147, 155
平 píng 14, 17, 18, 28, 36, 42, 56, 61, 65, 81, 83, 89, 91, 98, 107, 116, 126, 127, 130, 133, 134, 137, 141, 142, 143, 145, 156, 160, 161, 168, 176, 179, 185, 193
瓶 píng 45
苹 píng 4
萍 (*) píng 21
评 píng 36, 38, 41, 55, 59, 77, 95, 105, 106, 115, 139, 164, 181
坡 (†) pō 117
泼 pō 43
颇 (†) pō 114, 149
婆 pó 186, 187
朴 pò 85, 142
破 (†) pò 34, 45, 66, 83, 92, 101, 114, 142, 188, 191
迫 pò 74, 124, 143, 146, 170, 175, 177, 195
魄 pò 170, 174
剖 pōu 174
扑 (†) pū 140, 175
铺 (†) pū 114, 137, 188
葡 pú 21, 36, 193
蒲 (*) pú 88
普 pǔ 23, 31, 32, 61, 79, 85, 110, 154
朴 pǔ 85, 142
浦 (*) pǔ 141, 157
谱 pǔ 197
蹼 (*) pǔ 95
堡 pù 161, 167
曝 pù 109
瀑 pù 144
铺 (†) pù 114, 137, 188
七 (†) qī 3, 64, 109
凄 qī 184
妻 qī 10, 112
戚 qī 42
期 qī 6, 9, 11, 12, 18, 22, 42, 51, 52, 62, 65, 71, 72, 85, 89, 109, 110, 115, 116, 121, 123, 126, 133, 135, 140, 150, 152, 156, 157, 166, 192
欺 qī 146, 173
漆 qī 159, 186
其 qí 14, 15, 20, 26, 36, 37, 40, 59, 71, 73, 119, 142, 144, 149, 157, 175
圻 (*) qí 180
奇 qí 22, 72, 82, 114, 120, 128, 162, 167, 183
岐 (*) qí 159, 161
崎 (*) qí 181
旗 qí 114, 132, 172, 180
棋 qí 96
歧 qí 130, 131
淇 (*) qí 6
琦 (*) qí 138
琪 (*) qí 21
祁 (*) qí 161
祈 (*) qí 143
祺 (*) qí 171
骐 (*) qí 148
骑 (†) qí 20
齐 qí 43, 94, 124, 156, 158, 194
乞 qǐ 188
企 qǐ 48, 70, 74, 79, 87, 108, 110, 152, 155
启 qǐ 83, 101, 135, 167, 175
屺 (*) qǐ 196
岂 qǐ 198
杞 (*) qǐ 180
绮 (*) qǐ 156
起 qǐ 6, 9, 12, 20, 21, 24, 29, 43, 51, 63, 89, 95, 119, 120, 124, 127, 130, 135, 141, 146, 147, 150, 162, 170, 195
巫 (*) qì 164
器 qì 68, 73, 80, 87, 97, 126, 132, 140, 142, 147, 161, 166, 167, 174, 187, 198
契 (*) qì 177
妻 qì 10, 112
弃 qì 37, 153, 181
气 qì 5, 6, 22, 37, 45, 70, 77, 87, 90, 95, 108, 121, 127, 128, 131, 132, 143, 152, 157, 160, 164, 165, 167, 169, 172, 173, 174, 176, 179, 181, 184, 189, 192, 193, 195, 196, 198
汽 qì 12, 16, 24, 76
砌 (*) qì 168
迄 qì 146
掐 (†) qiā 169
卡 qiǎ 45, 92, 153, 179, 192
恰 qià 151, 177, 185
洽 qià 124, 168
千 (†) qiān 9, 36, 91, 119, 138, 141, 169
牵 (†) qiān 84, 168, 172, 177
签 qiān 42, 76, 107, 108
谦 qiān 89, 182
迁 qiān 145, 160, 174, 181
铅 qiān 24
阡 (*) qiān 192
乾 (*) qián 143
前 qián 6, 10, 12, 17, 22, 23, 24, 30, 31, 35, 41, 46, 48, 60, 65, 70, 78, 88, 91, 101, 109, 113, 116, 119, 127, 134, 140, 151, 154, 155, 158, 174, 188, 189, 196, 198
潜 qián 110, 127, 152, 166, 167, 182
钱 (†) qián 3, 24, 41, 90, 97, 128, 146, 160, 188, 192
钳 (*) qián 185
黔 (*) qián 81

浅 (†) qiǎn 74
谴 qiǎn 146
遣 qiǎn 135, 181
堑 (*) qiàn 182
嵌 qiàn 150
欠 (†) qiàn 75
歉 qiàn 40, 46
纤 qiàn 128
茜 (*) qiàn 155
呛 (*) qiāng 177
将 qiāng 38, 45, 72, 104, 116, 129, 144, 168
抢 (†) qiāng 64, 116, 152, 157
枪 (†) qiāng 71
羌 (*) qiāng 174
腔 qiāng 137
墙 (†) qiáng 34, 154
强 qiáng 52, 53, 58, 60, 61, 64, 66, 68, 79, 80, 86, 89, 91, 108, 126, 130, 131, 143, 164, 195
樯 (*) qiáng 197
强 qiǎng 52, 53, 58, 60, 61, 64, 66, 68, 79, 80, 86, 89, 91, 108, 126, 130, 131, 143, 164, 195
抢 (†) qiǎng 64, 116, 152, 157
呛 (*) qiàng 177
敲 (†) qiāo 43, 171, 183
乔 qiáo 69, 95, 188, 196
侨 qiáo 124
桥 (†) qiáo 31, 36, 118, 151
瞧 (†) qiáo 92
翘 (†) qiáo 164
巧 qiǎo 44, 47, 83, 126, 185
悄 qiāo 84
俏 (*) qiào 179
壳 qiào 189
峭 qiào 178, 189
窍 (*) qiào 95
翘 (†) qiào 164

Index

切 qiē 31, 41, 47, 61, 63, 74, 96, 101, 129, 144, 154, 171, 178, 182, 193, 198
茄 (*) qié 158
且 qiě 15, 32, 166, 186, 194
切 qiè 31, 41, 47, 61, 63, 74, 96, 101, 129, 144, 154, 171, 178, 182, 193, 198
怯 qiè 189
窃 qiè 138
锲 qiè 182
亲 qīn 32, 33, 42, 46, 63, 66, 89, 127, 135, 145, 154, 159, 167, 191, 195
侵 qīn 86, 114, 120, 130, 176
钦 qīn 161
勤 qín 82, 89, 133, 141, 181, 196
琴 qín 47, 149
禽 qín 197
秦 (*) qín 18
沁 (*) qìn 86
倾 qīng 128, 135, 137, 153, 192
卿 (*) qīng 43
氢 (†) qīng 166
清 qīng 19, 41, 71, 92, 106, 112, 113, 120, 125, 134, 136, 143, 145, 155, 157, 179, 193
轻 qīng 17, 19, 38, 95, 118, 144, 165, 177, 180
青 (†) qīng 55, 62, 63, 67, 77, 80, 83, 126, 127, 175
情 qíng 24, 25, 32, 35, 37, 38, 39, 42, 43, 44, 45, 55, 65, 74, 76, 82, 90, 93, 96, 111, 120, 121, 123, 126, 133, 139, 152, 157, 169, 173, 176, 177, 185, 187, 197

擎 qíng 128
晴 (†) qíng 11, 192
请 (†) qǐng 3, 30, 32, 45, 46, 72, 118, 127, 159, 163, 196, 198
亲 qìng 32, 33, 42, 46, 63, 66, 89, 127, 135, 145, 154, 159, 167, 191, 195
庆 qìng 60, 64, 68, 79, 94, 127, 131, 137
琼 (*) qióng 79
穷 (†) qióng 40, 144, 190, 197
丘 qiū 156
秋 (†) qiū 19, 157, 180
邱 (*) qiū 75
仇 qiú 196
求 qiú 13, 59, 67, 72, 92, 100, 122, 125, 132, 141, 153, 162, 176, 195, 197
球 qiú 12, 28, 40, 43, 44, 63, 77, 78, 95, 112, 115, 119, 135, 138, 157, 159
裘 (*) qiú 86
区 qū 39, 49, 56, 57, 59, 60, 61, 64, 79, 82, 85, 89, 90, 99, 100, 110, 113, 122, 124, 125, 131, 142, 145, 147, 148, 150, 153, 157, 161, 171, 183, 184, 188, 191, 193, 194, 198
屈 qū 88, 185, 190
曲 qū 136, 141, 173, 178, 179, 181, 189, 194
祛 (*) qū 159
趋 qū 62, 147, 190
驱 qū 178, 195
渠 qú 101, 187
瞿 (*) qú 24
衢 (*) qú 178
取 (†) qǔ 34, 53, 62, 63, 73, 74, 75, 84, 90, 97, 116, 132, 133,

144, 148, 150, 160, 178, 192, 195
娶 (†) qǔ 90
曲 qǔ 136, 141, 173, 178, 179, 181, 189, 194
去 (†) qù 2, 8, 12, 16, 37, 68, 74, 124, 133, 183
趣 qù 20, 41, 124, 133, 143, 173, 194
圈 (†) quān 59, 85, 195
全 quán 26, 28, 29, 30, 35, 37, 39, 40, 44, 46, 49, 63, 69, 71, 75, 78, 81, 88, 93, 103, 104, 109, 114, 116, 124, 128, 130, 143, 152, 156, 166, 168, 174, 176, 179, 183
拳 quán 96, 172
权 quán 58, 60, 72, 75, 77, 84, 85, 93, 97, 105, 111, 114, 120, 123, 125, 136, 141, 154, 156, 159, 173, 191
泉 quán 87, 144, 178, 184
铨 (*) quán 96
犬 (†) quǎn 146, 174
券 quàn 136, 141, 155, 188
劝 (†) quàn 77, 190
缺 quē 39, 43, 61, 130, 133, 138, 162
瘸 (†) qué 193
却 (†) què 26, 162, 197
确 què 32, 35, 51, 54, 66, 69, 90, 92, 100, 113, 140, 154, 184
群 (†) qún 30, 34, 64, 99, 136, 152
裙 qún 23
儿 r 5, 6, 22, 31, 66, 98, 126, 141, 146, 151, 190, 192, 194, 197, 198

然 rán 15, 16, 17, 18, 20, 29, 31, 32, 38, 39, 43, 44, 47, 57, 62, 65, 74, 82, 84, 86, 98, 108, 131, 142, 152, 160, 161, 162, 167, 178, 180, 186, 193
燃 rán 80
髯 (*) rán 196
冉 (*) rǎn 152
染 rǎn 33, 91, 113, 148
嚷 (†) rǎng 96
壤 rǎng 130
让 (†) ràng 7, 69, 116, 177
饶 ráo 196
扰 rǎo 46, 77, 126, 150
绕 rào 55, 185
惹 rě 195
热 (†) rè 4, 5, 24, 41, 63, 68, 81, 93, 126, 127, 134, 150, 162, 184, 191
人 (†) rén 1, 4, 5, 6, 10, 11, 12, 17, 19, 20, 24, 28, 29, 31, 32, 34, 37, 39, 43, 44, 49, 51, 55, 57, 58, 59, 61, 62, 63, 64, 65, 67, 72, 74, 76, 77, 78, 80, 81, 82, 83, 84, 88, 91, 93, 101, 104, 107, 108, 109, 111, 113, 115, 117, 119, 120, 121, 122, 123, 124, 126, 127, 128, 129, 132, 134, 135, 136, 137, 139, 140, 147, 153, 154, 155, 157, 158, 162, 163, 166, 167, 173, 176, 178, 179, 182, 184, 190, 191, 193
仁 rén 195, 197
忍 rěn 86, 168, 174, 182
仞 (*) rèn 192

I-25

Index

任 rèn 27, 28, 29, 37, 41, 42, 57, 72, 88, 89, 91, 102, 110, 115, 117, 121, 135, 136, 145, 147, 156, 162, 172, 185, 192
刃 (*) rèn 181
认 rèn 4, 13, 15, 37, 65, 66, 71, 73, 92, 108, 109, 136, 171, 173
韧 (*) rèn 191
韧 rèn 176
饪 rèn 138
扔 (†) rēng 43
仍 réng 32, 151
日 (†) rì 1, 3, 4, 6, 11, 17, 19, 21, 31, 33, 34, 44, 62, 64, 72, 81, 82, 94, 97, 106, 135, 138, 139, 150, 155, 158, 171, 178, 192
容 róng 17, 27, 78, 124, 126, 128, 135, 141, 147, 158, 170, 174, 176, 188, 195, 197
嵘 (*) róng 90
榕 (*) róng 82
溶 róng 180
绒 róng 192
荣 róng 60, 62, 67, 73, 85, 90, 155, 175, 189, 197
蓉 (*) róng 130
融 róng 92, 101, 102, 104, 108, 145, 150, 168
揉 (†) róu 161
柔 róu 88, 163
肉 ròu 12, 68, 77
儒 (*) rú 141
如 rú 13, 22, 31, 36, 44, 50, 52, 57, 70, 82, 122, 138, 143, 145, 147, 151, 156
乳 rǔ 162
女 rǔ 5, 6, 10, 57, 60, 69, 87, 88, 110, 126
汝 (*) rǔ 138

辱 rǔ 149
入 rù 26, 27, 31, 32, 41, 42, 46, 52, 72, 75, 76, 79, 89, 113, 118, 119, 122, 128, 138, 144, 145, 150, 163, 181, 185
软 (†) ruǎn 37, 46, 61, 75, 96, 97, 135, 177
阮 (*) ruǎn 77
瑞 (*) ruì 18, 129, 156
睿 (*) ruì 84
芮 (*) ruì 175
锐 ruì 88, 147, 155
润 rùn 45, 63
弱 (*) ruò 69, 86, 122, 141, 147, 164, 188
若 ruò 115
撒 sā 187
撒 sǎ 187
洒 (†) sǎ 85, 193, 195
萨 (*) sà 20, 41, 156
塞 sāi 160, 176, 197
腮 (†) sāi 181
塞 sài 160, 176, 197
赛 sài 16, 69, 70, 120, 123, 140, 165, 171, 197
三 (†) sān 1, 5, 9, 11, 71, 73, 75, 90, 117, 126, 140, 164, 174, 178, 185, 186, 188, 198
伞 (†) sǎn 23, 165
散 sǎn 45, 129, 135, 154, 164, 165, 191, 193
散 sàn 45, 129, 135, 154, 164, 165, 191, 193
丧 sāng 133, 177, 194
桑 sāng 192, 196
嗓 sǎng 94
丧 sàng 133, 177, 194
骚 sāo 190
嫂 sǎo 188
扫 sǎo 23
扫 sào 23
啬 sè 195
塞 sè 160, 176, 197

涩 (*) sè 153
色 sè 10, 17, 32, 45, 59, 64, 71, 87, 100, 111, 156, 157, 175, 176, 177, 179, 185, 195, 197
铯 (*) sè 47
森 sēn 36, 196
僧 (*) sēng 154
刹 shā 155, 184
杀 (†) shā 68, 82, 96, 185, 189
沙 shā 42, 46, 75, 85, 95, 97, 120, 158, 159, 196
砂 (*) shā 70, 174
纱 (*) shā 157, 158
莎 (*) shā 76
啥 (†) shá 129
傻 (†) shǎ 87
厦 shà 129
筛 shāi 141
色 shǎi 10, 17, 32, 45, 59, 64, 71, 87, 100, 111, 156, 157, 175, 176, 177, 179, 185, 195, 197
晒 (†) shài 72
删 shān 82
山 shān 24, 39, 58, 85, 87, 92, 98, 108, 138, 153, 161, 164, 167, 168, 171, 173, 175, 176, 178, 182, 185, 191, 193, 194, 196, 197, 198
扇 shān 185
衫 shān 23
掺 (*) shǎn 152, 188
闪 shǎn 92, 157, 161, 183, 196
陕 (*) shǎn 85, 117
单 shàn 17, 19, 23, 47, 48, 74, 75, 77, 82, 86, 89, 91, 119, 166, 168, 185, 186, 189, 195
善 shàn 50, 53, 71, 86, 120, 156, 187
扇 shàn 185

擅 shàn 131, 138
汕 (*) shàn 94
禅 (*) shàn 149
伤 shāng 45, 72, 97, 98, 116, 171, 197
商 shāng 6, 10, 18, 38, 42, 46, 54, 64, 67, 69, 79, 87, 106, 111, 113, 114, 117, 120, 122, 134, 136, 141, 150, 151, 160, 169, 172, 180
汤 (†) shāng 34, 185
上 shǎng 4, 6, 8, 10, 11, 12, 17, 18, 20, 23, 24, 30, 33, 36, 37, 38, 62, 66, 68, 71, 79, 86, 88, 98, 104, 108, 109, 115, 116, 118, 124, 127, 128, 130, 132, 136, 137, 144, 147, 148, 153, 158, 162, 180, 184, 188, 189, 190, 197, 198
赏 shǎng 69, 192, 193
上 shàng 4, 6, 8, 10, 11, 12, 17, 18, 20, 23, 24, 30, 33, 36, 37, 38, 62, 66, 68, 71, 79, 86, 88, 98, 104, 108, 109, 115, 116, 118, 124, 127, 128, 130, 132, 136, 137, 144, 147, 148, 153, 158, 162, 180, 184, 188, 189, 190, 197, 198
尚 shàng 60, 66, 131
捎 (†) shāo 183
梢 (†) shāo 188
烧 shāo 23, 80
稍 shāo 44
勺 sháo 97
少 (†) shǎo 3, 4, 30, 34, 39, 43, 63, 69, 70, 71, 86, 114, 136
召 shào 51, 95, 122, 125
哨 (†) shào 161

I-26

Index

少 (†) shào 3, 4, 30, 34, 39, 43, 63, 69, 70, 71, 86, 114, 136
绍 shào 8, 95
邵 (*) shào 21
奢 shē 143
折 shé 43, 96, 136, 150, 153, 154, 157, 159, 178, 183
舌 shé 94, 186
蛇 (†) shé 79, 197
舍 shě 78, 91, 172, 182
射 shè 87, 96, 112, 132, 140, 159, 171, 177
摄 shè 68, 73, 105, 128, 139, 160, 169, 184, 193
涉 shè 101, 156, 168
社 shè 25, 36, 38, 55, 59, 65, 99, 103, 105, 125, 126, 132, 134, 136, 149, 159, 164, 165, 178
舍 shè 78, 91, 172, 182
设 shè 48, 49, 54, 55, 58, 71, 73, 102, 103, 136, 156, 160, 183
谁 (†) shéi 4
伸 (†) shēn 82, 111
参 shēn 14, 33, 47, 50, 65, 83, 84, 115, 127, 163
呻 shēn 186
深 (†) shēn 31, 40, 44, 58, 76, 111, 124, 125, 149, 174, 176, 182, 183, 187, 192
申 shēn 30, 44, 106, 127, 134, 144, 159
砷 (*) shēn 147
绅 shēn 180
莘 (*) shēn 84
身 shēn 9, 21, 31, 41, 45, 47, 61, 76, 78, 83, 86, 87, 93, 95, 104, 109, 115, 123, 130, 131, 135, 137, 138, 151, 166, 175, 179, 183, 187, 196

什 shén 2, 6, 9, 67, 136, 141, 162
神 shén 26, 72, 77, 83, 88, 97, 128, 136, 142, 153, 157, 159, 168, 174, 177, 185, 186, 187, 192, 197
审 shěn 107, 111, 113, 115, 120, 123, 137, 154, 175, 180
沈 (*) shěn 5, 68, 141
慎 shèn 75, 144, 196
渗 shèn 128
甚 shèn 27
肾 (*) shèn 40, 92
升 (†) shēng 60, 62, 84, 134, 148, 169
声 shēng 19, 81, 97, 98, 106, 132, 133, 143, 152, 164, 183, 187
牲 shēng 114, 157
生 shēng 3, 4, 5, 6, 11, 12, 22, 26, 30, 32, 35, 36, 38, 42, 44, 46, 47, 48, 52, 59, 62, 67, 68, 72, 74, 77, 78, 79, 80, 83, 90, 100, 109, 112, 120, 122, 125, 126, 128, 132, 135, 136, 139, 141, 142, 147, 165, 167, 172, 184, 185, 192, 193, 195, 197, 198
绳 shéng 92
省 (†) shěng 25, 30, 35, 62, 66, 67, 76, 78, 97, 108, 112, 115, 117, 118, 120, 127, 133, 140, 146, 185
乘 shèng 39, 169, 176, 198
剩 (†) shèng 42, 83, 125
圣 shèng 136, 143, 167, 189
晟 (*) shèng 183

盛 (†) shèng 107, 145, 149, 165, 169, 178, 180, 185, 192
胜 shèng 62, 93, 169, 184, 187
失 shī 39, 41, 42, 46, 61, 68, 74, 88, 97, 128, 133, 138, 162, 164, 178, 182, 183
尸 shī 146
师 shī 4, 11, 18, 34, 41, 70, 71, 73, 82, 112, 122, 124, 198
施 shī 51, 55, 58, 59, 89, 99, 156, 167
湿 shī 45, 169
狮 shī 171
诗 (†) shī 62, 80, 144, 175
什 shí 2, 6, 9, 67, 136, 141, 162
十 (†) shí 3, 4, 5, 6, 10, 19, 21, 29, 71, 73, 108, 109, 114, 122, 126, 130, 137, 139, 148, 163, 185
实 shí 15, 20, 21, 28, 32, 33, 35, 43, 45, 48, 52, 53, 56, 60, 67, 70, 74, 82, 86, 93, 94, 95, 96, 99, 101, 104, 106, 107, 113, 116, 117, 118, 122, 125, 132, 134, 135, 137, 139, 142, 145, 150, 151, 157, 194
拾 shí 45
时 shí 3, 7, 9, 28, 29, 36, 39, 42, 45, 47, 48, 52, 60, 67, 68, 69, 74, 81, 86, 92, 96, 114, 117, 122, 125, 128, 136, 137, 139, 140, 141, 145, 148, 149, 151, 164, 172, 179, 187, 189, 192
石 shí 80, 85, 92, 104, 122, 141, 154, 158, 166, 169, 174, 175, 186, 188

蚀 shí 139
识 shí 4, 19, 30, 58, 78, 102, 136, 151, 194
食 shí 27, 30, 61, 64, 69, 91, 108, 111, 177, 192, 198
使 (†) shǐ 13, 18, 22, 23, 26, 33, 43, 44, 74, 98, 107, 129, 187, 195
史 shǐ 13, 73, 110, 118, 140, 146, 173
始 shǐ 7, 54, 125, 135
矢 (*) shǐ 81, 162
驶 shǐ 68, 75
世 shì 13, 24, 32, 35, 37, 38, 74, 91, 98, 114, 129, 137, 142, 143, 147, 151, 154, 167, 185, 186, 188, 192
事 shì 20, 42, 55, 57, 58, 60, 65, 69, 74, 76, 77, 81, 85, 96, 99, 100, 102, 104, 108, 110, 113, 114, 117, 119, 123, 125, 131, 141, 149, 154, 164, 167, 168, 177, 186, 187, 190
仕 (*) shì 71
势 shì 50, 55, 62, 78, 86, 124, 132, 138, 156, 159, 164, 175, 176
士 shì 34, 40, 41, 60, 77, 82, 88, 92, 101, 129, 133, 135, 160, 164, 172, 180
室 shì 12, 16, 23, 74, 80, 144
市 shì 13, 16, 17, 18, 21, 25, 29, 31, 34, 36, 44, 46, 60, 67, 68, 69, 76, 77, 87, 94, 109, 113, 115, 116, 120, 121, 124, 131, 133, 135, 141,

I-27

Index

146, 147, 150, 151, 154, 158, 165, 174, 180, 181, 184, 189, 196
式 shì 28, 45, 48, 52, 62, 79, 84, 88, 95, 100, 102, 113, 137, 141, 162, 165, 173
是 (†) shì 1, 3, 6, 8, 10, 14, 16, 17, 18, 33, 35, 37, 38, 39, 42, 52, 63, 66, 72, 76, 77, 114, 117, 125, 143, 145, 146, 171
柿 shì 42
氏 shì 139, 160, 193
示 shì 13, 51, 101, 112, 116, 135, 144, 150, 152, 163, 176
视 shì 3, 6, 28, 40, 59, 65, 73, 95, 109, 116, 121, 129, 131, 143, 150, 155, 164, 174, 180, 183, 189, 191
誓 shì 143, 190
试 shì 9, 10, 12, 57, 86, 90, 108, 111, 113, 122, 127, 150, 190
弑 (*) shì 183
适 shì 33, 34, 39, 71, 112, 133, 139, 140, 172
逝 shì 142
释 shì 33, 116, 165, 185
饰 shì 67, 80, 170, 174
收 shōu 26, 31, 35, 36, 40, 45, 47, 62, 65, 71, 72, 79, 91, 94, 106, 109, 111, 114, 116, 117, 142, 143, 145, 149, 167, 172, 173, 191
熟 shóu 35, 37, 83, 150
守 shǒu 69, 86, 140, 151, 156, 160, 178
手 shǒu 8, 11, 17, 24, 41, 42, 64, 65, 66, 75, 79, 84, 93, 96, 97, 116, 117, 128,

130, 139, 144, 145, 147, 156, 158, 160, 163, 168, 172, 174, 175, 179, 181, 185, 188, 189, 194, 197
首 shǒu 29, 31, 34, 41, 42, 45, 46, 72, 89, 116, 129, 132, 135, 136, 140, 145, 155, 175, 185, 186, 196
兽 shòu 197
受 shòu 27, 39, 40, 43, 44, 45, 54, 56, 60, 70, 72, 74, 116, 117, 118, 120, 135, 154, 161, 168, 175, 195
售 shòu 46, 50, 67, 69, 86, 164, 174
寿 shòu 80, 137, 186
授 shòu 30, 111, 139, 147, 156
瘦 (†) shòu 21
书 (†) shū 3, 5, 20, 33, 39, 63, 73, 74, 78, 95, 99, 101, 106, 117, 118, 121, 124, 130, 155, 159, 169, 173
叔 shū 23
抒 shū 188
梳 shū 98, 130
殊 shū 56, 155
淑 (*) shū 21
疏 shū 172, 191, 192
舒 shū 23, 71, 157, 182, 192
蔬 shū 61
输 (†) shū 37, 58, 76, 133, 181
孰 (*) shú 159
熟 shú 35, 37, 83, 150
属 shǔ 56, 65, 69, 73, 77, 113, 121, 125, 127, 137, 156, 157, 162
数 shǔ 22, 31, 32, 42, 54, 69, 71, 81, 84, 90, 109, 110, 112, 125, 131, 140, 162, 165, 170, 173, 196

暑 shǔ 47
署 shǔ 102, 108, 111
蜀 (*) shǔ 135
鼠 shǔ 88, 89
墅 shù 116
庶 (*) shù 94
恕 shù 196
数 shù 22, 31, 32, 42, 54, 69, 71, 81, 84, 90, 109, 110, 112, 125, 131, 140, 162, 165, 170, 173, 196
术 shù 25, 27, 35, 36, 57, 65, 68, 76, 81, 132, 134, 160, 174, 176, 179
束 shù 16, 118, 154, 183
树 (†) shù 17, 89, 105, 152
沭 (*) shù 185
竖 (†) shù 159, 170
述 shù 87, 95, 104, 113, 127, 152, 170, 172
刷 shuā 23, 132, 188
耍 (†) shuǎ 160
刷 shuǎ 23, 132, 188
摔 (†) shuāi 88
衰 shuāi 137, 157, 170
甩 (†) shuǎi 87
帅 (†) shuài 36
率 shuài 62, 63, 81, 82, 86, 88, 90, 93, 94, 123, 127, 129, 135, 138, 168, 182
涮 shuàn 197
双 (†) shuāng 16, 47, 51, 73, 164, 173, 197
霜 shuāng 184
爽 shuǎng 171
水 (†) shuǐ 2, 11, 12, 14, 23, 24, 85, 86, 87, 91, 94, 96, 97, 98, 108, 120, 123, 130, 133, 136, 139, 142, 144, 148, 149, 152, 154, 156, 159, 160, 163, 173, 175,

181, 184, 188, 192, 193, 195, 198
睡 shuì 6, 176
税 (†) shuì 50, 62, 65, 67, 80, 116, 120, 125, 126, 190
说 shuì 5, 6, 32, 38, 42, 63, 70, 75, 84, 87, 94, 97, 98, 117, 140, 146, 166, 181, 185
舜 (*) shùn 140
顺 shùn 32, 43, 46, 84, 168, 174, 178, 194, 198
说 shuō 5, 6, 32, 38, 42, 63, 70, 75, 84, 87, 94, 97, 98, 117, 140, 146, 166, 181, 185
数 shuò 22, 31, 32, 42, 54, 69, 71, 81, 84, 90, 109, 110, 112, 125, 131, 140, 162, 165, 170, 173, 196
朔 (*) shuò 167
烁 shuò 161
硕 shuò 40, 128
丝 sī 70, 84, 145, 175, 185, 194
司 sī 7, 19, 34, 68, 104, 115, 126, 137, 140, 143, 170, 173, 178
思 sī 11, 50, 60, 63, 79, 85, 91, 108, 112, 132, 157, 158, 166, 169, 172, 177
撕 (†) sī 91, 190
斯 sī 180, 181, 184, 193, 194, 196, 197
私 sī 72, 77, 89, 95, 96, 135, 167, 172
死 (†) sǐ 34, 42, 110, 168, 173, 184
伺 sì 183
似 sì 62, 78, 87, 110, 130
四 (†) sì 2, 6, 10, 93, 116, 139, 148, 149, 171, 172, 188, 192, 198

I-28

Index

寺 sì 82, 195
肆 sì 156, 178
食 sì 27, 30, 61, 64, 69, 91, 108, 111, 177, 192, 198
饲 sì 149
松 sōng 38, 72, 92, 190, 191
耸 (†) sǒng 188
宋 (*) sòng 10
讼 sòng 117
诵 sòng 174, 178
送 (†) sòng 9, 47, 75, 125, 131, 170
颂 sòng 145
搜 sōu 115
艘 (†) sōu 117
嗽 sòu 43
苏 sū 186
酥 (*) sū 157, 191
俗 sú 89, 122, 140, 152, 178, 190
塑 sù 45, 118, 121
宿 sù 78, 136, 172, 179
素 sù 55, 85, 102, 111, 112, 118, 132, 190, 191, 198
肃 sù 66
诉 sù 9, 63, 117, 122, 134, 163, 166
速 sù 31, 32, 37, 39, 56, 59, 93, 111, 137, 142
酸 (†) suān 37
算 suàn 20, 21, 22, 39, 61, 95, 96, 100, 124, 152, 174, 189, 192, 196
蒜 (*) suàn 86
尿 (*) suī 151
虽 suī 15
绥 (*) suí 89, 98
隋 (*) suí 45
随 suí 28, 33, 42, 69, 122, 123, 136, 141, 149, 151, 163
岁 (†) suì 2, 93, 96, 118, 134, 192
碎 (†) suì 83, 86, 160
遂 (*) suì 21

隧 suì 122
孙 sūn 85, 89, 138
损 sǔn 61, 92, 98, 109, 119, 135, 147
笋 (*) sǔn 150
唆 suō 198
嗦 suō 194
缩 suō 73, 77, 85, 136, 149, 158, 170, 198
莎 (*) suō 76
所 suǒ 8, 10, 11, 28, 37, 59, 62, 63, 65, 68, 77, 83, 85, 108, 122, 125, 141, 143, 144, 150, 157, 162
索 suǒ 101, 115, 118, 125, 144, 149, 166, 176
锁 (†) suǒ 78, 129, 152
他 (†) tā 1, 2, 14, 111, 194
塌 (†) tā 174
她 (†) tā 2
它 (†) tā 8, 20, 107
塔 (†) tǎ 61, 193
拓 tà 109, 171
沓 (*) tà 189
踏 tà 150, 180, 196
蹋 tà 191
胎 tāi 127, 173
苔 (*) tāi 167
台 (†) tái 28, 32, 36, 46, 65, 68, 73, 85, 86, 94, 106, 115, 124, 136, 137, 143, 148, 152, 156
抬 (†) tái 42
苔 (*) tái 167
太 (†) tài 3, 21, 86, 96, 130, 136, 145, 150, 164
态 tài 33, 58, 88, 100, 114, 115, 121, 127, 128, 139, 168, 177
汰 tài 117, 184
泰 tài 181
摊 tān 197
滩 tān 85, 163
瘫 tān 156

贪 tān 125, 154, 175, 190
坛 tán 100
弹 tán 47, 124, 144, 156
潭 (*) tán 135
痰 (*) tán 162
覃 (*) tán 84
谈 (†) tán 31, 34, 61, 66, 114, 124, 126, 143, 144
谭 (*) tán 71
坦 tǎn 94, 168, 177, 192
毯 tǎn 85, 183
叹 tàn 160, 195
探 tàn 101, 112, 146, 153, 159, 166, 175, 181, 193
炭 tàn 64
碳 tàn 148
汤 (†) tāng 34, 185
趟 (†) tāng 75
唐 táng 175
堂 táng 147, 165, 170, 190
塘 táng 179
棠 (*) táng 142
糖 (†) táng 19, 197
膛 táng 191
躺 (†) tǎng 41
烫 tàng 88
荡 tàng 151, 185, 189
趟 (†) tàng 75
叨 tāo 182
掏 (†) tāo 139
涛 tāo 188
滔 tāo 187
桃 (†) táo 71, 81, 164
淘 táo 117, 192
萄 táo 21, 36, 193
逃 (†) táo 75, 88, 157
陶 táo 103, 162
讨 tǎo 31, 46, 112, 113, 126, 158, 160, 182
套 (†) tào 56, 66, 93, 102, 195
特 tè 14, 30, 56, 59, 60, 64, 74, 76, 82, 84,

91, 94, 100, 121, 147, 151, 160
滕 (*) téng 163
疼 (†) téng 22, 96, 174
腾 téng 153, 166, 167, 188
藤 (*) téng 143
剔 tī 169
梯 tī 20
踢 tī 12
提 tí 13, 14, 26, 35, 60, 66, 69, 71, 76, 96, 112, 113, 116, 118, 123, 127, 138, 140, 142, 147, 198
绨 (*) tí 198
题 tí 7, 11, 12, 20, 68, 76, 81, 100, 104, 110, 113, 142, 166, 196
体 tǐ 9, 17, 18, 21, 32, 34, 40, 43, 44, 52, 55, 58, 63, 71, 78, 85, 87, 90, 94, 97, 99, 108, 110, 111, 115, 119, 121, 122, 124, 146, 147, 149, 167, 170, 172, 180, 188, 191, 195
嚏 tì 98
屉 tì 94
弟 tì 11, 69, 86, 146, 166
惕 tì 130
替 tì 41, 170
涕 tì 193, 198
天 tiān 3, 5, 6, 9, 19, 20, 23, 40, 41, 61, 73, 84, 85, 87, 88, 90, 98, 108, 119, 128, 130, 139, 145, 147, 148, 151, 152, 155, 157, 165, 166, 173, 187, 188, 197
添 tiān 125, 126, 197
填 tián 47, 137
甜 (†) tián 20
田 tián 91, 98, 121, 129, 169, 171, 173, 181

I-29

Index

钿 (*) tián 189
舔 (†) tiǎn 192
挑 tiāo 57, 169, 174, 196
条 (†) tiáo 13, 23, 24, 27, 60, 96, 118, 127, 175, 176, 179, 181, 198
调 tiáo 19, 21, 24, 27, 35, 50, 52, 53, 76, 90, 91, 96, 98, 108, 110, 116, 118, 139, 141, 156, 158, 159, 161, 168
挑 tiǎo 57, 169, 174, 196
跳 tiào 12, 170
帖 tiē 198
贴 tiē 93, 94, 96, 103, 140
帖 tiě 198
铁 tiě 20, 33, 58, 70, 72, 176, 188
帖 tiè 198
厅 tīng 70, 76, 98, 122
听 (†) tīng 4, 34, 70, 92, 94, 116, 135, 149, 170, 194
汀 (*) tīng 144
亭 tíng 189
停 tíng 35, 78, 84, 161, 180, 182, 189
婷 (*) tíng 126
庭 tíng 53, 122
廷 tíng 75
霆 tíng 138
挺 (†) tǐng 38, 175
艇 tǐng 156, 182
听 (†) tìng 4, 34, 70, 92, 94, 116, 135, 149, 170, 194
通 tōng 23, 24, 25, 28, 30, 31, 34, 37, 39, 40, 57, 65, 68, 69, 84, 112, 118, 122, 132, 133, 137, 140, 147, 153, 157, 175, 178, 192
同 tóng 5, 8, 18, 19, 20, 21, 22, 27, 38, 40, 44, 48, 58, 65, 69, 70, 71, 74, 78, 84, 95, 99, 115, 122, 127, 133, 144, 163, 168, 169, 170, 181, 197
肜 (*) tóng 88
桐 (*) tóng 163
童 tóng 31, 141, 163
铜 (†) tóng 69, 198
桶 tǒng 46
甬 (*) tǒng 140
筒 tǒng 187
统 tǒng 49, 52, 60, 77, 90, 97, 103, 121, 155, 162, 168, 179, 187
同 tòng 5, 8, 18, 19, 20, 21, 22, 27, 38, 40, 44, 48, 58, 65, 69, 70, 71, 74, 78, 84, 95, 99, 115, 122, 127, 133, 144, 163, 168, 169, 170, 181, 197
痛 tòng 76, 92, 182
通 tòng 23, 24, 25, 28, 30, 31, 34, 37, 39, 40, 57, 65, 68, 69, 84, 112, 118, 122, 132, 133, 137, 140, 147, 153, 157, 175, 178, 192
偷 tōu 90, 96
头 tóu 21, 23, 44, 72, 80, 84, 90, 91, 92, 93, 94, 95, 97, 98, 119, 122, 124, 134, 160, 172, 173, 175, 178, 179, 183
投 tóu 48, 52, 63, 112, 116, 142, 143, 144, 171, 188, 189
透 tòu 70, 82, 128, 136, 176, 178
头 tou 21, 23, 44, 72, 80, 84, 90, 91, 92, 93, 94, 95, 97, 98, 119, 122, 124, 134, 160, 172, 173, 175, 178, 179, 183
凸 tū 185
秃 (†) tū 191
突 tū 18, 54, 101, 114
图 tú 20, 21, 34, 63, 78, 87, 122, 123, 132, 152, 163, 169, 177, 193
徒 tú 156, 166, 195
涂 tú 93, 165
途 tú 77, 78, 86, 90, 108, 197
吐 (†) tǔ 79, 156
土 tǔ 51, 75, 80, 130, 145, 150, 162, 163, 176
兔 tù 90
吐 (†) tù 79, 156
团 (†) tuán 53, 65, 78, 88, 99, 103, 106, 111, 119, 125, 136, 155, 182, 193
推 (†) tuī 31, 45, 48, 56, 65, 70, 97, 134, 148, 149, 152, 153, 160, 187, 188
腿 (†) tuǐ 20, 164, 184
退 tuì 59, 97, 113, 145, 157, 170, 176
吞 tūn 195
囤 (*) tún 153
屯 (†) tún 75
托 tuō 67, 78, 80, 98, 110, 131, 153, 185, 186
拖 tuō 161
脱 (†) tuō 40, 126, 131, 180
陀 (*) tuó 185, 194
驮 (*) tuó 182
妥 tuǒ 120, 168, 187
椭 tuǒ 193
唾 tuò 195
拓 tuò 109, 171
哇 (†) wā 180
挖 wā 113
娃 wá 146, 197
瓦 wǎ 184, 190
袜 wà 46
哇 (†) wa 180
歪 (†) wāi 92, 173
外 (†) wài 8, 17, 24, 30, 32, 33, 35, 42, 54, 67, 68, 71, 77, 78, 81, 88, 92, 93, 112, 114, 116, 119, 124, 143, 146, 147, 153, 154, 155, 166, 173, 180, 186, 188, 192
弯 (†) wān 80, 97
湾 wān 167, 170, 180
丸 (†) wán 145
完 (†) wán 9, 14, 29, 50, 66, 69, 130, 136, 163
玩 (†) wán 9, 43, 77, 109, 191, 194
顽 wán 130, 175
惋 wǎn 173
挽 wǎn 144, 146
晚 wǎn 10, 19, 21, 84, 184
皖 (*) wǎn 12
碗 (†) wǎn 22, 98
万 (†) wàn 13, 20, 22, 36, 58, 85, 89, 93, 163, 185, 189
腕 (*) wàn 142
汪 (*) wāng 68
亡 wáng 110, 173, 186
王 wáng 80, 81, 188
往 (†) wǎng 32, 33, 82, 97, 107, 110, 118, 137, 143, 149, 162, 168
枉 wǎng 182
网 wǎng 18, 21, 27, 29, 30, 32, 37, 43, 72, 78, 88, 92, 99, 101, 120, 149, 194
妄 wàng 184
忘 wàng 20, 135, 152
旺 wàng 167
望 wàng 8, 42, 73, 91, 113, 117, 126, 131, 134, 142, 158, 159, 173, 175, 178, 198
王 wàng 80, 81, 188

I-30

Index

危 wēi 34, 65, 105, 108, 197
委 wēi 67, 72, 88, 94, 100, 101, 104, 107, 109, 117, 125, 156, 177
威 wēi 66, 111, 138, 160, 163, 165, 172, 173, 178, 182
微 wēi 44, 51, 75, 77, 157, 178, 181, 182
薇 (*) wēi 70, 176
为 wéi 7, 9, 11, 13, 14, 17, 19, 20, 25, 39, 48, 50, 63, 76, 78, 92, 110, 116, 117, 121, 124, 133, 135, 136, 145, 146, 149, 153, 172, 181, 185
唯 wéi 62, 172
围 wéi 28, 37, 55, 94, 108, 140, 143
圩 (*) wéi 85
桅 (*) wéi 98
维 wéi 53, 75, 109, 112, 115, 128, 172
违 wéi 64, 85, 95, 123, 138, 196
韦 (*) wéi 73
伟 wěi 55, 68, 91, 127, 164
伪 wěi 139, 150, 177, 186
唯 wěi 62, 172
委 wěi 67, 72, 88, 94, 100, 101, 104, 107, 109, 117, 125, 156, 177
娓 (*) wěi 90
尾 wěi 94
炜 (*) wěi 142
玮 (*) wěi 42
纬 wěi 180
苇 (*) wěi 172
为 wèi 7, 9, 11, 13, 14, 17, 19, 20, 25, 39, 48, 50, 63, 76, 78, 92, 110, 116, 117, 121, 124, 133, 135,

136, 145, 146, 149, 153, 172, 181, 185
位 (†) wèi 13, 18, 35, 39, 43, 45, 48, 57, 59, 62, 77, 79, 80, 89, 101, 102, 106, 125, 128, 129, 138, 155, 166, 185, 186
卫 wèi 80, 91, 109, 120, 122, 126, 140, 149, 165, 172
味 wèi 39, 44, 79, 103, 138, 143, 151, 152, 162, 168, 191
喂 (†) wèi 6
慰 wèi 88, 112, 138
未 wèi 50, 66, 71, 73, 80, 112, 180, 197
畏 (†) wèi 81, 89, 188
胃 (†) wèi 67, 92, 159, 167
蔚 (*) wèi 136, 181
谓 wèi 59, 68
魏 (*) wèi 37
温 wēn 39, 41, 42, 71, 88, 101, 108, 138, 145, 160, 171, 173
文 wén 13, 32, 38, 47, 55, 59, 64, 65, 77, 79, 80, 90, 95, 97, 104, 108, 109, 115, 148, 152, 164, 180, 189, 191
纹 wén 150, 198
蚊 (*) wén 156
闻 wén 14, 23, 47, 70, 72, 78, 115, 124, 163, 165, 185, 188
雯 (*) wén 134
吻 (†) wěn 84
稳 wěn 51, 73, 83, 84
紊 wěn 181
问 wèn 7, 11, 12, 24, 32, 64, 71, 72, 76, 81, 89, 112, 113, 118, 154, 166, 168, 176, 182, 192
翁 (*) wēng 140
窝 (†) wō 114
我 (†) wǒ 1, 3, 10

卧 wò 80
握 wò 42, 59, 60
沃 wò 179
乌 wū 187
屋 wū 91
巫 (*) wū 175
污 wū 33, 85, 125, 189
诬 wū 187
吴 (*) wú 4, 93, 179, 193
吾 (*) wú 80, 172
无 (†) wú 27, 30, 31, 43, 44, 45, 69, 73, 77, 79, 84, 93, 114, 119, 128, 134, 137, 145, 150, 151, 155, 159, 168, 178, 181, 182, 185, 188, 189, 190, 192, 193, 194, 196, 197
毋 (*) wú 93
五 (†) wǔ 2, 6, 33, 131, 194
伍 wǔ 102
侮 wǔ 149
午 wǔ 4, 6, 152, 178
捂 (*) wǔ 92
武 wǔ 68, 76, 81, 83, 96, 119, 141, 186, 197, 198
舞 wǔ 12, 36, 76, 117, 129, 188
务 wù 11, 13, 16, 18, 20, 23, 27, 38, 42, 51, 64, 73, 75, 78, 85, 87, 88, 89, 99, 103, 104, 106, 108, 112, 119, 125, 145, 159, 169, 190, 193
勿 (†) wù 144
恶 wù 78, 141, 146, 171, 182, 185, 187, 190, 198
悟 wù 159, 167, 193
晤 wù 136
寤 (*) wù 197
物 wù 18, 19, 21, 22, 33, 36, 38, 43, 58, 59, 60, 61, 76, 77, 86, 89, 90, 104, 109,

112, 119, 121, 127, 134, 145, 169, 177, 178, 180
误 wù 45, 67, 86, 93, 128, 131, 141, 171
雾 (†) wù 83
兮 (*) xī 151
吸 xī 31, 44, 46, 65, 74, 150, 178
夕 xī 93, 176
希 xī 8
息 xī 10, 18, 29, 49, 83, 95, 132, 185, 191, 194, 195
悉 xī 37, 63, 103, 158, 170
惜 xī 41, 77, 97, 144, 173
昔 xī 139
晰 xī 112
曦 (*) xī 158
析 xī 53, 135, 174
溪 (†) xī 120, 129, 150, 176
熄 xī 183
熙 (*) xī 43, 86
牺 xī 114
稀 xī 160, 181
膝 xī 162
西 xī 4, 11, 20, 23, 24, 33, 38, 42, 44, 46, 47, 64, 101, 108, 117, 118, 124, 145, 150, 170, 186, 198
锡 (*) xī 72, 196
习 xí 2, 18, 22, 23, 47, 70, 135, 152, 179
媳 xí 157
席 xí 51, 67, 72, 101, 143, 151, 162, 185
袭 xí 139
喜 xǐ 4, 137, 141, 165, 174
徙 xǐ 174
洗 (†) xǐ 10, 22, 24, 41, 83, 141, 163, 175
玺 (*) xǐ 175
戏 xì 15, 76, 141, 152, 167, 190

I-31

Index

系 xì 6, 13, 29, 49, 58, 91, 97, 98, 99, 101, 111, 137, 144, 159, 162, 171, 196
细 xì 34, 38, 42, 43, 64, 120, 125, 129, 147, 189, 192
隙 xì 178
瞎 (†) xiā 93
虾 (*) xiā 141
侠 xiá 141
峡 xiá 140, 158, 196
狭 xiá 153, 184
辖 xiá 134
霞 (†) xiá 115, 184
下 (†) xià 2, 4, 5, 6, 9, 19, 20, 21, 24, 32, 34, 37, 38, 66, 70, 75, 80, 113, 114, 123, 125, 131, 132, 133, 140, 160, 175, 190
厦 xià 129
吓 (†) xià 80, 165
夏 (†) xià 17, 37, 84, 123, 157, 175
仙 xiān 174
先 xiān 3, 17, 29, 44, 63, 81, 88, 91, 100, 107, 111, 121, 137, 157, 158, 163, 168, 178, 191
掀 xiān 120, 173
纤 xiān 128
鲜 xiān 20, 73, 83, 87, 114, 135, 146, 174, 192
咸 (†) xián 40
嫌 (†) xián 141, 142, 171
弦 (†) xián 150
衔 xián 124
贤 xián 192
闲 xián 60, 77, 95, 196
冼 (*) xiǎn 160
显 xiǎn 51, 52, 65, 66, 105, 123, 128
险 xiǎn 34, 36, 57, 63, 67, 70, 86, 174, 181

鲜 xiǎn 20, 73, 83, 87, 114, 135, 146, 174, 192
县 (†) xiàn 49, 94, 126, 172, 185, 187, 188, 193, 194, 197, 198
宪 xiàn 121
献 xiàn 53, 90, 107, 115, 132
现 xiàn 2, 6, 14, 19, 28, 32, 37, 48, 54, 55, 56, 67, 83, 84, 98, 99, 104, 106, 112, 123, 128, 137, 150, 179
线 xiàn 98, 106, 112, 114, 117, 118, 128, 137, 143, 151, 154, 169, 175, 184, 190
羡 xiàn 44
见 xiàn 6, 10, 11, 12, 20, 27, 68, 92, 97, 117, 121, 123, 148, 153, 163, 164, 165, 170, 185, 188, 194
限 xiàn 34, 35, 42, 77, 115, 119, 123, 139, 150, 151, 159
陷 xiàn 119, 130, 182, 185, 187
馅 xiàn 197
乡 xiāng 72, 102, 103, 111, 123, 134, 143
厢 xiāng 80
湘 (*) xiāng 70, 161
相 xiāng 17, 19, 24, 38, 40, 48, 56, 57, 58, 59, 68, 78, 79, 81, 91, 95, 104, 128, 137, 145, 154, 166, 168, 186, 190, 198
箱 xiāng 20, 24, 42
襄 (*) xiāng 136
镶 xiāng 150
香 xiāng 23, 98, 115, 160, 191, 194
庠 (*) xiáng 97
祥 xiáng 152, 184, 198
翔 xiáng 178
详 xiáng 34, 189

降 xiáng 30, 32, 39, 74, 90, 150, 166, 171, 172
享 xiǎng 56, 65, 69, 72, 160, 167
响 xiǎng 14, 18, 22, 23, 75, 123, 160, 162, 183
想 (†) xiǎng 2, 11, 23, 34, 50, 70, 86, 95, 111, 116, 136, 140, 159, 160, 162, 175, 182, 184, 194
像 xiàng 39, 73, 123, 130, 145, 193
向 (†) xiàng 13, 18, 19, 24, 30, 44, 73, 84, 113, 119, 132, 134, 137, 141, 153, 155, 167, 175, 180, 198
巷 (†) xiàng 131, 177
橡 xiàng 94
相 xiàng 17, 19, 24, 38, 40, 48, 56, 57, 58, 59, 68, 78, 79, 81, 91, 95, 104, 128, 137, 145, 154, 166, 168, 186, 190, 198
象 xiàng 37, 54, 60, 70, 73, 85, 95, 96, 121, 139
项 xiàng 48, 56, 75, 93, 110, 111, 125
削 xiāo 147, 170
宵 xiāo 177, 185, 196
消 xiāo 29, 31, 52, 63, 70, 74, 80, 82, 100, 111, 123, 125, 130, 133, 160, 174, 181
萧 (*) xiāo 143
销 xiāo 50, 60, 66, 67, 83, 112, 124, 143, 145, 152, 166, 168, 169, 181
潇 xiáo 176
小 (†) xiǎo 2, 5, 9, 21, 32, 38, 41, 61, 68, 69, 73, 75, 79, 81, 86, 90, 95, 96, 98, 108, 122, 127, 139,

148, 152, 153, 162, 169, 176, 177, 182, 184, 192
晓 xiǎo 153, 155, 185, 188
筱 (*) xiāo 94
啸 xiào 187
孝 xiào 174
效 xiào 29, 41, 45, 62, 67, 94, 104, 105, 110, 120, 136, 188
校 xiào 3, 19, 38, 59, 90, 96, 109, 117, 153
笑 (†) xiào 10, 43, 44, 77, 172, 188, 197
肖 xiào 145
些 (†) xiē 5, 8, 10, 17
歇 (†) xiē 87, 188, 189
协 xié 53, 56, 69, 78, 80, 100, 103, 106, 114, 158, 161, 168, 193, 196
叶 xié 45, 46, 192, 193
携 xié 127
斜 (†) xié 85, 128
胁 xié 66
谐 xié 100
邪 (*) xié 153
鞋 (†) xié 21, 92, 165
写 (†) xiě 3, 45, 78, 79, 80, 84, 123, 194
卸 xiè 182
屑 (†) xiè 172, 191
械 xiè 108, 161
泄 xiè 140, 151, 154, 173, 196
泻 xiè 146
蟹 (*) xiè 85
解 xiè 14, 22, 33, 58, 64, 70, 71, 81, 97, 111, 116, 127, 134, 141, 148, 157, 165, 167, 174, 180, 181, 184, 192
谢 xiè 5, 33, 149, 173, 178
心 xīn 17, 19, 20, 21, 33, 38, 39, 42, 43, 45, 47, 48, 52, 60,

I-32

Index

67, 68, 71, 76, 78, 81, 82, 83, 91, 93, 94, 98, 109, 115, 122, 125, 131, 140, 144, 145, 146, 151, 156, 158, 159, 171, 174, 176, 177, 181, 187, 190, 193, 194, 196, 197, 198
新 (†) xīn 7, 10, 12, 14, 19, 20, 23, 33, 35, 60, 64, 70, 72, 78, 80, 82, 85, 88, 99, 103, 109, 113, 115, 117, 124, 125, 129, 138, 141, 142, 145, 148, 149, 153, 158, 159, 162, 180, 188, 190
昕 (*) xīn 152
欣 xīn 69, 138, 175
芯 (*) xīn 81, 128
莘 (*) xīn 84
薪 xīn 154, 192
辛 xīn 40, 141
鑫 (*) xīn 70
锌 (*) xīn 138
馨 (*) xīn 87, 138
信 (†) xìn 16, 17, 18, 33, 37, 45, 49, 66, 69, 74, 80, 84, 91, 96, 97, 110, 114, 119, 123, 132, 136, 148, 149, 156, 160, 162, 173, 184, 195, 197
芯 (*) xìn 81, 128
衅 xìn 174
兴 xīng 5, 11, 20, 39, 69, 83, 111, 113, 116, 124, 161, 167, 170, 172, 182, 190, 192
星 xīng 6, 11, 61, 98, 126, 143, 159, 174, 184, 192, 198
腥 (†) xīng 170
刑 xíng 114, 131, 156
型 xíng 55, 59, 60, 106, 110, 118, 122, 128

形 xíng 49, 52, 54, 55, 78, 84, 89, 120, 121, 137, 165
行 xíng 10, 15, 16, 21, 24, 25, 38, 39, 49, 50, 51, 53, 54, 65, 67, 69, 75, 76, 84, 85, 88, 100, 101, 103, 104, 116, 118, 121, 123, 124, 127, 131, 134, 136, 139, 143, 144, 149, 157, 158, 163, 164, 168, 173, 183, 186
邢 (*) xíng 83
省 (†) xǐng 25, 30, 35, 62, 66, 67, 76, 78, 97, 108, 112, 115, 117, 118, 120, 127, 133, 140, 146, 185
醒 xǐng 35, 125, 164, 171, 186
兴 xìng 5, 11, 20, 39, 69, 83, 111, 113, 116, 124, 161, 167, 170, 172, 182, 190, 192
姓 (†) xìng 10, 34, 58, 120, 160
幸 xìng 31, 77, 85, 96, 158, 171
性 xìng 40, 42, 43, 45, 47, 57, 67, 69, 73, 75, 77, 81, 85, 91, 112, 113, 121, 123, 135, 136, 142, 144, 152, 158, 160, 161, 162, 166, 169, 176, 177, 178, 190, 191, 192, 196
杏 (*) xìng 147
行 xìng 10, 15, 16, 21, 24, 25, 38, 39, 49, 50, 51, 53, 54, 65, 67, 69, 75, 76, 84, 85, 88, 100, 101, 103, 104, 116, 118, 121, 123, 124, 127, 131, 134, 136, 139, 143, 144, 149, 157,

158, 163, 164, 168, 173, 183, 186
兄 xiōng 69
凶 xiōng 172, 178, 198
匈 (*) xiōng 155, 156
汹 xiōng 188
胸 (†) xiōng 74, 146, 176, 191
熊 xióng 21
雄 xióng 63, 91, 98, 141, 179, 190, 191, 193
休 xiū 10, 59, 60
修 (†) xiū 33, 41, 42, 46, 62, 63, 81, 84, 115, 119, 120, 122, 157, 163, 174
羞 xiū 46, 193
宿 xiū 78, 136, 172, 179
朽 xiǔ 171
嗅 xiù 181
宿 xiù 78, 136, 172, 179
秀 xiù 28, 144, 161, 180
绣 (†) xiù 126, 198
臭 (†) xiù 83, 168, 171
袖 xiù 119
锈 xiù 193
吁 xū 111
墟 xū 157, 191
虚 xū 89, 91, 126, 147, 180, 185, 186, 189, 198
需 xū 13, 88, 100, 125, 135, 183
须 xū 15, 95, 177
徐 (*) xú 4, 173
许 xǔ 28, 36, 39, 110, 116, 193, 196
叙 xù 87
序 xù 43, 56, 64, 155, 163, 179, 188
恤 xù 84
旭 xù 38
畜 xù 149, 157
绪 xù 65, 172

续 xù 27, 36, 40, 54, 57, 64, 66, 93, 117, 193
蓄 xù 155, 179
酗 xù 186
宣 xuān 50, 57, 67, 134, 138, 139, 143, 158, 165, 194
喧 xuān 190
轩 (*) xuān 137
悬 xuán 127, 170, 189, 197
旋 xuán 142, 156, 189
璇 (*) xuán 174
选 xuǎn 15, 19, 22, 42, 59, 61, 97, 105, 108, 116, 119, 137, 141, 161, 162, 184, 192
旋 xuàn 142, 156, 189
炫 (*) xuàn 87
削 xuē 147, 170
薛 (*) xuē 129
学 xué 2, 3, 4, 5, 6, 10, 11, 12, 22, 23, 24, 26, 32, 36, 39, 40, 41, 47, 57, 62, 63, 64, 69, 70, 71, 74, 77, 80, 82, 88, 89, 90, 93, 96, 97, 110, 118, 126, 130, 134, 137, 138, 140, 143, 148, 149, 153, 159, 165, 169, 173, 179, 189, 191, 195
穴 xué 173, 183
雪 (†) xuě 10, 128, 159, 180, 184
血 (†) xuè 35, 42, 89, 125, 134, 144, 154, 158, 160, 182
勋 (*) xūn 139
熏 xūn 162
寻 xún 65, 72, 178, 181
巡 xún 130, 160
循 xún 112, 123, 158, 163
询 (*) xún 192
旬 xún 96, 132
浔 (*) xún 192
荀 (*) xún 193

I-33

Index

询 xún 59, 64, 95
巽 (*) xùn 186
训 xùn 61, 74, 75, 100, 178
讯 xùn 69, 113, 163, 174, 175, 176, 188
迅 xùn 56
逊 xùn 182
压 yā 30, 42, 136, 146, 154, 158, 162, 164, 175, 180, 184, 192, 198
哑 yā 194
押 yā 182, 195
鸭 yā 85, 180, 197
崖 yá 189
牙 yá 23, 46, 156, 198
芽 yá 163
哑 yǎ 194
雅 yǎ 189
亚 yà 33, 42, 71, 86, 96, 111, 115, 124, 126, 131, 151, 154, 159, 174, 180, 185, 192
压 yà 30, 42, 136, 146, 154, 158, 162, 164, 175, 180, 184, 192, 198
娅 (*) yà 148
讶 yà 142
呀 (†) ya 40
咽 yān 195
殷 (*) yān 79, 191
淹 yān 152
烟 yān 44, 68, 72, 86, 124, 143, 186, 198
焉 (*) yān 83
燕 (*) yān 36
严 yán 29, 30, 46, 66, 80, 120, 128, 129, 130, 134, 137, 142, 159
妍 (*) yán 149
岩 yán 169
延 yán 72, 110, 111, 117, 131, 161, 166, 167
沿 yán 116, 117, 131, 169

炎 yán 150, 167, 186, 190, 191
盐 (†) yán 38
研 yán 35, 37, 39, 40, 43, 57, 62, 111, 113, 120, 126, 144, 163
言 yán 36, 62, 64, 115, 126, 146, 154, 158, 161, 164, 168, 174, 179, 182, 183, 191
闫 (*) yán 41
阎 (*) yán 23, 196
颜 yán 10
掩 yǎn 154, 155, 170
演 yǎn 18, 21, 33, 63, 81, 114, 115, 118, 128, 135, 136, 146, 149, 163, 182
眼 yǎn 11, 22, 46, 78, 123, 133, 147, 151, 153, 154, 185, 197, 198
衍 yǎn 184, 197
厌 yàn 46, 183, 187
咽 yàn 195
宴 yàn 87, 145
彦 (*) yàn 71
晏 (*) yàn 83
沿 yàn 116, 117, 131, 169
焰 yàn 171
焱 (*) yàn 172
燕 yàn 36
砚 yàn 93
艳 yàn 83
雁 yàn 151
验 yàn 28, 58, 67, 74, 94, 105, 108, 111, 117, 130, 151, 160
央 yāng 99, 101, 106, 116, 117, 124, 143
殃 yāng 189
扬 yáng 44, 116, 135, 146, 148, 159, 165, 187
杨 (*) yáng 3, 180, 191
洋 yáng 33, 86, 130, 190, 198
羊 yáng 12

阳 yáng 21, 35, 44, 68, 86, 94, 113, 119, 131, 141, 148, 167, 176, 181, 186, 193, 196, 198
仰 yǎng 119, 163, 197
养 yǎng 42, 55, 60, 67, 68, 69, 122, 124, 132, 149, 151, 162, 164, 183, 192
氧 yǎng 148, 167
痒 (†) yǎng 87
样 yàng 5, 6, 8, 16, 21, 23, 42, 67, 80, 88, 97, 112, 128, 131, 144, 153, 155, 169, 184
妖 (*) yāo 177
约 yāo 36, 37, 45, 79, 112, 117, 118, 120, 142, 151, 182
腰 (†) yāo 70
要 (†) yāo 13, 17, 18, 19, 31, 42, 63, 64, 76, 89, 92, 95, 97, 107, 114, 118, 120, 137, 140, 141, 164, 172, 175, 178, 179, 184, 186
邀 yāo 32, 134
姚 (*) yáo 20
尧 (*) yáo 136
摇 (†) yáo 78, 79, 91, 129, 173, 183
窑 (*) yáo 75, 155
肴 yáo 160
谣 yáo 146
遥 yáo 143, 177
咬 (†) yǎo 81, 97, 198
耀 yào 154, 157, 168
药 (†) yào 9, 19, 61, 62, 86, 167, 180
要 (†) yào 13, 17, 18, 19, 31, 42, 63, 64, 76, 89, 92, 95, 97, 107, 114, 118, 120, 137, 140, 141, 164, 172, 175, 178, 179, 184, 186
椰 (*) yē 91

耶 (*) yē 6, 196
爷 yé 22, 97
耶 (*) yé 6, 196
也 (†) yě 7, 36, 38, 117, 165
冶 (*) yě 90, 91
野 yě 91, 121, 141, 156, 172, 177, 194
业 yè 20, 22, 23, 27, 31, 36, 45, 47, 48, 49, 51, 54, 65, 67, 68, 69, 70, 74, 76, 79, 83, 84, 87, 93, 96, 99, 101, 102, 108, 110, 113, 127, 129, 137, 142, 148, 150, 151, 152, 169, 177, 189
叶 yè 45, 46, 192, 193
咽 yè 195
夜 (†) yè 67, 95, 144, 155, 158, 161, 178, 196, 198
拽 (†) yè 171
液 yè 87, 125, 158
烨 (*) yè 22
谒 (*) yè 183
页 (†) yè 39, 45, 120, 142
耶 (*) ye 6, 196
一 (†) yī 1, 4, 5, 7, 8, 9, 14, 15, 16, 18, 19, 20, 21, 22, 28, 31, 33, 34, 35, 37, 40, 42, 47, 52, 58, 62, 63, 66, 69, 79, 80, 82, 83, 86, 89, 91, 92, 93, 98, 106, 108, 109, 110, 112, 114, 117, 118, 119, 121, 123, 124, 125, 131, 132, 134, 135, 138, 140, 142, 143, 146, 149, 151, 152, 154, 161, 162, 166, 168, 170, 171, 175, 176, 178, 185, 187, 189, 191
伊 (*) yī 19, 180

Index

依 yī 57, 104, 107, 110, 115, 120, 121, 143, 181
医 yī 2, 4, 5, 6, 11, 17, 41, 56, 62, 70, 80, 85, 127
壹 (*) yī 146
漪 (*) yī 92
衣 yī 5, 24, 41, 141, 170, 176, 184, 186
仪 yí 102, 142, 177
夷 (*) yí 178
姨 yí 22
宜 yí 11, 69, 96, 124, 133, 157, 196, 198
彝 (*) yí 170
怡 (*) yí 78
沂 (*) yí 172
疑 yí 39, 76, 87, 142, 151, 189
移 yí 54, 71, 72, 84, 86, 104, 160, 166, 191
遗 yí 72, 108, 109, 146, 153, 164
颐 (*) yí 144
乙 (†) yǐ 81
以 yǐ 7, 8, 9, 11, 16, 17, 19, 33, 37, 39, 48, 51, 66, 70, 74, 106, 110, 114, 130, 131, 133, 135, 139, 143, 156, 159, 165, 170, 177
倚 (*) yǐ 46
尾 yǐ 94
已 yǐ 7, 113, 127, 132, 176
椅 yǐ 6
矣 (*) yǐ 132
苡 (*) yǐ 197
义 yì 55, 59, 64, 75, 88, 94, 108, 117, 128, 129, 135, 139, 140, 149, 153, 161, 165, 187, 193, 197, 198
亦 (†) yì 107
亿 (†) yì 25, 85
奕 (*) yì 139

异 yì 115, 116, 129, 158, 181, 185, 188, 195
役 yì 123, 145, 150
忆 yì 37, 70
意 yì 11, 17, 18, 22, 27, 35, 38, 39, 44, 55, 56, 71, 72, 76, 78, 85, 91, 97, 102, 103, 123, 127, 132, 138, 139, 141, 145, 147, 148, 149, 152, 156, 166, 167, 170, 171, 174, 176, 181, 187, 194, 196
抑 yì 122, 162
易 yì 17, 21, 59, 90, 102, 153, 157, 180, 191
毅 yì 160, 166, 197
溢 (*) yì 41
疫 yì 139, 148
益 yì 50, 61, 104, 105, 106, 111, 118, 133, 176, 178, 179, 181, 182
绎 yì 118, 162
翼 (†) yì 125, 176
艺 yì 27, 35, 36, 65, 81, 93, 109, 126, 151, 178, 179
艾 (*) yì 11
衣 yì 5, 24, 41, 141, 170, 176, 184, 186
裔 yì 87
议 yì 14, 51, 73, 77, 78, 80, 84, 96, 103, 107, 109, 122, 142, 144, 147, 158, 177, 193
译 yì 39
谊 yì 35, 187
轶 (*) yì 179
逸 (*) yì 82, 176
邑 (*) yì 158
驿 (*) yì 176
因 yīn 7, 27, 28, 39, 55, 72, 133
姻 yīn 66
殷 (*) yīn 79, 191
茵 (*) yīn 169, 192

阴 (†) yīn 11, 36, 44, 131, 151, 168, 196
音 yīn 17, 19, 42, 81, 134, 141, 147, 158, 160, 170, 188, 191
吟 yín 186
寅 (*) yín 167
银 yín 16, 24, 90, 195
尹 (*) yǐn 73
引 yǐn 29, 31, 32, 33, 43, 64, 67, 101, 128, 139, 172, 190, 192
殷 (*) yǐn 79, 191
瘾 yǐn 183, 189
隐 yǐn 109, 135, 142, 151, 182
饮 yǐn 35, 43, 110, 111, 133, 144, 187
印 yìn 37, 42, 46, 117, 132, 146, 151, 170, 171, 176, 190
荫 (*) yìn 152
隐 yìn 109, 135, 142, 151, 182
婴 yīng 126, 141, 190
应 yīng 14, 16, 17, 33, 34, 35, 56, 65, 80, 84, 90, 104, 120, 123, 134, 135, 159, 162, 166, 194
瑛 (*) yīng 137
缨 (*) yīng 46
英 yīng 63, 74, 79, 82, 91, 93, 125, 137, 179, 186, 190
莺 (*) yīng 181
鹰 yīng 135, 179
楹 yīng 89
滢 yīng 194
瀛 yīng 176
盈 yíng 117, 177, 184
荧 yíng 155
莹 (*) yíng 85
营 yíng 50, 56, 60, 62, 64, 68, 83, 95, 96, 175, 182
赢 (†) yíng 39, 72
迎 yíng 9, 70, 167, 183, 198

影 yǐng 3, 14, 18, 19, 22, 23, 68, 78, 88, 109, 130, 138, 140, 144, 151, 181, 184, 197
颖 yǐng 138, 152, 183
应 yìng 14, 16, 17, 33, 34, 35, 56, 65, 80, 84, 90, 104, 120, 123, 134, 135, 159, 162, 166, 194
映 yìng 29, 128
硬 (†) yìng 36, 47, 73, 94, 147, 169, 177, 188
哟 yō 197
哟 yo 197
佣 yōng 91
墉 (*) yōng 196
庸 yōng 178
拥 yōng 85, 88, 101, 133
镛 (*) yōng 24
雍 (*) yōng 157
勇 yǒng 42, 77, 122, 137, 153, 160
咏 (*) yǒng 148
永 yǒng 34, 38, 97, 138
泳 yǒng 11, 24, 98
涌 yǒng 123, 188
甬 (*) yǒng 140
踊 yǒng 138
佣 yòng 91
用 (†) yòng 13, 14, 17, 22, 23, 26, 37, 44, 45, 50, 54, 56, 60, 64, 70, 77, 94, 96, 97, 100, 108, 115, 123, 127, 132, 133, 137, 139, 144, 150, 156, 160, 163, 169, 180, 192, 195, 197
优 yōu 28, 32, 34, 41, 50, 59, 66, 79, 92, 107, 129, 131, 148, 179, 184, 188
幽 yōu 42
忧 yōu 156, 167, 193
悠 yōu 80, 146, 171
尤 yóu 37, 135

I-35

Index

油 yóu 43, 47, 73, 76, 91, 94, 104, 115, 129, 131, 133, 159, 179, 180, 191, 194
游 yóu 7, 9, 11, 12, 15, 20, 40, 74, 88, 114, 127, 139, 146, 167, 178
犹 yóu 89, 138
由 (†) yóu 25, 26, 61, 65, 90, 98, 111, 175, 183, 187
邮 yóu 23, 42, 84, 95, 160
友 yǒu 4, 18, 31, 35, 41, 82, 144, 153, 164
有 (†) yǒu 1, 3, 4, 5, 6, 8, 9, 10, 15, 19, 22, 28, 29, 32, 34, 35, 39, 41, 44, 45, 63, 69, 70, 71, 72, 74, 75, 80, 83, 85, 89, 92, 93, 97, 101, 111, 114, 115, 116, 117, 133, 136, 141, 154, 156, 157, 158, 159, 172, 181, 184, 188, 191, 197, 198
佑 (*) yòu 144
又 (†) yòu 13, 80
右 yòu 12, 24, 100, 181
幼 yòu 66, 141, 151, 176
诱 yòu 130, 155
釉 (*) yòu 154
淤 (*) yū 170
瘀 (*) yū 151
与 (†) yú 48, 50, 69, 73, 74, 84, 175, 178, 184
予 yú 101, 106, 111, 114, 138, 173, 180
于 yú 15, 17, 18, 26, 33, 38, 44, 45, 49, 56, 58, 62, 66, 67, 71, 76, 77, 101, 112, 117, 119, 122, 130, 132, 133, 138, 147,

153, 170, 188, 193, 195, 198
余 yú 71, 83, 88, 93, 97, 133
俞 (*) yú 42
娱 yú 57
愉 yú 42, 152
愚 yú 183, 191
渔 yú 137, 141
渝 (*) yú 42
瑜 (*) yú 144
舆 yú 103
虞 (*) yú 88, 98, 187
逾 (*) yú 71
隅 (*) yú 161, 195
鱼 (†) yú 10, 147
与 (†) yǔ 48, 50, 69, 73, 74, 84, 175, 178, 184
予 yǔ 101, 106, 111, 114, 138, 173, 180
宇 yǔ 87
屿 yǔ 147
禹 (*) yǔ 149
羽 yǔ 44, 192
语 yǔ 6, 23, 36, 42, 46, 74, 90, 96, 98, 141, 191
雨 yǔ 6, 39, 41, 45, 89, 95, 126, 130, 168, 194
与 (†) yù 48, 50, 69, 73, 74, 84, 175, 178, 184
吁 yù 111
喻 yù 153, 154, 164
域 yù 49, 73, 88, 100, 124
寓 yù 76, 149, 191, 193
御 yù 132, 141
愈 (†) yù 126, 146
欲 yù 142, 190
浴 yù 157
煜 (*) yù 171
熨 (*) yù 189
狱 yù 134
玉 yù 78, 125, 176, 192
粥 (†) yù 121

育 yù 17, 25, 43, 75, 96, 104, 127, 132, 134, 144, 153, 198
蔚 (*) yù 136, 181
裕 yù 119
誉 yù 62, 81, 120, 136, 143
语 yù 6, 23, 36, 42, 46, 74, 90, 96, 98, 141, 191
谷 yù 140, 158, 174, 195
豫 yù 89
遇 yù 18, 63, 101, 109, 181
郁 yù 167
预 yù 47, 57, 60, 81, 84, 86, 100, 109, 115, 128, 133, 148, 155, 161, 165, 168, 194
鹬 (*) yù 98
冤 yuān 182
元 (†) yuán 25, 35, 52, 76, 82, 85, 111, 116, 132, 157, 177, 185
原 yuán 28, 33, 39, 45, 55, 63, 68, 73, 94, 95, 120, 125, 134, 136, 137, 142, 143, 144, 187
员 yuán 11, 16, 24, 33, 45, 46, 49, 56, 63, 75, 76, 88, 90, 97, 100, 103, 107, 110, 111, 118, 122, 125, 140, 148, 152, 155, 159, 169, 193
园 yuán 17, 21, 45, 59, 66, 117, 121, 164, 169, 187
圆 (†) yuán 11, 117, 193
垣 (*) yuán 95
媛 (*) yuán 81
援 yuán 110, 111, 150
源 yuán 49, 53, 65, 76, 94, 95, 97, 100, 138, 139, 144, 146, 148, 150, 152, 161

缘 yuán 93, 140, 179
袁 (*) yuán 37
远 (†) yuǎn 9, 34, 78, 92, 119, 143, 146, 162, 163, 164, 165, 191
媛 (*) yuàn 81
怨 yuàn 132, 175, 179, 182
愿 yuàn 18, 22, 63, 70, 73, 74, 165
苑 (*) yuàn 69
远 (†) yuàn 9, 34, 78, 92, 119, 143, 146, 162, 163, 164, 165, 191
院 yuàn 2, 6, 10, 23, 32, 34, 37, 38, 39, 40, 41, 58, 67, 87, 99, 112, 113, 128, 130, 134, 140, 148, 153, 168
曰 (*) yuē 39, 46
约 yuē 36, 37, 45, 79, 112, 117, 118, 120, 142, 151, 182
乐 yuè 10, 17, 24, 57, 66, 71, 85, 87, 123, 133, 148, 165, 166, 192, 195, 197
岳 yuè 171, 187, 189
悦 yuè 141, 152
月 (†) yuè 1, 22, 23, 31, 36, 74, 75, 85, 90, 118, 145, 148, 158, 173, 177, 192
粤 (*) yuè 129
越 (†) yuè 16, 23, 110, 113, 115, 120, 124, 126, 131, 156
跃 yuè 69, 86, 98, 138, 163, 170
钥 yuè 43
阅 yuè 25, 46
晕 (†) yūn 90
云 (†) yún 16, 44, 64, 82, 118, 172
匀 yún 86
允 yǔn 36

I-36

Index

孕 yùn 127, 134, 144, 153, 156
晕 (†) yùn 90
熨 (†) yùn 189
蕴 yùn 154
运 yùn 9, 56, 58, 60, 64, 65, 68, 71, 77, 81, 83, 87, 90, 101, 122, 131, 145, 148, 174, 178, 186, 195
酝 yùn 134
韵 (*) yùn 134, 162
扎 (†) zā 110, 113, 134, 150, 159, 165, 177
咱 zá 41
杂 zá 33, 35, 90, 161, 175, 176, 185
砸 (†) zá 128
咋 (†) ză 154
哉 (*) zāi 146
栽 zāi 153, 182
灾 zāi 66, 90, 110, 117, 129, 131, 138, 166, 169, 173
仔 zăi 38, 92, 161
宰 (†) zăi 177
载 zăi 75, 93, 111, 112, 118, 127, 163, 192
再 zài 6, 10, 40, 90, 135, 158, 163, 164, 179
在 (†) zài 1, 2, 8, 10, 11, 18, 35, 40, 50, 63, 64, 78, 106, 122, 127, 129, 134, 152, 166, 172, 180
载 zài 75, 93, 111, 112, 118, 127, 163, 192
咱 zán 41
攒 (†) zăn 153
暂 zàn 39, 44, 76, 186
赞 zàn 81, 82, 92, 115, 133, 148, 160
脏 zāng 78, 82, 87, 92
赃 (*) zāng 189
脏 zàng 78, 82, 87, 92
葬 zàng 179
藏 zàng 98, 101, 106, 138, 154, 168, 184
糟 zāo 89, 191

遭 zāo 109, 120, 121, 189
凿 (*) záo 156
早 zăo 11, 12, 71, 113, 128, 147, 161
枣 (*) zăo 130
澡 zăo 22
噪 zào 141, 152, 166
灶 zào 191
燥 zào 42, 166
皂 zào 94, 98
躁 zào 179, 191
造 zào 32, 52, 53, 62, 67, 74, 75, 77, 79, 110, 118, 139, 146, 149, 153, 157, 158, 163, 189, 191
则 zé 37, 42, 46, 55, 64, 131, 143, 161, 168, 171
咋 (†) zé 154
择 zé 15, 188
泽 zé 190
责 zé 27, 28, 33, 72, 95, 121, 129, 146, 156, 181, 185, 197
贼 (†) zéi 154
怎 zěn 4, 5, 76
谮 (*) zèn 197
增 zēng 26, 27, 39, 45, 53, 66, 80, 81, 124, 125, 138, 152, 177, 178
曾 zēng 57, 91
缯 (*) zēng 150
综 zèng 50, 77, 93
缯 (*) zèng 150
赠 zèng 131, 175
扎 (†) zhā 110, 113, 134, 150, 159, 165, 177
查 zhā 15, 23, 24, 27, 46, 64, 78, 85, 90, 107, 132, 141, 151, 154, 165
渣 (†) zhā 155
扎 (†) zhá 110, 113, 134, 150, 159, 165, 177
炸 zhá 94, 123, 167

闸 (*) zhá 141, 176
眨 (†) ză 183
砟 (*) ză 184
咋 (†) ză 154
榨 zhà 192
炸 zhà 94, 123, 167
诈 zhà 127, 146, 171
侧 zhāi 139
摘 (†) zhāi 79, 137
斋 (*) zhāi 140
宅 zhái 111
窄 (†) zhăi 42, 153
债 zhài 136, 152, 159, 187, 192
寨 (*) zhài 20, 85
祭 (*) zhài 150
占 zhān 98, 114, 132, 133
沾 zhān 198
瞻 zhān 163
粘 zhān 93
詹 (*) zhān 87
展 zhăn 25, 29, 36, 37, 38, 60, 61, 99, 101, 104, 106, 109, 114, 115, 127, 130, 134, 156, 160, 181
崭 zhăn 125
斩 zhăn 188
盏 (*) zhăn 145
占 zhàn 98, 114, 132, 133
战 zhàn 57, 61, 79, 81, 82, 89, 91, 96, 99, 108, 113, 120, 122, 123, 134, 138, 145, 154, 163, 178, 180, 181, 194
湛 (*) zhàn 94, 142
站 zhàn 6, 27, 43, 75, 127, 152, 160, 166, 195
张 (†) zhāng 7, 34, 68, 70, 97, 119, 159, 164, 165, 198
彰 zhāng 105, 123, 189
章 zhāng 32, 85, 92, 123, 131, 163, 168, 189
掌 zhăng 45, 59, 190

涨 (†) zhăng 66, 71, 140
长 (†) zhăng 8, 9, 10, 11, 19, 20, 23, 26, 32, 34, 35, 38, 40, 59, 65, 68, 70, 72, 73, 76, 78, 81, 86, 91, 92, 101, 104, 106, 107, 109, 113, 118, 120, 125, 132, 136, 137, 138, 142, 143, 146, 147, 152, 154, 157, 163, 170, 172, 174, 188, 189, 194, 196
丈 zhàng 10
仗 zhàng 159
帐 zhàng 150
幛 (*) zhàng 197
杖 zhàng 187
涨 (†) zhàng 66, 71, 140
胀 zhàng 133
账 zhàng 70, 95, 143, 168, 171
障 zhàng 99, 105, 113, 124, 147
嘲 zhāo 188
招 zhāo 38, 67, 88, 91, 120, 142, 143, 175, 196
昭 (*) zhāo 126
朝 (†) zhāo 65, 73, 83, 95, 113, 119, 146, 173, 192, 198
着 (†) zhāo 7, 12, 23, 28, 32, 45, 75, 98, 103, 129, 130, 131, 133, 144, 159, 171, 184
着 (†) zháo 7, 12, 23, 28, 32, 45, 75, 98, 103, 129, 130, 131, 133, 144, 159, 171, 184
找 (†) zhăo 9, 10, 65, 79, 141, 181
沼 zhăo 190
兆 zhào 194

I-37

Index

召 zhào 51, 95, 122, 125
照 zhào 17, 19, 20, 21, 24, 27, 75, 81, 85, 94, 115, 127, 130, 137, 163, 168, 169, 170, 194
罩 zhào 169
赵 (*) zhào 9, 176
折 zhé 43, 96, 136, 150, 153, 154, 157, 159, 178, 183
遮 zhē 165
乙 (†) zhé 81
哲 zhé 70
折 zhé 43, 96, 136, 150, 153, 154, 157, 159, 178, 183
辙 zhé 197
者 zhě 15, 19, 24, 25, 31, 33, 38, 42, 43, 44, 62, 63, 66, 84, 90, 97, 102, 108, 112, 122, 129, 140, 146, 154, 155, 159, 166, 171, 176, 179, 184
浙 (*) zhè 129
这 (†) zhè 1, 2, 4, 5, 6, 8, 12, 15, 18, 74, 111
着 (†) zhe 7, 12, 23, 28, 32, 45, 75, 98, 103, 129, 130, 131, 133, 144, 159, 171, 184
侦 zhēn 193
斟 zhēn 185
珍 zhēn 77, 115, 153, 160
甄 (*) zhēn 147
真 (†) zhēn 8, 15, 29, 42, 43, 60, 78, 90, 128, 153, 155, 170, 179, 185
贞 (*) zhēn 23
针 zhēn 46, 54, 107, 183, 191
枕 zhěn 93
诊 zhěn 73, 77, 91, 92, 120

振 zhèn 93, 116, 136
镇 zhèn 103, 115, 155, 169, 179, 180
阵 (†) zhèn 69, 127, 135
震 zhèn 65, 143
争 zhēng 30, 61, 62, 63, 77, 81, 91, 107, 109, 111, 123, 158, 178, 196
征 zhēng 64, 67, 73, 109, 120, 125, 155, 163, 183
挣 zhēng 90, 159
正 zhēng 8, 10, 28, 29, 32, 41, 47, 79, 89, 90, 93, 107, 117, 118, 121, 122, 133, 138, 143, 157, 161, 164, 170, 172, 173, 180, 186, 188, 196
症 zhēng 115, 125, 198
睁 (†) zhēng 92
蒸 zhēng 160
铮 (*) zhēng 76
整 zhěng 37, 43, 50, 53, 55, 58, 60, 66, 124, 161, 163, 164
帧 (*) zhèng 172
挣 zhèng 90, 159
政 zhèng 48, 51, 56, 57, 60, 62, 64, 71, 73, 76, 81, 82, 83, 84, 88, 99, 100, 103, 108, 110, 114, 116, 123, 125, 130, 143, 153, 157, 177, 190, 196
正 zhèng 8, 10, 28, 29, 32, 41, 47, 79, 89, 90, 93, 107, 117, 118, 121, 122, 133, 138, 143, 157, 161, 164, 170, 172, 173, 180, 186, 188, 196
症 zhèng 115, 125, 198
证 zhèng 29, 33, 37, 39, 42, 67, 75, 96, 97, 107, 115, 117, 121, 122, 130, 136,

145, 155, 161, 164, 165
郑 zhèng 159
之 (†) zhī 25, 28, 30, 35, 37, 43, 45, 65, 66, 81, 96, 107, 129, 138, 145, 148, 156, 159, 168, 183, 184, 192, 193, 194, 197
只 (†) zhī 14, 15, 16, 31, 32, 41, 138, 162
支 zhī 26, 62, 75, 84, 89, 90, 102, 103, 105, 110, 126, 133, 150, 151, 159
枝 (†) zhī 123, 194
氏 zhī 139, 160, 193
汁 zhī 22, 193
知 zhī 30, 34, 51, 58, 117, 121, 123, 143, 150, 151, 155, 162, 168, 177, 183, 187, 192
织 zhī 25, 129, 159, 167, 183, 198
肢 zhī 171
脂 zhī 119, 133
芝 (*) zhī 69, 70, 88
值 zhí 34, 43, 53, 77, 80, 120, 129, 140, 143, 145, 170, 181
执 zhí 51, 53, 76, 81, 82, 85, 110, 144, 153, 183
植 zhí 38, 86, 152
殖 zhí 155, 184
直 zhí 15, 28, 68, 69, 82, 114, 132, 135, 148, 149, 179, 185, 194
职 zhí 31, 33, 40, 78, 85, 88, 103, 105, 106, 110, 127, 134, 140, 150, 153, 156, 160
只 (†) zhǐ 14, 15, 16, 31, 32, 41, 138, 162
址 zhǐ 38, 149
指 (†) zhǐ 30, 52, 58, 84, 89, 102, 110,

115, 116, 129, 130, 149, 159, 173, 174, 177, 185, 191
旨 zhǐ 112, 161, 194
止 zhǐ 35, 45, 47, 82, 107, 126, 133, 134, 136, 146, 165
纸 zhǐ 10, 24, 96, 163, 172, 191
制 zhì 32, 34, 49, 52, 53, 57, 62, 64, 67, 72, 73, 76, 108, 112, 117, 120, 122, 125, 128, 134, 135, 140, 146, 149, 151, 164, 169, 170, 172, 175, 177, 191, 193
峙 (*) zhì 183
帜 zhì 114
志 zhì 35, 58, 63, 70, 95, 99, 127, 162, 195
挚 zhì 142, 153
掷 zhì 188
智 zhì 64, 106, 129, 131, 169, 172, 182
栉 (*) zhì 194
治 zhì 51, 56, 60, 66, 76, 77, 82, 88, 102, 103, 108, 111, 131, 146, 156, 157, 178, 179
滞 zhì 151, 161
炙 (*) zhì 182
秩 zhì 64
稚 zhì 176
置 zhì 59, 63, 71, 77, 103, 113, 114, 130, 142, 145
至 zhì 27, 33, 34, 59, 66, 80, 102, 110, 132, 165, 182
致 zhì 53, 62, 66, 71, 85, 121, 125, 129, 132, 133, 136, 156, 161, 165, 168, 173, 177, 178, 191, 198
识 zhì 4, 19, 30, 58, 78, 102, 136, 151, 194

I-38

Index

质 zhì 28, 34, 39, 58, 69, 73, 78, 88, 90, 94, 95, 102, 105, 115, 117, 132, 137, 147, 162, 169, 177, 178, 195
中 zhōng 1, 3, 4, 5, 6, 11, 12, 17, 18, 19, 26, 36, 38, 39, 40, 41, 45, 46, 48, 53, 59, 68, 71, 74, 76, 81, 85, 90, 94, 96, 97, 98, 99, 100, 101, 103, 104, 106, 107, 108, 111, 114, 116, 117, 120, 125, 128, 132, 133, 134, 138, 142, 143, 150, 151, 155, 158, 162, 165, 167, 172, 175, 184, 193, 194, 195
忠 zhōng 118, 138, 151, 186
盅 (*) zhōng 194
终 zhōng 18, 30, 54, 112, 123, 136, 148, 162, 181
衷 zhōng 125, 138, 188
钟 zhōng 4, 12, 93, 153, 192
冢 (*) zhǒng 173
种 (†) zhǒng 15, 20, 28, 33, 62, 72, 75, 120, 165, 169, 170, 171, 172, 182
肿 zhǒng 113
中 zhòng 1, 3, 4, 5, 6, 11, 12, 17, 18, 19, 26, 36, 38, 39, 40, 41, 45, 46, 48, 53, 59, 68, 71, 74, 76, 81, 85, 90, 94, 96, 97, 98, 99, 100, 101, 103, 104, 106, 107, 108, 111, 114, 116, 117, 120, 125, 128, 132, 133, 134, 138, 142, 143, 150, 151, 155, 158, 162, 165, 167, 172, 175, 184, 193, 194, 195
仲 (*) zhòng 72, 192
众 zhòng 30, 35, 43, 58, 59, 99, 116, 143, 152, 163
种 (†) zhòng 15, 20, 28, 33, 62, 72, 75, 120, 165, 169, 170, 171, 172, 182
重 zhòng 13, 15, 24, 26, 28, 29, 32, 33, 42, 46, 60, 68, 73, 80, 81, 82, 90, 104, 107, 109, 110, 114, 133, 136, 138, 141, 143, 144, 155, 159, 161, 162, 165, 173, 180, 182, 184, 193
周 zhōu 21, 37, 38, 46, 87, 100, 105, 123, 132, 134, 143, 149, 156, 163, 178, 189
州 (†) zhōu 105, 106, 108, 117, 118, 122, 159, 170
洲 zhōu 33, 102, 115, 188
粥 (†) zhōu 121
舟 (†) zhōu 128, 147, 168
轴 (*) zhóu 82
肘 zhǒu 145
宙 zhòu 87
昼 zhòu 158
皱 zhòu 150
轴 (*) zhòu 82
骤 zhòu 79
朱 (*) zhū 4, 68
株 (†) zhū 133
潴 (*) zhū 195
猪 (†) zhū 32, 68
珠 zhū 153
诛 (*) zhū 165
诸 zhū 186
术 zhú 25, 27, 35, 36, 57, 65, 68, 76, 81, 132, 134, 160, 174, 176, 179
烛 zhú 96
竹 zhú 93, 162, 198
竺 (*) zhú 165, 166
逐 zhú 33, 44, 56, 131, 144, 178, 195
主 zhǔ 13, 17, 18, 20, 28, 31, 42, 44, 51, 55, 56, 59, 67, 68, 76, 77, 79, 84, 88, 89, 91, 93, 98, 100, 101, 102, 103, 104, 108, 110, 111, 119, 120, 128, 136, 140, 143, 148, 149, 161, 165, 171, 175, 187, 197, 198
嘱 zhǔ 89, 149
属 zhǔ 56, 65, 69, 73, 77, 113, 121, 125, 127, 137, 156, 157, 162
拄 (†) zhǔ 189
渚 (*) zhǔ 45
煮 (†) zhǔ 72
瞩 zhǔ 147, 148
住 (†) zhù 3, 17, 43, 86, 106, 109, 111, 136
助 zhù 9, 65, 66, 111, 114, 115, 117, 127, 133, 136, 147, 156, 159, 179, 196
柱 zhù 150
注 zhù 17, 43, 63, 104, 118, 140, 141, 145, 148, 150, 164, 165, 168, 174, 181
祝 (†) zhù 20, 22, 38, 60, 74
筑 zhù 53, 77, 176
著 zhù 30, 77, 105, 117, 157, 173
铸 zhù 153, 198
驻 zhù 177, 178
抓 zhuā 74, 106, 118
拽 (†) zhuāi 171
拽 (†) zhuǎi 171
拽 (†) zhuài 171
专 zhuān 27, 31, 37, 49, 56, 91, 96, 103, 104, 129, 132, 135, 136, 137, 148, 149, 150, 151, 161, 174
砖 zhuān 190, 192
转 zhuǎn 53, 59, 65, 76, 80, 84, 87, 97, 104, 112, 116, 131, 138, 140, 145, 150, 156, 164, 174
传 zhuàn 43, 49, 50, 52, 63, 65, 67, 75, 76, 78, 90, 91, 93, 95, 96, 107, 120, 124, 133, 137, 148, 153, 156, 158, 183, 184, 186, 192
撰 (*) zhuàn 172, 182
赚 (†) zhuàn 39, 41
转 zhuàn 53, 59, 65, 76, 80, 84, 87, 97, 104, 112, 116, 131, 138, 140, 145, 150, 156, 164, 174
妆 zhuāng 137
庄 zhuāng 134, 152, 154, 161
桩 (*) zhuāng 77
装 (†) zhuāng 56, 63, 66, 67, 71, 93, 96, 103, 107, 119, 148, 160, 174, 182
壮 zhuàng 144, 151, 167, 179
幢 (†) zhuàng 142
撞 (†) zhuàng 41, 196
状 zhuàng 58, 84, 88, 112, 115, 184
椎 zhuī 183
追 zhuī 59, 111, 144, 178, 190
锥 (*) zhuī 184
隹 (*) zhuī 24
坠 (*) zhuì 43
缀 zhuì 158
屯 (*) zhūn 75
准 zhǔn 9, 26, 35, 45, 57, 113, 131, 134, 149, 172
拙 zhuō 196
捉 zhuō 155, 197
桌 zhuō 6, 132

I-39

Index

卓 zhuó 124
浊 zhuó 191
琢 zhuó 158
着 (†) zhuó 7, 12, 23, 28, 32, 45, 75, 98, 103, 129, 130, 131, 133, 144, 159, 171, 184
酌 zhuó 185
仔 zī 38, 92, 161
兹 (*) zī 78
咨 zī 59
姿 zī 86, 128
滋 zī 151, 164, 165, 194
资 zī 30, 47, 48, 49, 55, 61, 65, 67, 70, 102, 104, 105, 112, 113, 114, 121, 124, 125, 138, 140, 152, 155, 157, 158, 161, 163, 164, 169
仔 zǐ 38, 92, 161
子 zǐ 5, 6, 8, 10, 12, 19, 22, 23, 24, 34, 38, 42, 45, 46, 62, 77, 80, 83, 85, 86, 88, 89, 90, 91, 92, 93, 94, 95, 97, 98, 110, 112, 120, 131, 137, 146, 151, 152, 153, 154, 156, 164, 171, 175, 178, 179, 182, 183, 185, 188, 189, 194, 197
梓 (*) zǐ 160
籽 (*) zǐ 45
紫 (†) zǐ 67, 186
字 (†) zì 4, 5, 10, 12, 24, 32, 76, 80, 96, 108, 154, 176, 191, 195
自 zì 10, 12, 13, 23, 29, 31, 52, 56, 61, 63, 66, 74, 75, 76, 77, 82, 86, 89, 93, 95, 98, 101, 108, 118, 123, 131, 139, 142, 152, 157, 167, 179, 181, 183, 186, 190

子 zi 5, 6, 8, 10, 12, 19, 22, 23, 24, 34, 38, 42, 45, 46, 62, 77, 80, 83, 85, 86, 88, 89, 90, 91, 92, 93, 94, 95, 97, 98, 110, 112, 120, 131, 137, 146, 151, 152, 153, 154, 156, 164, 171, 175, 178, 179, 182, 183, 185, 188, 189, 194, 197
宗 zōng 69, 93, 112, 161
棕 zōng 177
综 zōng 50, 77, 93
踪 zōng 115, 138, 180
总 zǒng 18, 32, 33, 36, 43, 54, 60, 65, 77, 79, 81, 82, 83, 95, 109, 110, 118, 120, 126, 137, 149, 161, 164, 168, 183, 187
从 zòng 43, 44, 57, 58, 71, 73, 75, 76, 83, 88, 120, 138, 151, 195
纵 zòng 149, 152, 170
邹 (*) zōu 80, 197
走 (†) zǒu 8, 18, 34, 36, 47, 72, 78, 89, 113, 135, 136, 168, 197
奏 zòu 133, 149, 189
揍 (†) zòu 189
租 zū 6, 116
卒 zú 92
族 zú 29, 41, 71, 93, 106, 114, 125, 146, 153, 157, 171, 172, 182, 184, 187
足 zú 12, 56, 57, 78, 80, 92, 113, 115, 122, 130, 131, 165, 181, 192, 197
祖 zǔ 60, 88, 159
组 zǔ 25, 32, 66, 68, 72, 103, 116, 130, 142, 150, 159, 160, 167, 177
阻 zǔ 82, 136, 170, 185

钻 zuān 122, 163
赚 (†) zuàn 39, 41
钻 zuàn 122, 163
嘴 (†) zuǐ 40, 172
最 (†) zuì 7, 10, 12, 17, 19, 29, 30, 32, 71, 140
罪 zuì 92, 102, 177, 195
醉 (†) zuì 72, 155, 198
尊 zūn 32, 79, 130
樽 (*) zūn 97
遵 zūn 69, 123
俊 zùn 93
昨 zuó 3, 4
琢 zuó 158
佐 (*) zuǒ 82, 97
左 zuǒ 12, 100, 190, 194
作 zuò 1, 6, 11, 14, 20, 22, 33, 36, 38, 43, 48, 51, 57, 65, 69, 73, 77, 86, 89, 102, 103, 105, 108, 113, 114, 115, 117, 123, 130, 141, 155, 158, 163, 164, 166, 169, 180, 185, 193
做 (†) zuò 2, 6, 11, 32, 33, 44, 108, 131, 168, 171, 175, 182, 197
凿 (*) zuò 156
唑 (*) zuò 191
坐 (†) zuò 4, 39, 146, 193
座 (†) zuò 28, 43, 61, 75, 97, 181, 185

Made in the USA
San Bernardino, CA
15 June 2014